The Jim Russell Story

by Norman Greenway

The Jim Russell Story

by Norman Greenway

Transport Bookman Publications

ACKNOWLEDGEMENTS

I would like to sincerely thank all the people who have given their time to recount and, in some cases, write about their memories of times with Jim or at the Jim Russell Racing Drivers School, including ...

Chris Alford, Derek Bell, Alex Bremner, Claude Bourgoignie, Bob Butte, David Clarke, Mark Cole, Jacques Couture, David Cuff, Freddy Dack, Tim Elkins, Brian Feltham, Ralph Firman, Sid Fox, Frank Gardner, John Giles, Ron Howe, Bill Inholes, Malcolm Kingham, John Kirkpatrick, Mike Knight, Richard Knight, David Lefley, Vince Loughran, John Lyon, Alan Mertons, Peter Merrylees, Tiff Needell, John Paine, Teddy Pilette, Rod Pither, Marcus Pye, Anthony Reid, Peter Russell, John Schofield, Graham Scotton, Richard Sefton, Carol Shelby, Colin Stokes, Andrew Stronack, Danny Sullivan, Simon Taylor of Autosport, Trevor Taylor, Kelly Tipps, Mervyn Trundle, Dave Walker, Ted Walker, Mike Warner, James Weaver, Anne and Edward Williams, Graham Williams, Alan Wood and the many others who helped. Finally, I would like to thank Jim and Jennifer Russell for all their help and for authorising the contents of this book.

Every effort has been made to trace the copyright holders of photographs and we apologise in advance for any unintentional omissions. We would be pleased to insert the appropriate acknowledgement in any subsequent edition of this publication.

Published by Transport Bookman Publications Ltd.
8, South Street, Isleworth, Middlesex TW7 7BG, England

ISBN 0-85184-058-2

Design: Silke Fahnert + Uwe Koch, Cologne
Production: Uwe Kraus GmbH, Murr/Stuttgart
Printed in Italy by Musumeci, Aosta

Foreword

I would like to pay tribute to Jim Russell and the Jim Russell Racing Drivers School whom I was fortunate enough to join at a vital stage in my career.

The school has introduced many hundreds of young people to motor racing and now has a long list of successful pupils. To anybody thinking of taking up motor racing as a hobby or as a career, my advice is to start at the Jim Russell Racing Drivers School where they will receive professional training and gain valuable experience in learning to drive a racing car.

EMERSON FITTIPALDI F1 World Champion 1972/74. IndyCar Champion 1989

Many congratulations to the Jim Russell Racing Drivers School which has done so much over the years to allow potential drivers to either progress to the heady heights within the sport or for others to clear their heads of dreams not to come true, but to still enjoy the thrill and pleasure of driving a racing car around a track.

JACKIE STEWART F1 World Champion 1969, 1971 & 1973.

I have known Jim Russell since our racing days in the 50s when we were both driving Cooper Cars. It was during that era that he opened his first racing school at Snetterton. Over the years he has given thousands of young people the opportunity to go motor racing inexpensively.
I congratulate him on his many years of successful schooling.

SIR JACK BRABHAM F1 World Champion 1959, 1960 & 1966.

I think that everyone who wants to race should start at a racing drivers school. Not only will they gain valuable experience but they will learn the essential track disciplines which are vital to successful racing. The Jim Russell School is where I started and in my opinion, it's the best in the world.

DEREK BELL OBE World Sports Car Champion 1985/86. Le Mans Winner 5 times

Jim Russell knows what he is talking about, I can vouch for that having raced against him He has applied the same professional standards to a school which has proved to be one of the most successful worldwide. He has given people the chance to become champions – or contented spectators.

KEN TYRRELL

I have to thank my patron, Dr Frank Faulkner, for insisting that, if I was going to try to go motor racing, I had to enrol in "the only school", the Jim Russell Racing Drivers School in England. Not for the first time was the good doctor right. One thing's for certain .... the basic training I received at the Jim Russell Racing Drivers School has stood me in good stead, whether I've been racing on road circuits, ovals, tri-ovals, or even the parking lot in Las Vegas.
DANNY SULLIVAN Cart PPG Indy Winner 1985.

Many thanks for a great deal of real help and encouragement in the early stages and a lot of sound advice over the years.
JAMES HUNT F1 World Champion 1986.

Congratulations for all the good work you have done for young people starting out in this difficult profession.
JUAN MANUEL FANGIO F1 World Champion 1951, 1954, 1955, 1956 & 1957.

Contents

Chapter 1   Rescued from Le Mans

"Careful, we've got a dying man here." Almost subconsciously, Jim Russell heard those words and joined the very small exclusive list of people who had. He was laying on a stretcher as it was being manoeuvred into a small aircraft at Le Mans airfield for the flight back to England.

What had started out as a very promising drive in the 1959 Le Mans 24 hour race, had turned into a life-threatening nightmare. He had very badly burnt arms, a broken leg, broken ribs and fractured wrists but, when he heard those words, he said to himself, "No way", and probably started his recovery at that moment.

Things had been going so well for Jim that year. He was successfully running his own team, racing his Cooper in the European F11 Championship alongside a programme of sports car races in his Cooper Monaco. He was well on course to become the F11 Champion and had taken both cars to Le Mans, where his co-driver was Bruce McLaren, so that the team could carry on to Clermont Ferrand, further south in France, for the next F11 race before returning home.

Fate had struck a devastating blow late on Saturday evening as Jim was causing everyone to sit up and take notice. After heading his class in practice, the Monaco engine had failed to 'fire-up', after the usual driver dash across the circuit. He had eventually started behind the entire field of 52 cars Some five hours later, his sensational drive through the field had brought him into the lead of his class. By 9 pm, he was some six seconds ahead of the next car in the class, which was the 'works' Ferrari Suddenly, disaster struck. As he rounded the blind White House Corner flat out, he was confronted by the Whitehouse/Naylor Aston Martin, which had spun on some oil seconds earlier. It was completely blocking the road and Jim could do nothing but plough helplessly straight into it. Before he could move, a Stanguellini came round the corner at full speed. The driver had the same problem and hit the back of the Monaco before exploding into a ball of flames. With, in those days, no seat belts, Jim dived out of the car and immediately fell down. He hadn't realised that his leg was broken Crawling as quickly as possible he reached the grass, where a couple of spectators rushed forward and placed him on a straw bale. He was in a lot of pain with his broken leg and ribs and he looked at his arms thinking that bandages were hanging from them. Actually, it was skin! Like nearly every other driver in the race, he was wearing a short-sleeved sports shirt ... no flame-proof overalls then As it dawned on him that the blackened strips hanging from his arms were skin, his mind flashed back to a Benghazi hospital during the war. It was there, while recovering from an operation, that he had seen badly burnt soldiers being brought in. They were foaming at the mouth, in fact they were already past saving. He kept saying to himself, "Don't foam at the mouth, whatever you do", convinced that this was imperative for his survival. When the ambulance turned up, he was placed on the bottom bunk with the very poorly Stanguellini driver above him. Jim was drifting in and out of consciousness and, when he was conscious, he longed for the nurse, who was holding the hand of the man above, to do the same for him. He was hazily aware of being in the bed at the infamous Le Mans hospital and sometimes recognised his crew and the other drivers, when they popped in to see him.

It is debatable whether he would have survived had it not been for the prompt emergency action of his brother Peter back home in Norfolk. Like everyone else in the family and the staff at Jim's garage, which Peter ran, they had followed the radio reports of the race. By 9 pm, John Bolster was predicting that the little Russell team might even win the race. Then came the news of the crash and, at first, Jim was reported to have only minor injuries.

However, at about 4 pm on the Sunday afternoon, Jim's mechanic, Mervyn Trundle, rang Peter to say that Jim was far from all right. In fact, he was suffering from third degree burns, in addition to his other injuries, and needed urgent attention. An English doctor at Le Mans had strongly advised Mervyn to get Jim brought back to the East Grinstead Burns Unit in Sussex as soon as possible.

The team were in a quandary with no idea how this could be done. Peter said, "Give me your telephone number and, whatever you do, stay by the phone". He had no idea how he could arrange things but knew that something had to be done ... but quickly. Pondering the matter, he decided to start with the family doctor. When he rang Dr Gibb, he struck lucky. A friend, who was also a doctor, was with him that afternoon. He spoke to Peter and said, "Forget East Grinstead, we've got a very good burns unit in the West Norfolk Hospital. I'll book him a bed and you get him there. I'll await details after you've arranged things".

"That's the hospital fixed," thought Peter, "Now for the difficult task of getting him there". He thought of all the local airports and, remembering that Marshalls at Cambridge did some charter flying, he rang them. Hearing the urgency of the matter, they gave Peter the manager's home telephone number. As soon as he heard the story, the manager, with no hesitation, said, "Give me half an hour and I'll see what I can do." In less than ten minutes, he had phoned back to say that a plane and pilot would be ready to take off at 10 am the following morning and would Peter make sure that a nurse was there to go with them. Once again, Peter did some head scratching which led him to phone the British Red Cross. They were also very helpful and passed on the telephone number of a nurse who immediately agreed to go. A call back to Mervyn in France arranged for Jim to be stretchered to the nearby Le Mans airfield to meet the plane the following morning. Then it was just a case of alerting R.A.F. St Faiths near

Norwich who were also very ready to co-operate. The West Norfolk Hospital was informed of the arrangements and they confirmed that their ambulance would meet the plane.

Peter's hard work paid off. Everything went according to plan , except for the matter of the narrow plane door causing the "jarring" to the stretcher, which brought the spine chilling warning mentioned earlier. It was much easier at St Faiths where it was removed with no drama.

Jim was conscious at this time and was amazed to see, that by a very strange coincidence, the RAF Officer in charge was none other than Squadron Leader Billy Drake, who had served with him in North Africa during the war.

Unfortunately, the problems were not over. The hospital's ambulance door was another narrow one Again, they needed to tip the stretcher and Jim, in his light-headed state was getting extremely agitated. He was convinced that he would be tipped off in the process. Eventually, rather than upsetting him further, they removed the door of the ambulance before carefully loading him and taking him to the burns unit. He later learnt that the treatment he had initially received in the Le Mans hospital meant a delay of three weeks before any treatment could be started in Norwich. It was three months before he could take his first short trip outside the hospital and realise that he had been very lucky to survive and to have a caring brother like Peter.

Chapter 2   The Early Years

Jim Russell was born and brought up in the market town of Downham Market in Norfolk. He was one of six children with brothers Ossie, Fred, Jack and Peter plus his sister, Dorothy. They lived over their parents' fish and chip shop in the town.

Downham was a place steeped in history. Around 1650, King Charles, disguised as a clergyman and hiding from Oliver Cromwell's troops, had stayed in an old hostelry, later to become the Swan Inn. Another legendary figure was Lord Nelson who had stayed with his father in the town and had attended a local school where one of his school contemporaries had been Captain Manby, inventor of the rocket apparatus for saving life at sea. Little were Jim's parents to know that their fourth son would also bring fame to the little town.

Silent films at the local cinema attracted just about all the children and when Jim was just four years old, the cinema ran a competition which gave him his first ever chance to stand out from the crowd. The film was one of the early Charlie Chaplin epics which also starred the very young Jackie Coogan and the competition was for the best impression of Coogan. Jim was entered and beat eight other little boys to win His prize was free admission for the next six Saturdays at a value of one and a half pence each He soon shone in sports at school, winning the Junior Victor Ludoram when he was nine years old.

He desperately wanted a bicycle and, when he was thirteen, his first one was purchased from Fells Cycle Shop in the town for ten shillings (just 50p). It was paid for on Friday and collected on Saturday so he could use it over the weekend.

Off he went with three pence in his pocket to watch a football match in Kings Lynn. However, a bigger boy on a trade bike smashed into him and damaged his new bike. Instead of going to the football ground, Jim found a garage and used the three pence to pay for repairs to his bike before going home. His father never knew.

On the Monday, a carrier was fitted to it ready for Jim to join his other brothers delivering fish and chips around the local villages. Even at that age, he was looking for ways to make money and realised that his father's bulk buying of potatoes for the chip shop could be turned to his

Starting early ... as Jackie Coogan in "The Kid".   **11**

The smallest in the photo with his Victor Ludoram Shield at the age of nine.

advantage. His father was buying them at two shillings a hundredweight. Jim persuaded him to buy some extras which he could sell. He found an old galvanised bath in which to wash them, scrubbing them with a sweeping brush. He would then take them around the local houses in a wheelbarrow, selling them at sixpence for seven pounds. He further supplemented this income with half penny bundles of kindling wood which he got from chopping up the fish boxes.

He was now one of the family team regularly delivering fish and chips. They were packed in sixpenny (two and a half pence in latter day money) bags and the boys earned one penny commission on each shillings-worth sold. He soon sorted himself out a special deal for Saturday evenings by taking his wares to the local Denver Sluice Public House. Here, after selling eleven packets of fish and chips, he could gamble the last one on a game of darts ... either coming away with a shilling, which would double his take, or nothing.

One of the jobs his father gave him to do was supplying off-cuts of fish to the Gardner sisters, who kept a lot of cats. Every week he would deliver to them and collect sixpence for his father. One day, they offered to sell him a K B Radio for two shillings. He wanted it, but had to say that he hadn't got the money to pay for it. They said he could take it away and pay by supplying their fish free for the next four weeks. Accepting this offer, he took the radio and secretly did the necessary repairs before selling it to a neighbour for a pound. He gave his father, who had been constantly urging him to collect the money owed by the Gardners, the two shillings owing and made a handsome profit of eighteen shillings for himself, plus, of course, the two pence commission owing on the transaction His father could never understand why the Gardner sisters, who had always paid promptly, had fallen so far behind in their weekly payments.

His parents couldn't afford the apprentice fee of seven shillings per week for him to achieve his ambition of going into the garage trade. He became very restless and one day his father suggested that he look for a job. Eventually, he found one at Wade Wrights – the local ice cream firm. He was given a three wheeled bicycle with a sidecar cold box and sent out to sell their products. He soon started trick riding, which helped to sell lollipops and penny ices. One Sunday night, he was travelling back past the local golf club giving his pals a ride on the bike, unaware that a director of the firm was at the club (Co-incidentally, many years later, Jim was to sponsor the Jim Russell Grand Prix Tournament at that very club) Eager to report that, for the very first time, he had sold completely out, he walked into the factory. He was met by a furious Mr Wade Wright. "You're fired", he yelled, "for giving rides and trick riding on our bicycle". Jim pleaded to no avail and was given his cards on the spot. Within a few days,

however, Mr Wade Wright came round to offer him his job back, providing he travelled daily to Lincolnshire. This he did in a car driven by Jack Grange, towing a trailer loaded with barrels of ice cream. On arrival, the cool box on the three wheeled cycle was filled up and Jim went off for the day – returning about 6 pm for the lift back to base. By the time he had walked back home, it was generally about 10 pm. This made it a fourteen hour day, seven days a week, for just twenty-one shillings plus about three or four shillings commission.

Starting to win races already!

During this period, Jim tried his hand at driving a car for the first time and it ended in tears. He used to wait in the pub yard while Jack had his daily drink and one day, he slid into the driving seat and attempted to drive the car complete with trailer. Naturally, he failed miserably and Jack ran out and thumped him very hard. However, after he had calmed down, he began to regret his action and pointed out that Jim was too young to drive, officially. In recompense, the following week he took him into Boston to collect an old car he had bought, letting him steer and brake on tow all the way home. This was completed with no dramas and, as he never had any further tuition, it was always joked that he was taught to drive by Jack Grange.

He was, and remained, a passionate follower of football. Not only as a spectator, but as a player too. Like his brother Jack, he had become a most useful goal keeper and they both played for local Downham Market teams most weekends. In Jim's case, it was when his work schedule allowed. However, things were about to change when the ice cream job came to an abrupt end.

Jim buckled the front wheel of the bike and Mr Wade Wright, who always reminded Jim of Oliver Hardy, of Laurel and Hardy fame, gave him an ultimatum ... "You can pay for the wheel or leave my employment" He took the latter course, confident that he would get another job. However, after a week in the ranks of the unemployed, he wasn't quite so sure.

An opportunity came when a friend, Ted Aldred, who was stationed in the Army at Ipswich, offered to give him a lift there one Saturday evening. His bemused mother helped him to pack a few belongings into a carrier bag and off he went with Ted to find his brother Fred in Ipswich. By the time they got there, it was too late to look for him that night and Jim stayed in the Sailors rest home, near the docks, for just sixpence (two and a half pence).

The next morning, he located Fred and started to look for a job. It was 1938 and work was scarce but, nevertheless, he got fixed up as a general handyman, cleaning up and stoking the boilers among other things, at Limmers & Pipe High Class Restaurant in the middle of town.

Clutching the ball in his school football team.

Although he was with him at weekends, his elder brother was away all week working as a foreman with a firm of contractors in Kent. It wasn't long before he had persuaded Jim that earning £3.10.0 with him was better than the 19 shillings he was getting at the restaurant. So Jim gave his notice and was soon journeying to Kent with Fred. Little did he realise that things were about to change dramatically again. Hitler's peace agreements had proved to be worthless and, when war broke out, the Kent job came to a sudden halt. Jim returned to

Ipswich and, swallowing his pride, applied to Limmers & Pipe for his old job back. He must have been a good odd job man as they re-employed him. His position looked shaky when, while putting up the blackout curtains, he smashed a large glass sign To his relief, he was forgiven and remained in their employment. All the time, however, wartime fever was biting and, one day in 1940, he jumped on the trade bike and rode off to volunteer for the RAF.

His long-time ambition to get involved in the motor trade helped him to be assigned to the transport section and his footballing skills soon had him playing for an RAF team. He was based in the Sheffield area and found that the majority of the players, unlike him, were ex-professionals. The same thing applied to most of the teams they

Keeping goal for his R.A.F. team playing an Italian team at the end of the war.

played against. One good example was a crack Army X1 who gave them a very hard time. Despite all their efforts, they lost 3-0. The last goal came from a 25 yard free kick which goal keeper, A/C Russell J didn't see at all. No wonder really as it came from the foot of the famous International, Bill Shankly.

His job in the transport section took him to North Africa with 260 Fighter Squadron. One of his regular chores was to drive the transporter full of the pilot's equipment to the various airstrips. How he envied those pilots, but it was twenty-five years before he got a pilot's licence and flew his own plane. After three years in the desert, he took part in the invasion of Sardinia before moving to the Italian mainland and from there to England. By the end of the war, he was a Flight Sergeant and came out with the standard demob suit and a few pounds in 1946.

While Jim was abroad in the RAF, he bought a tiny puppy for a few pence in Syria. To his horror, shortly afterwards, it was announced that all dogs on the camp were to be shot before the unit left for Palestine. Jim went to plead for his dog to the Commanding Officer whose reply was, "It's no bigger than a revolver, put it in your pocket" The dog was saved and went all over the place with Jim, but she always seemed to be having a litter of pups at the wrong time. When the unit moved to Italy and took over some stables as a repair and salvage depot, the dog was about to have another litter. Jim was upstairs in the Sergeants Mess when someone yelled out that the Warrant Officer's dog was fighting Jim's little bitch. Jim flew down the stairs to find his dog in a sorry state with her stomach torn open. Not knowing what to do, he was being advised to put the dog out of her misery. Luckily, the CO had another solution. His girlfriend was an American nurse and, fortunately, she was nearby. Seeing how upset Jim was, she offered her help. The Medical Orderly known as Fritz due to his lack of hair, was asked to open the Medical Room. "Right", said the nurse, "Who has anaesthetised a dog before"? Naturally, there was no answer to that but, after putting on a pair of rubber gloves, she instructed someone to administer the ether on cotton wool. "Goddammit", she exclaimed, "I can't work in these gloves", and promptly took them off before pulling the dog's torn flesh together and stitching up her stomach. To everyone's astonishment, just seven days later, she produced six pups Unfortunately, due to the operation, she only had three teats so it was essential to put down three of the pups straight away. When the CO and his girlfriend arrived to see the dogs, she took his peaked cap off, turned it upside down on the ground and placed the three remaining pups in it. As she took a photo, it was decided to christen them, Catgut, Ether and Acraflavin. All three were found new owners before Jim was sent down to Naples to start his journey home. He had previously joined the Spratts Dog Club back home and this meant that they would bring the dog back and look after her in quarantine on his behalf. Jim went to the service police and asked them to look after her until she was collected by Spratts.

Shepreth Motors ... Jim's first car sales site.

He gave them about £25 to pay for her keep but when he phoned back from England, they told him that the dog had run away He didn't believe that story and reflected that, after trying to do everything correctly, he should perhaps have tried to smuggle her into the country after all!

In the last few months of his service career, he started to buy and sell a few second-hand cars and it seemed a good idea to continue after his demob. He had made some friends in Hitchen and decided to stay there. He rented a room in a council house and ran a little car sales business from there, keeping the cars in a little cul-de-sac next to the house. Amazingly, no-one complained. A friend of his, named Jim Stannion, kept talking to him about a partnership. After a while, they decided to form one and rented a little garage in Shepreth, near Cambridge.

For a while, things seemed to be going nicely. Jim had a simple dress method ... when he was out buying cars, he always wore his uniform complete with medals and, with the war still fresh in people's minds, this worked in his favour. Back at the garage, however, he would change into his demob suit to sell cars. Gradually, Jim realised that he was doing the lion's share of the work and began thinking that the partnership was a mistake. "I must be mad," he thought, "I would be better off on my own." He was also beginning to feel a little homesick. So, he dissolved the partnership and soon afterwards piled all his equipment onto his lorry before heading back to Downham Market.

By now, brother Fred had a public house at Tottenhill, opposite what was to become Martin Brundle's family garage. Jim took over the barn at the back. Strangely, while the pub still operated with hurricane lamps, he had electric lights thanks to this generator. Buying and selling cars needed trade plates, but to get them it was necessary to have a staff of three. He had a word with the friendly local policeman,

PC Scott, who quickly said, "Now you've got this lad working for you, brother Fred helps out now and then and I've been known to give a hand occasionally – so get the form filled in". As soon as the plates arrived, he was able to buy much further afield. Bury St Edmunds market was a regular trip and he used to employ part-time drivers who left off work at the gasworks at 4 pm. They all piled into the ex-Army pick-up with cans of petrol and oil and went off to collect the cars Jim had bought earlier in the day. The non-runners had to be towed home as well – as long as they could be made road-worthy, they were acceptable. By this time, he had bought an acre and a half field and had erected a Nissen hut as a workshop. However, Sid Rix, a local character who helped out, told Jim of a main road site. It was a wooden shack on the London road and Jim rented it from the owner, a widow with five children, for £1 plus a cwt of coal per week. It proved to be a most important decision; it's been the site of the Jim Russell garage ever since.

Brother Peter was in the navy at that time. He had rejoined in 1948 for a three year term but when the Korean war started, he was caught up for another year and a half. When he eventually came out, he got a job in the Post Office and very soon Jim was suggesting that he could do with Peter in his garage business. However, the Post Office had just arranged for Peter to be taught to drive and, never one to 'look a gift horse in the mouth', Jim said, "Stay there until you've got your driving licence" The day after this happened, Jim poached him for the garage. It was to be a long and successful association and, of course, after Jim started to race, Peter became indispensable as he ran the garage while Jim was away racing.

They started to think about a petrol station and Peter spoke to the Esso representative who was most receptive. Before long, they had submitted plans to the council which were passed.

The first Downham Market garage.

Needing to re-house Sarah Trundle, the widow who was still living in a bungalow on the site, they went to see her. She agreed to Jim's offer to find her another place to live. A cottage was found and bought for £700 and Sarah as given a further £150 to fit it out. She happily moved from the bungalow and it very soon became the garage office. Much later, it was demolished to make way for the panel beating shop. As for the Trundle family, Jim kept in touch and Mervyn, the eldest son, later became Jim's racing mechanic.

Plans were soon drawn up and passed for the new petrol station which was to replace the old wooden shack on the main road site. Included were three 1,000 gallon petrol tanks and the necessary holes had to be dug for them. Jim and Peter decided to dig the holes themselves to save money and set to work with a couple of spades When this mammoth task was completed, Jim arranged for some local builders, the Barker Brothers, to do the building work. This had to be done piecemeal as he still couldn't afford to pay for the whole job in one go. So, as he sold a car or two, they came back to carry on with the work. Obviously, this meant a rather drawn out job but, eventually, it was finished. Then came the need for an inspection pit in the work-shop. Again, it would mean a hand-digging job. This time, Sid Rix agreed to help and they decided to mark out the area and dig it out with one starting at each end. After tossing a coin to decide which end each would start, Jim suggested that they had a bet on who would be the first to finish. The stake was fixed at £1 to the winner.

A couple of hours went by and Jim said, "I think we should have a short break now but make sure we drop our spades at the same time". By then, they had both dug down some way leaving a section, rather like a dividing wall, between them. Before Sid could turn round, Jim had dropped on his knees and was just able to look over the divider. Sid's face dropped at this sight as he thought he was really being left behind. He was most relieved when Jim stood up. From then on, they continued to dig with very few rest periods, and at the finish Jim was just ahead. As Sid handed over the £1, he said, "I can't believe it. I've just paid you £1 for the pleasure of digging your pit!".

Jim was by now making his name in motor racing and the brothers used his successes to great effect. The local media were continually giving Jim plenty of exposure, especially on their sports pages, all of which helped to promote the Downham Market garage. One local news-man, Ron Howe, the Editor of the Kings Lynn News, became an ardent fan, and followed Jim's every race with glowing reports. Not only that, he became a good friend in the process.

During this time, it was decided that the garage needed a new car agency. They decided to approach Vauxhall Motors and were accepted as Vauxhall dealers in 1957. Looking for ideas to further sales of the new cars, again it was decided to use Jim's motor racing connection and came up with the idea of doing a 24 hour run in one of the standard Vauxhall models at the local Snetterton circuit.

In actual fact 1957 became, arguably, the most important year in Jim's life.

In the May, he had launched his racing drivers school and, by the end of the season, he had won the British FIII Championship for the third successive time. With all this going on, media and public interest was very high when he carried out the 24 hour run in August. He had a target to go for as a Morris Oxford had covered 476 laps, a total of 1,291.8 miles, at an average speed of 53.8 mph in 1954. This had effectively set a production saloon record which Jim was aiming to beat. He decided to use his own road car, a standard Vauxhall Victor, which had covered about 9,000 miles. Apart from a full service, new brake linings and tyres, the car had no special preparation.

He enlisted the help of fellow racer, Dennis Taylor, to share the driving and at 7 pm on Friday 16th August 1957, the run got under way. All went well, with regular pit stops, overseen by brother Peter, for fuel and driver changes, until the early hours when co-driver Dennis felt ill. This left Jim having to do all the driving for about fifteen hours. However, knowing that he was on course to take the record, Jim's adrenaline was flowing so well that he fought off tiredness.

The start of the 24 hour record breaking run in a Vauxhall at Snetterton.

Pit stop ... Peter Russell cleans the screen ... Mervyn Trundle checks the oil and Johnny Giles oversees the operation.

Oliver Sear, Dennis Allen and Jack Sears congratulate Jim and Dennis after their successful day and night run ...

When the chequered flag fell at 7 pm, the car had completed 501 laps which totalled 1,357 miles at an average speed of 58.6 miles per hour. It had easily established a new production car record and the elated team was congratulated by a large crowd of well-wishers and press which included Jack Sears, Oliver Sear and Commander Philip Heseltine, who at the time was Chief Marshal at Snetterton. He had decided to present a trophy for the fastest 24 hour time by a production car and so Jim was the very first recipient of the Commanders Trophy. It was to be won many times more in the future including during the Willhire 24 hour races in the 1980s.

Ron Howe, continued to help promote Jim's racing successes. One day, he came to Jim and said, "I'd like you to give a talk to the Round Table at Kings Lynn". "You've got to be joking," replied Jim. "I'd rather go into the first corner with no damned brakes" "Wait a minute ... what if we go together and I just ask you questions?" Jim agreed to this and the question and answer session went well. Before long, they did the same for the Kings Lynn Motoring Club. Next, it was a lunch time meeting of the Rotarians who had brought their sons and daughters along especially to hear Jim. This time, however, before Ron could ask questions, Jim was away and talking without any prompting. As they left, Ron said, "You don't need me anymore, Jim". He was right and from then on, Jim travelled all over East Anglia giving talks about motor racing.

In 1960, Jim learnt that the 11 acre field next to his garage was for sale. It had previously been leased to a certain George Hartley as grazing for his animals. He attended the sale at the Town Hall and was just going to get the land for £1,500 when Hartley stepped in and took the price up until Jim finally got it for £2,500. When Jim arrived back at the garage, he received a phone call from Hartley asking if he could now lease the land from the new owner. Jim, still feeling aggrieved at the way Hartley had pushed the price up said, "You've just cost me £1,000 ... you haven't got enough money to lease that land from me".

Jim put in planning permission for 66 bungalows on eight acres of his newly acquired land and, as soon as permission was obtained, he sold it off to the local builders, Barker Brothers, for £8,000. To put this price into perspective, it has to be remembered that, at the time, three bedroomed bungalows were selling at around £2,000 and two bedroomed ones were even less.

However, Jim's plan had worked well. He now had a prime main road three acre plot on which to develop his garage and over £5,000 to pay for it. Then, another 12 acres came up for sale behind the existing 11 acre plot and Tom, one of the Barker Brothers, told Jim that he was interested in buying this land. "So am I", said Jim, "it could increase the price but, remember, I'm always prepared to do a deal".

Coincidentally, Jim and the Barkers had the same Solicitor, a Mr Walton, and when Jim arrived rather late at the sale, he saw him sitting with Tom at the front. Jim stood at the back, just inside the door and entered into the bidding eventually buying the land for £3,500. When the auctioneer said, "Sold to Mr Russell", Tom and Walton swung round and, before Jim could move, they were with him. "You bought it," said Tom accusingly. "I told you I was going to buy it," replied Jim. "What are you trying to say, Tom? Would you like to buy it?" "You know I would," was Tom's instant retort. "Well ... give me £500 profit and it's yours", Jim said with some relish. Off they went to Mr Walton's office and completed the necessary paperwork. Some time later, Jim returned to the garage very satisfied with his profitable morning's work.

Barker Brothers ended up building a further one hundred houses on this new plot and, in addition to the profit he had made, Jim had a further on-going bonus from these deals as most of the new house owners became regular customers at his garage.

While this was going on, the plans were approved for Jim to build his new garage, show-room and forecourt on two acres of his remaining land. He also included a special building to house the racing school. The remaining acre was left. A year or so later, Bullards, a local brewery showed interest and wanted to buy it in order to build one of their public houses. They agreed to Jim's asking price of £4,000 which, to say the least, showed a fair profit on his original purchase price. Then they changed their plans and let the sale drop. Much to Jim's surprise, the following year they came back and paid Jim's new asking price of £5,000. The strange saga didn't end there. They never built the public house and eventually they put the land back on the market and Barker Brothers bought it for about £11,000!

When the new garage complex was nearly ready, Peter thought they could do with a celebrity to officially open it and suggested that they approach Billy Cotton to do the honours. Apart from being one of the country's top dance band leaders, he was also a well known racing driver at the time. Peter, quite rightly, thought the connection to Jim's racing career made him a good choice. However, after finding out that the band leader would charge £300 to officially declare the garage open, Jim had second thoughts. "What do we want to spend that kind of money for?" he reasoned. "I know who will do it ... let's ask Jack Grange ... he's a well known local character and it will only cost us a bottle of scotch" Jack, who was over eighty by then, had kept in touch with Jim since their days together at the ice cream factory. He was thrilled to be asked and Jim was equally thrilled to have saved £300.

In the end, the forecourt opening probably got as much publicity as it would have if a national celebrity had carried it out.

Suddenly, the garage achieved national notoriety for the way they marketed the last of the then current Vauxhall Cresta models. Vauxhall, needing to dispose of large numbers of these to make way for the new model, released dealers from their contracts. This gave them a free hand in the way they sold them. Peter, seeing the opportunity to sell a lot of them at a small profit, took the unprecedented step of knocking £100 of the price. This was a huge discount off the retail price at the time. National reports and advertising brought customers to the garage

from all over the country and, one day, the famous Giles cartoon in the Daily Express showed a transporter loaded with Crestas and the driver saying, "They are so cheap at the Russell Garage that I've bought a load!".

Before long. other dealers were complaining to Vauxhall Motors and Jim received a phone call from the factory which said, "There is little we can do about it, but PLEASE, no more publicity if you can help it ... and how many more Crestas do you want?" They needed to move them and Jim's garage certainly did more than their fair share.

In the early 70s, they took on the Alfa Romeo franchise which fitted in with their sporting image very well. In fact, they held the franchise for about ten years. 1972 was a very important year for the garage as it heralded the start of a long and successful partnership with Mercedes. Jim was delighted when he had the chance of this

Jack Grange arrives to open Jim's garage.

prestigious franchise alongside the Vauxhall dealership, giving him the opportunity of supplying an even wider range of customers. From then on, despite the recessionary years, the growth was steadily upwards.

Jim's partner through all these growth years had been brother Peter who, in addition to being an efficient manager, had proved invaluable especially during Jim's racing career and when Jim was involved in racing school days. While Peter was managing the garage, brother Jack was the accounts director for nearly thirty years. Both retired in the 80s but, luckily, all of Jim's children were keen to follow in his footsteps. Mercedes were not happy with Jim's dual franchise and it became obvious that one had to go.

It was a very difficult decision to discontinue the Vauxhall connection after nearly forty years and many happy memories but, after a lot of heart searching, Jim and his family decided that becoming exclusive Mercedes dealers was the right way forward.

Then, in 1991, came the chance for them to take on the Mercedes truck franchise for Norfolk. The only stipulation was that they would have to find suitable premises in Norwich. In his usual fashion, Jim wasted no time and had found premises near Norwich Airport within just 48 hours. Mercedes soon approved the new truck depot and his eldest son James took over.

At the same time, daughter Amanda became Dealer Principal. His youngest son, Robert, became Service Manager in 1993 and, with Jim easing back to become Company Consultant, the Jim Russell Garage remains very much a family business.

Jim's first Cooper 500 c.c. FIII car.

Chapter 3   Jim Goes Motor Racing

Almost by accident, Jim discovered motor racing in 1952. He was 32 years old and was devoting his time to his garage business. A friend suggested that they went to a race meeting at their local Snetterton Circuit on Whitsun Bank Holiday Monday.

It was all new to him as they entered the circuit alongside the main Norwich road. They walked around and settled for a place on the outside of a fast sweeping Coram Curve. As complete novices, they had luckily selected a very good spot. Jim was fascinated by the sight and sound of motor racing.

He was especially taken by the 500cc FIII cars. These little open wheeled single seaters, powered by their 58 bhp motor cycle engines, captured Jim's imagination. They seemed to tear round very quickly like a load of angry bees. As he watched Don Parker's winning drive, he was completely 'hooked' and he made his mind up there and then to get involved in the action.

He soon found out about Autosport, the weekly magazine devoted to motor racing, and became a regular reader. Through it's pages he found the details of the Cooper Car factory, whose products were absolutely dominating FIII racing. Burning with desire to start racing, he rang the factory and, in typical motor trade fashion, he asked if they had any good second-hand models for sale They hadn't, but offered him a good deal on a new Cooper fitted with a JAP engine. He then had to find the money and this he did by selling his almost new Vauxhall Wyvern road saloon. The money from the sale bought him a pick-up tow vehicle and trailer. Off he went to the Cooper factory in Surbiton, Surrey and was soon on his way back home with his new racing car on the trailer.

Rudy Gates, a local trainee mechanic, was a motor racing enthusiast and when he heard that Jim was starting to race, he volunteered to be his race mechanic free of charge. Naturally, Jim was delighted to accept the offer.

His next problem was learning to drive it and he looked around locally for a suitable place. An old airfield on the outskirts of Downham was chosen and very soon the air was filled with the raucous sound of his JAP engine as he drove it up and down the old runway. It didn't seem to worry the locals except for one. Unfortunately, he was the resident farmer. Despite Jim's protestations, Mr Cox was adamant and kicked him off. He probably regretted his decision when Jim later became the toast of Downham Market.

So, it was in at the deep end and he entered his first race. Then he discovered the need for a medical before he could get a racing licence. He was very worried that being 32 years old would stop him getting the necessary certificate of fitness. With great relief, he walked out of the local doctor's surgery clutching the precious piece of paper which allowed him to get his licence.

His first few races, and the mistakes he made as a complete novice, were to later give him the idea of opening a school for people in the same circumstances.

He was constantly being told that he was too old by all kinds of friends and acquaintances which made him even more determined to succeed. When he was involved in a five car pile-up on one of his first visits to Brands Hatch, he did begin to wonder if he was doing the right thing. "Now give up", was the cry as he towed his very bent racing car back into Downham. However, reasoning that the accident had not been his fault, he dismissed such thoughts and ordered the parts necessary to repair his car. Soon it was rebuilt and he was racing again.

Around that time, he was talking about motor sport to a friend, Peter Brighton, over a drink in their 'local'. Peter was keen to join the Kings Lynn Motor Club and Jim agreed to go along. Very soon they were members and, as the main occupation of the club was rallying, started to enter events with Jim driving a Ford Zephyr and Peter doing the navigating. On one occasion, the competitors were set the task of getting from one place to another in the shortest number of miles. All the speedometer mileages were checked before everyone started to study maps and plan their best routes. Jim had a better way ... he just drove certain sections in reverse so that the speedometer didn't register Despite the 'ploy', they failed to win that one. They did, however, win one event later, before Jim felt that rallying and racing didn't mix. This was the Hunstanton Rally, in which they came first.

Peter brought up the matter of restricted speeds and said, "Can't you judge your speeds?" "I'll show you", said Jim, slowing the car, this time a Ford Consul, down to about 30 mph. "Now put your hands over the speedo so that I can't see it and I'll bet you I can hold the car right on 60 mph." Peter did so, Jim accelerated and when he was cruising steadily, Peter re-moved his hands. Sure enough, the car was recording 60 mph. "A fluke", said Peter. "all right, I'll do it again", was the confident reply. He let the car lose speed, Peter repeated the covering up and Jim accelerated. Once again, the result was the same. "Just to convince you", Jim told his astounded passenger , "This time I'll hold it on 68 mph". They went through the same procedure and when Peter took his hands off the speedo face, it read exactly 68 mph. It was some time before Jim told him about the slight vibration on the car's propeller shaft which he could feel starting at 60 mph and disappearing at 68 mph, however, with his increasing com-mitments in motor racing, Jim Russell Rally Driver became history.

His very first race at Snetterton and he made sure that he was next to champion Don Parker in the paddock. He wanted to be able to watch what the little man did and look to him for advice. Sure enough, Parker said to him, "What a lovely car ... it would be a shame to bend it, so just make sure you finish. Oh, and by the way, make certain you wire up the carburettor tops ... they have a habit of working loose during the race." He went on to win the race and Jim was pleased to bring his car home in one piece for ninth place. On the 'cooling down' lap, Parker's Keift stopped on the Norwich straight and had to be towed in. "What happened?" asked Jim. "Oh, I forgot to wire up the carb tops", sheepily replied Parker. Incidentally, another novice having his first race that day was Ken Tyrrell ... little did he and Jim realise at the time that one would be running a Formula I team and the other an International Racing Drivers School years later. Or, for that matter, that there would one day be a Russell Corner and a Tyrrell's Restaurant at the circuit. After a while, Jim started to win a few JAP races but, of course, all the leading drivers were using Norton engines and he wanted to follow suit. The top Norton engine tuner was Steve Lancefield, notoriously a tough man who didn't suffer fools gladly. He was extremely careful to supply his products only to drivers who he thought were worthy of them. "What makes you think you can bloody well drive?" was his terse response when Jim approached him about an engine for 1953. "It will cost you £300 with no carburettors", he added. Jim, trying very hard to lighten up the conversation made a frivolous remark which only seemed to incur further displeasure from the far from amused Lancefield. "That will be a further £30 for the carbs", was his only reaction. Still obviously concerned for his good name, he expressed his lack of confidence in Jim's set-up and suggested that the fitting was done at Don Parker's workshop. Jim, seeking to please him, agreed to go there. At that time, Don was undoubtedly the 'star' of FIII racing and the visit proved invaluable. He oversaw everything and checked that all the work was carried out correctly. When they finished, he invited Jim and his mechanic, Hudy Harrison, into the house for a cup of tea. Hudy was taken aback by the large

display of trophies. He couldn't have been more wrong however, with his prediction ... "Look at those Russell, you'll never win anything like that as long as you live"!

A few weeks later at the Snetterton August meeting, Jim won his first senior race using the new engine. He went on to several more victories before the 1953 season finished.

A new model Cooper was purchased and fitted with the new engine ready for the 1954 season. A news item early that year had Jim sitting up and taking notice. He read that Don Parker had split from Lancefield over the oil to use. Lancefield had a long-standing policy of using castor based oil and Parker had signed a new agreement to run on Shell Oils which was extremely lucrative. Jim saw an opportunity and drove down to South Norwood. He had to find Lancefield's house first and finally, with great trepidation, he rang the door bell. Introducing himself, he reminded the engine tuner of his engine purchase the previous year and asked if he would concentrate his support on the Russell team as a replacement for Parker. This brought a barrage of belittling remarks and a dismissive, "Let me know if you have any problems with that engine", before the door was shut. Off went Jim towards Norfolk with his tail 'well and truly' between his legs.

At the time, Jim was getting some support from Shell who were supplying him with free fuel and oils for his racing. Peter had now joined Jim to manage the garage and they had started to plan for a petrol filling station on the site. When the Esso representative called in, Peter discussed the proposed project with him. He suggested that Esso took over and supplied their products to the garage and Jim for racing. When he heard this, Jim was excited. He had heard good things about Esso's Motor Sport Manager, Reg Tanner. "I like the idea, so let's arrange a meeting soon", he said to Peter. "They might be better for the garage and for my racing." Several meetings later, a deal was struck. Esso took over the forecourt planning application at the garage and advanced money based on the projected profit over the next 21 years trading. This was the start of their on-going agreement ever since.

They also made a separate racing agreement with Jim to supply him oils and fuel plus pay him bonuses on his successes. It became Peter's job to send them a telegram every Monday morning with Jim's weekend results. They would send a cheque based on £30 for a win, £15 for a second place and £5 for a third place. Before long, they were also using Jim's results in their national advertising, boasting that he had won using Esso fuel and oils.

Some of the leading drivers at the Snetterton opening meeting of the 1954 season were using the new and very expensive nitro methane fuel. It was costing them about £12 a gallon while the alcohol used by Jim and the others was just 7/6d (about 37p) a gallon. Fortunately, the situation was resolved very quickly when the use of nitro methane was banned within a couple of weeks.

During this first race of the season, Jim had an on-going scrap for the lead with Les Leston. Jim led through the corners but Les took over on the straights to finally win by about a length.

28

Chasing Les Leston to the line in his first race with a Norton engine at Snetterton.

Jim was still anxious to be accepted by Lancefield and rushed to the phone to report his success. "Who won?", he asked. "Leston," replied Jim. "Where was Parker?" queried Lancefield. "Way back in third place", was Jim's triumphant reply. "Thanks for calling," said the engine tuner, replacing his phone.

In 1953, Jim had been refused an entry for the Silverstone International Trophy meeting. Now that he was established, there was no problem and his entry form was accepted by John Eason Gibson.

It still meant that he would be racing on the full Grand Prix circuit for the first time at 34 years old. Using the same, as yet unstripped engine, he qualified on the outside of the front row alongside Moss and Leston. Lancefield came over and said, "Don't take too much notice of the official times ... I didn't bother to time you. Have a good race but don't kid yourself you're that good". Jim was glad to be on the front row with 'superstar' Moss. He hoped someone would take a photo of them and he wasn't disappointed.

During practice, he had learnt a very important lesson from following Stirling. He realised that he had been going too quickly into the corners and therefore not getting the power on early enough on the exit to use all the road. The lesson proved invaluable both for his racing career and for the basics of the racing school later on.

In the race, the positions remained unchanged but he was delighted to finish third in his first big International race. Lancefield, still not relaxing his stony attitude, commented, "It could have been a flash in the pan ... let's see how you do at Aintree".

Aintree, near Liverpool, was internationally famous for its horserace course, home of the notorious Grand National steeplechase. The motor racing circuit ran around the outside of the horserace track.

Another feature were the magnificent grandstands, put there for the horse racing, but giving unusual luxury viewing to motor racing fans who were not used to such splendour in those days.

It was a really wet day for Jim's first visit to this circuit but he soon learnt his way round, qualifying for the front row of the grid, again alongside Moss. Stirling led away but Jim shadowed him every inch of the race. For lap after lap, there was hardly any daylight between them. Then, as they went into the very last corner, the slippery conditions nearly caught him out and his car slipped sideways. This was very quickly corrected, but it allowed the following Don Parker to get alongside with sufficient power to beat Jim to the line by half a wheel's length. Still Jim was over the moon with his result in such exalted company. After all, he had only been beaten by his hero Moss and the reigning champion, Parker. He was soaking wet but very happy with the reception he received in the paddock where there were plenty of requests for his autograph. As he was busy signing, and towelling himself at the same time, Lancefield came up to him. Looking over his glasses he said, "Will you come and see me when you're finished?" "Yes, Mr Lancefield", was Jim's exuberant reply. When they met, he asked what had gone wrong. "I didn't expect you to beat Moss but why, oh why, did you let that little man Parker through?" "I suppose it was lack of experience and then when I had that slide on the wet corner, he just 'pipped me' to the line". "Well, why don't you get yourself a little drier, and then we'll have a cup of tea." Jim was excited by the upturn in Lancefield's attitude and returned as quickly as he could. "Now", said Lancefield, as they sipped their tea, "we're really going to town. I know your engine hasn't been touched since you bought it. I'm going to build you up a new one for the Daily Telegraph International Trophy at Brands Hatch in August." This, Jim knew, was the big one. It was the Blue Riband of FIII racing with a big prize fund. The first prize was £250 which was a large amount in those days and there were bonuses as well. With the kudos of winning such an event, it was little wonder that everyone in FIII wanted to win.

Brands Hatch, just south of the River Thames in Kent, had first been designed as a motor cycle scramble course, before having a tarmac race circuit laid down. The original circuit, just over a mile long, is in a natural bowl giving unrivalled viewing all the way round. No wonder it has always been very popular with the spectators.

The new engine was built and fitted ready for practise on the August Saturday. Lancefield, in his usual authoritative way, stressed that if Jim felt the engine judder at all, he should come straight into the pits. It duly happened and Jim dutifully came in. After some adjustments had been made, he went out to continue practise. In a few laps, the trouble started again. "That's it", said Lancefield, "We might as well pack up and go home". Desperately disappointed, Jim suggested that, perhaps, they could fit the old engine. Lancefield, knowing that this would mean Jim missing the official practice and losing the chance of qualifying for a good grid position, turned down the idea. However, the team felt differently and were soon heading back to Downham Market where they fitted the older engine overnight before retracing the route back to Kent. Obviously, Jim had missed the official practice and this gave him a formidable task in his heat. There were so many entries that there were four heats run, from which the top few in each one would qualify to race in the final. As he sat at the very back of the grid in his heat, Jim was determined to do his best for his team who had done so much to get him a start at all. Head down, he shot off like a rocket passing half a dozen or so before the first bend. Continuing to carve his way through the field, he was actually leading the race at the finish line.

In the paddock, Lancefield suddenly arrived to assume control. He came up to the car, 'shooed' everyone away and promptly had a chain put around the area. "Now then", he said, "don't let anyone bother you. I'm checking everything over before the final". Jim was only too pleased to have Lancefield's backing again and concentrated his mind on the fact that his fastest heat had meant that he would start from 'pole' position. He had, in fact, easily been the fastest heat winner with his time, over 4 seconds quicker than champion Parker's heat win. The other heats had been won by Adrian Cowley and Charles Headland and Moss had been demoted to a second row position for the final.

Stuart Lewis-Evans, who was already showing the form which would take him to Grand Prix driving, shot through to take the lead at the start. Jim was having none of that and very quickly disposed of Stuart while Ivor Bueb, soon to become Jim's greatest pal, came through into second place. This was short-lived because his car developed trouble and he retired to let Stirling Moss into second place. Now the pressure was on and from then on, it was a two car race. Jim, however, was in great form and determined to keep the much more experienced Moss at bay. Gradually, he eased away from the younger man as the 40 lap race neared its conclusion. When he had a lead of 10 seconds, Lancefield held out the 'Ease up' board to him, which was obeyed. A very anxious Rudy Gates kept a close eye on the gap between his driver and the second place Moss. When the gap started to come down, Rudy, who was getting worried, went to hang out the 'Speed up' sign. Lancefield angrily pulled the mechanic back. "I'm in charge of things", he warned as he carefully kept an eye on the situation. When he finally thought that Moss was getting a little too close for comfort, he urged Jim on to win by around 7 seconds. A jubilant driver and team had succeeded in overcoming the setbacks of practice day and Jim had beaten the best in the Formula to take the coveted Daily Telegraph Trophy for the first time.

At the pre-race driver's briefing, Clerk of the Course, Ken Gregory, had stressed that only

△ The lap of honour.

◁ Stirling Moss congratulates Jim on winning the Daily Telegraph Trophy at Brands Hatch 1954.

◁ Smiles all round afterwards.

▷ Back at the garage with the trophies.

the winner of the race should come round to the start line for the presentation. Still very much flushed with success, Jim arrived and to his amazement, found that Moss was standing next to him Not only that, after Jim's garland had been placed over his head, he saw the same thing happening to the second place man. It puzzled him for a moment and then it dawned on him ... Gregory was Stirling's manager and had seized the opportunity to promote his man. Immediately afterwards, this second garland was taken away for the winner of the next race However, despite the surprise, Jim was elated that, at the age of 34, he was not only racing against and beating his hero, he was now standing next to him at the presentation. In those days, the winners didn't waste the champagne by throwing it around and it was a very proud Norfolk man who offered the trophy to Stirling first. "No thanks", he replied, "I'm teetotal".

Still very much on a high, the whole team were delighted with the next week's issue of Autosport ... not only was a photo of Jim leading on the front cover, the double page report inside was headlined, "Russell Wins the Daily Telegraph Trophy". It was to be the first of many such headings.

Jim won the Trophy again for the next three years to claim it forever. In fact, by also winning the British FIII Championship in 1955, 56 and 57, not only had he won all the major trophies he had admired in Don Parker's house, he had won them outright.

Back to August 1954 and the Oulton Park 75 mile race the following week. Oulton Park in Cheshire was in direct contrast to Brands Hatch. Twisting and turning, much of the time through the trees, the circuit presented a completely different challenge. Again, Jim beat Moss away and it was Les Leston, like Moss to later get into Grand Prix racing, who slotted in between

them. However, trouble struck and caused him to retire, leaving the way open for Moss to close on leader Russell. Bent on taking his revenge, Stirling pulled out all the stops and began to close on Jim. His efforts brought him onto the tail of Jim's Cooper and looking for a way past. After several abortive attempts, he saw his chance and went for the lead around the outside of Jim on a long sweeping left handed bend. Good driving by both of them saved a coming together and after that Jim had to contend with the determined

33

At the West Essex C.C. International Snetterton meeting 1954.

efforts of Don Parker who tried to take the second place from him all the way to the finish. In fact, there was only half a second between them at the flag. Afterwards, Stirling came up and said, "I hope I wasn't too naughty with the way I passed you". He was obviously the man to beat at that time and Jim had acquitted himself well although he was a little disappointed that he hadn't won on this occasion.

The following Saturday's meeting was another International one and, what's more, it was back at Jim's home circuit, Snetterton. This was one of the many ex-wartime airfield tracks which had been converted in the late 1940s. It had been an American bomber base and, in those early 50s, very little had been added. Nevertheless, the three mile circuit had some daunting features not the least of which was the hairpin which came at the end of the almost one mile Norwich straight The meeting, which had a separate Friday practice day, contained races for Formula I, Formula Libre, Sports cars and, naturally, FIII cars. Following his recent successes, Jim was very much the local boy made good. The locals turned out in their droves and Saturday's large crowd were treated to glorious sunshine. The 20 lap FIII race had Parker, Russell and Bueb on the front row. Unfortunately for Parker, something broke in the gearbox of his Keift as he went to move off and he took no further part. In the meantime, Jim set off at a cracking pace, intent on giving his fans a good show. No question about that. He led all the way while firstly Bueb and Bicknell disputed second place until the former retired to let Leston close. There was no holding Jim, however. He kept his red Cooper some 15 or so seconds ahead all the way to be cheered to the echo as he passed the flag. His lap time of 1 minute 58.6 seconds which equated to a speed of 81.96 mph was the fastest of the race.

The very hectic August schedule gave none of them any respite as the following weekend they were all at Silverstone for the Commander Yorke Trophy meeting. Silverstone, yet another ex-airfield, near Northampton, was to become the almost permanent home of the British Grand Prix later on. At the time, the facilities were, to say the least, just about adequate. For the drivers of these little single seaters, it was a very exhausting circuit to drive, especially down the long straight where vibration and wind buffeting was accentuated by the screaming two stroke engine just behind the driver's head. Naturally, this was even worse in long distance races and the Yorke Trophy was over 100 miles Apart from anything else, this was an endurance race The

34

huge entry meant that there were two races and the winner would be the driver setting the fastest time on the day.

Jim was in the second race and watched the first one get under way. Charles Headland, Les Leston and Ivor Bueb initially fought over the lead. Leston retired around half distance and Bueb suddenly had a charging Colin Davis (son of the famous Sammy) on his tail. He was not to be denied and snatched second place from Ivor before the finish. Jim knew exactly what he had to do to win. He had to better a time of 1 hour, 23 minutes and 29.4 seconds which had been set by winner, Charles Headland in that first heat.

It was certainly not going to be easy as he was lined up against Don Parker, Stuart Lewis-Evans, Reg Bicknell, Dennis Taylor and Ken Tyrrell. In fact, it was the diminutive Parker in his light-weight Keift who shot off into the lead chased by Jim and the rest. Lewis-Evans was driving the 'works' Cooper but presented no threat after the early laps. He was beset by an engine problem which caused his early retirement. It took Jim until the round of fuelling stops to get to the front but, after that, there was no catching his red Cooper. Kept informed by his pit signals with the object of driving to win, without going too slow, he took the chequered flag in a time of 1 hour, 23 minutes and 25.8 seconds ... 3.6 seconds better than Headland's time, to win the coveted Yorke Trophy for the first time. Parker's vain chase had come to an end when his drive chain snapped and the next finisher was therefore Ken Tyrrell, a full two laps in arrears.

Saturday 28th August saw most of them in the West Country for the National Race Meeting at Castle Combe. Another ex-airfield circuit, this one was 1.8 miles long and set in the rolling cornfields of Wiltshire. It was a glorious day as the 500cc cars came out for the first race, which opened the programme. Don Parker was determined to turn the tables on Jim after being defeated in the York Trophy race the previous weekend. Sure enough, they started a 'tooth and nail' struggle which went suddenly wrong for Jim when gearbox trouble started. He had, however, been going quick enough to shatter the lap record which had previously been held by non other than Stirling Moss His time of 1 minute 19.8 seconds (83.01 mph) was a second and a half quicker than Parker's Keift in their second race. After his retirement, Jim's mechanics worked miracles to get his car ready for Event 6 where he again fought for the lead throughout the entire race with the Keift driver. Unfortunately, he had to take care with the repaired gearbox but still finished just half a second behind Parker.

The following Sunday, back at Brands Hatch, to quote Autosport, "Jim Russell, the most prominent of this year's Formula III drivers", was in sparkling form. No mechanical bothers this time at the meeting which was run especially for the benefit of the Half-Litre Club which, as it's name implied, was predominantly for 500cc owners and drivers. There was no prize money that day as all profits were to help carry out further improvements to the circuit. Jim was in the first heat and was caught out at the start by a hard charging Charles Headland who led off at a cracking pace in his Martin. By the third lap, Jim had successfully challenged and passed him to keep him behind for the rest of the way. These two pulled well away from the rest and third man home, Tommy Bridger, was over 12 seconds adrift at the end. Dennis Taylor (Staride) was the surprise winner of the second heat with Don Parker second and Adrian Cowley third. After a short respite, most of them lined up for a Senior Race. Jim led off the line, holding off Taylor and Parker. On the sixth lap, the latter had passed Taylor and was trying to get to grips with Jim who was really motoring and was determined to stay in front. His efforts brought him the fastest race time of the day and he also broke the 500cc lap record with a time of 61.2 seconds (72.84 mph). The final of the Open Challenge was the last race on the packed programme, and after the flag fell, several cars collided. In the ensuing confusion, Taylor was able to snatch the lead from Jim, but not for long. By the second lap, it was business as usual and, as the others squabbled over the minor placings, Jim kept out of trouble to comfortably take his third win of the day.

The Half-Litre Club was also responsible for his next meeting at the pretty little Crystal Palace circuit in the heart of London. This unique setting had come about after the actual Crystal Palace had burnt down. The almost all glass structure, originally built for the Great Exhibition in Hyde Park in 1851, had been re-erected in a Park in Sydenham in the 1930s. The circuit, to say the least, was very daunting. It was narrow and nearly all the way round it was lined with walls made of railway sleepers. With these just about a foot away from the road and plenty of trees down through the Glades, there was very little margin for error. Naturally, passing was very difficult and racing was always close.

Three heats were necessary to trim the large entry down for the final of the Redex Challenge Trophy and Jim was in the second one. His main rivals in this race were Stuart Lewis-Evans, another destined for Formula I, and the wily little Don Parker. He knew he had his work cut out and made a storming start to lead them away. Before the end of the lap, Parker had scraped past him but this was short-lived, the little man spinning down to third, and Jim keeping Lewis-Evans at bay until the flag. So to the final which, to quote Autosport, was "not only the best on the programme, but also one of the hardest fought 500cc events ever staged" Eighteen very determined drivers were unleashed and Jim, again, snatched the lead hounded by Bueb, Lewis-Evans, Bicknell, Allison (later to drive for Ferrari in FI) and Leston. Parker was making up ground from a poor start and by the fifth lap was fifth. Up front, however, Bueb had finally found a way past Jim who, after a few laps trying to retake the lead, found the hard-charging Parker trying to take him The ultra close three car battle for the lead couldn't possibly last the distance and, sure enough, on lap eight the latter two touched and spun off. Jim's engine stalled and caused his immediate retirement, Bueb went on to win the race and Parker got going again to finish fifth.

Before the big International meeting at Aintree at the beginning of October, a practice session was arranged at Snetterton. Steve Lancefield phoned Jim and said, "Meet me at 10 am, I'm bringing up two new engines for you." The day didn't start too well as Jim was 15 minutes late which didn't go down at all well with the engine tuner. This didn't improve the situation as the engine started to 'miss' straight away. So they fitted the second engine only for the same thing to happen. "Right", said Lancefield, "we'll have to take them to your workshop and find out what's going wrong with them". So off they went to Downham Market where Lancefield played hell about the state of Jim's workshop. Used to a spotless workshop, more like an operating theatre, there was no way he would strip down one of his precious engines until the workshop had been thoroughly cleaned Eventually this was done and throughout the evening, both engines were stripped down and checked over. Nothing appeared wrong on either of them and around midnight, one was fitted into the car in readiness for the trip to Aintree the next day.

His practice session was disastrous as the engine kept cutting out. As the engine 'died', so Jim immediately pulled out the ignition switch for safety. Suddenly, to his surprise, the engine burst into life. Back in the pits, Johnny Giles found the trouble. It was a brand new ignition switch and the vibration on the track was causing a 'short'. "See", said Lancefield, "never trust anything, not even new switches or plugs". This problem had cost him the chance to put in even one decent practice lap, so he was forced to start from the very last row of the large grid of cars. His loss was the crowds' gain While Stirling Moss shot off into a lead he was never to lose, Jim's red Cooper was the centre of attraction. From the first few yards, he was obviously determined to make a good showing and he certainly did. Weaving his way through the back markers, he had passed no less than 17 in the first two laps While Moss sat comfortably in the lead and Bueb (wearing his usual grin) fought for second with Parker, Leston and Bicknell, Jim was continuing to move through the field. Amazingly, by lap 5 he was up to sixth place and pressing Allison for fifth. This achieved, he set off after Don Parker's fourth place and was alongside him almost locking wheels before long. Both were determined not to give way and on the very limit. Inevitably something had to happen. Sure enough, they touched wheels and Jim hurtled onto the grass, just missing the straw bales before recovering and rejoining the race. This lost him any chance of taking any further places but, nonetheless, it was a tremendous performance to start from the back and finish fifth against such quality opposition. His drive had, without doubt, been the highlight of the race and just to emphasise the point, he shared the fastest lap of the race with the winner, Moss.

Back at Snetterton a couple of weeks later, the Eastern Counties MC Meeting was the circuit's season closer. It had another 'battle royal' lined up in the FIII race especially as the main protagonists were vying for the 1954 British 500 Championship. Reigning champion, Parker, was looking over his shoulder at Leston, just 1.5 points behind him and Jim was a close third. Parker and Leston initially led the local star but soon Jim was past Leston and hauling in the little champion. Gradually he got closer until he was a little too close to the leader – as he challenged on a bend, his front wheel just touched the rear wheel of Parker's car and he was off onto the grass. Again, he recovered but had no time to make any further effort for the lead. Nonetheless, he finished second and shared the fastest lap with the winner. Despite the time lost on the grass, he was still nearly twenty seconds ahead of third man, Leston.

No sooner had this Saturday meeting finished than they were all packing up and preparing for the next day's meeting at Cadwell Park. Always a favourite circuit with the drivers, this pretty little Lincolnshire track, although narrow, had plenty of demanding corners and the foreboding 'mountain' to keep everyone on their toes. For many of the 500cc drivers, including Jim, Ivor and even Parker, this was their first visit to the circuit. So practice was even more essential, and to make matters worse, heavy mist and a greasy track during the morning increased their problems. However, the sun came through and dried everything out for the racing. This was another meeting for 500cc cars, organised by the Half-Litre Club, consisting of three heats and the final. The real excitement all happened in the third heat which contained all the favourites plus the circuit lap record holder, one S Bloor. After taking the lead, Jim was caught out by the 'mountain' as he became airborne and, in the process, dropped to third place behind Bueb and Parker. From then on until the finish, this three car scrap pulled further and further away from the rest of the field but the positions, although very close indeed, stayed the same.

The final saw the same three out front changing places continually. By the start of the penultimate lap, Jim had taken control and was heading Bueb by a couple of lengths. Looking all set for victory, he suddenly overdid things at the Esses and spun, clouting the bank sufficiently to overturn the car. Except for his pride, he was unhurt and clambered out in time to watch Bueb go past to take the win followed home by Parker. As he did so, he thought, "this is definitely not the way to end a season". Despite losing out on this almost certain win, he still finished third in the National 500cc Championship and was shortlisted by Autosport as one of a handful of future Grand Prix prospects.

His efforts had not gone unnoticed by John Cooper who promptly signed him up with Ivor as Cooper 'works' drivers in 1955. Jim's deal was a bit special as he only agreed to have a Cooper rolling chassis and all necessary parts supplied providing it could be maintained in his Downham workshop with the engines continuing to be supplied by Steve Lancefield.

Chapter 4

The Champion Years

Early in 1955, Jim and Ivor were eager to get their new cars ready for the start of the season. As was the practice, they sent their own mechanics down to the Cooper factory at Surbiton to build up the cars. Jim's regular mechanic, Johnny Giles, was joined by Ivor's man, Pip Preece. The arrangement was for them to stay down near the factory all week and return home for the weekend. After a while, they began to notice that certain parts had 'vanished' over the weekend. It soon became clear that this was no accident; they were obviously being 'borrowed' to help out Cooper's customers. To solve the problem, Jim and Ivor supplied their men with a large lockable box apiece. From then on, each Friday afternoon, they took off all the removable parts from the cars and locked them away in the boxes until their return on Monday. Jim recounted this story to his brother-in-law, Van Diemen boss Ralph Firman, many years later who said, with a smile, "Oh yeah, nothing's changed – it happens in my factory these days".

The cars were completed in time for the season opener on Saturday March 19th. This was the Irish 500cc Championship, a single race event held on the ex-airfield circuit at Kirkistown, County Down. The reigning champion, Don Parker, headed the entry with Stuart Lewis-Evans, Dennis Taylor, Cliff Allison and the new Russell/Bueb partnership in their brand new Mk9 Coopers. Unfortunately, the new models had a single disc brake system which started to give them problems. Nevertheless, after the usual early lap 'sort outs', it was Bueb leading Jim by

Jim's typical crouching style.

the fourth lap of the 25 lap race. Bueb had a couple of moments but just managed to keep things under control. Then, after both Lewis-Evans and Allison had retired, Jim had a real braking problem which saw him go straight on at the hairpin and into the straw bales. By the time he had extracted his car and returned to the fray, he was down to fourth place with no time to regain even third. His one consolation that day was finding that he had shared the fastest lap with no less than four other drivers. So Bueb became the 1955 Irish Champion and Jim focused on the next race which was back at this home Snetterton circuit the following week.

As in Ireland, the weather was bright but windy as the cars came out for the second race on the programme. From the off, Jim led narrowly from Ivor with Parker, Lewis-Evans and Taylor making up a quintet which soon left everyone else behind. By lap six, Jim had lapped his old red Mk8 Cooper which was having its first race in the hands of a novice named D Heath. Despite all the pressure from Ivor, Jim stayed ahead. Then Ivor suffered a burst tyre and the local hero was left to take a comfortable victory.

With meetings at Castle Combe, Brands Hatch and Goodwood over the Easter weekend, the Cooper team decided to split the events between them. Jim took the West Country Saturday meeting and the Brands Hatch Monday meeting while Ivor went to Goodwood for Monday's racing.

There were two 500cc races at Castle Combe ex-airfield circuit in Wiltshire and both of them featured a three car battle. In the first one, Jim fought with Parker, swapping the lead until his engine started to falter which allowed Dennis Taylor to get by. From then on, Jim concentrated on nursing his ailing engine and the positions remained unchanged. Frantic work in the paddock had his car back on full song for the second race and what a titanic struggle that produced. This time, Taylor could only sit in third place and watch the lead continually change as first Parker and then Russell took over. Lap after lap, it was anybody's race but Parker managed to be in front for the last corner and led across the line to win by about a car's length. Parker went off to Goodwood, where he was beaten by Bueb in the only 500cc race on their 1955 calendar. Meanwhile at Brands, Jim had a field day He was in the first of the four heats and initially had to contend with a challenge from the up-and-coming Mackenzie-Low before asserting himself to lead over the line. The other heats were won by Cliff Allison, George Wicken and Dennis Taylor which ensured a hard fought final. It certainly was with Allison and Taylor getting off the line very smartly, some thought a little too smartly, to lead. Jim sat in third place for several laps until he made his move. Sweeping past them both, he took his second win of the day.

On May Day, Ivor and Jim were at the now long defunct Ibsley airfield circuit near Ringwood in Hampshire. Except for the oil drums, marking the edge of the circuit, and the statutory lines of straw bales in front of the spectators, the place was still very much an airfield. After four years of running their solitary meeting, the local club had decided to charge admission for the first time. Despite this, a very large crowd paid the 2s 6d (12.5p) admission price. The eight race programme certainly provided them with variety. There were races for sports cars from 750cc to unlimited, Vintage cars and saloons, in those days called 'closed cars', plus FIII and Formula Libre single seaters.

Jim and Ivor dominated their race leading off the line for a race long scrap. As they swapped the lead, so Lewis-Evans and Parker did likewise for third place with a hard trying Ken Tyrrell behind them. Reg Bicknell, in the Revis 500, gave everyone a 'heart stopping' moment when the rear suspension collapsed on his car sending it into the straw bales before turning over across the circuit, no seat belts, of course then, and Reg was thrown out onto the tarmac. Miraculously, he was almost unhurt and was able to pick himself up before limping to safety and the First Aid tent The race meanwhile stayed just as close and Ivor almost snatched the win on the last corner when, with a very late braking manoeuvre, he came alongside his team mate. Jim was better placed for the exit, however, and held him off by half a length across the line. It was another 1 2 for the pair and Ivor broke the lap record.

The Hon Gerald Lascelles, cousin of the Queen, was for many years a senior official at race meetings and, as such, was at Ibsley. His wife presented the awards. Jim was delighted when she kissed him and even more so when someone said, "There's a moment to cherish ... not many people can say they've had a kiss from Royalty".

The very next day, they were at Brands Hatch. It was a terrible day with the persistent rain ensuring a streaming wet track all day. They missed practice, due to being at Ibsley on the

The Hon. Mrs Gerald Lascelles presents the trophy to Jim at Ibsley.

The Arnott. Jim's Le Mans car.

Saturday and had to start from the back of the grid for their heat. It didn't take them long to carve their way through the field and by the end of the first lap, Ivor was challenging, and soon passing, Stuart Lewis-Evans for the lead Jim was right behind him and 'slotted' into third place which was obviously good enough for a good grid position for the final.

He decided not to risk going for second place in the final but when Ivor's car developed a fault, so Lewis-Evans inherited the lead and just beat Jim to the line.

Next, it was the Daily Express International Trophy Meeting at Silverstone on May 13th and, as seemed to be so often the case, the FIII race was last on the programme. Those people who elected to miss this one for a quick exit from the circuit were the poorer. It turned out to be even more of a fraught event than usual Practice had been held in the wet and the grid line-up was decidedly strange with Jim well down the order. However, after a couple of hectic laps, he was fourth behind Bueb, Lewis-Evans and Leston. On the next lap, he took third place and before long it became a three man fight at the front as Jim and Ivor swapped the lead and the lap record almost every lap. It was exciting stuff and the win was in doubt until the last corner, with Jim leading again as they started the last lap. It now looked as if he would be ahead at the flag, but no. Ivor put in a last ditch effort, took the lap record back and passed Jim going into the last corner, Woodcote, for the last time to win by a 'whisker'.

Motor racing enthusiast, Daphne Arnott, who had for some time entered her own Arnott 500cc car in FIII events, had built a special Arnott 1100cc sports car for the Le Mans 24 hour race. She asked Jim to be her No 1 driver for this most prestigious International. It was a most rewarding time for him as his many successes were bringing all kinds of accolades. 'Autosport' had been running a weekly driver feature called Portrait Gallery and, to his delight, he was No 24 the week before Le Mans. On a high, he arrived for practice at the French circuit but soon found that the new car 'wandered' at speed and needed the drivers' utmost concentration to keep it on the road. When he came into the pits, he warned his co-driver, Peter Taylor, of this, stressing that no way should he even take one hand off the wheel. However, as Taylor went past the pits, he gave his team a 'thumbs-up' and sure enough, seconds later, he had lost control. The car ended up being destroyed when it hit the Dunlop Bridge and the driver was very lucky indeed to get out uninjured. So Jim was a non-starter through no fault of his own. He was by now a very good friend of his Cooper team mate, Ivor Bueb. The quietly amusing, large man from Cheltenham, who always looked as if his body had been forced into the 500cc cockpit, was one of the Jaguar team drivers that year, co-driving with Mike Hawthorn. Jim spent a lot of time with the team but was not sorry to have missed driving on the day that the terrible accident happened involving Mike Hawthorn and Lance Macklin, among others. The awful effects of a race car ploughing into the crowd and killing more than eighty unfortunate spectators reverberated around the world. For a while, reactions were so bad that the future of motor racing appeared to be in doubt and it certainly looked as if Le Mans was finished. However, the officials decided not to stop the race and in fact, the Hawthorn/Bueb car scored what had to be a rather hollow victory.

In the end, it was only the French Government which took any drastic action over the tragedy. They cancelled race meetings until new spectator safety precautions had been carried out.

Ivor and Jim took the two Cooper 1100cc sports cars over to Dunrod in Ireland for another sports car race shortly after the Le Mans tragedy. They were staying at the same hotel as Tony Rolt and Duncan Hamilton who soon started their usual horseplay Things got rather out of hand and Hamilton, to say the least a hefty man, picked up Rolt and threw him at the wall with such force that he went straight through it The noise quickly brought the hotel owner to the scene. He was horrified at the damage and demanded payment there and then. "OK", said Hamilton. "We'll pay, no problem, but please let us show this off first. We must get to the circuit and round up the other drivers. They've just got to see this before it's repaired".

With just about everyone in the race from Fangio and Moss at the top end, it was a large field for the start at Dunrod. A feature of the circuit was Deers Leap. This was at the top of a steep climb and after going over the top in practice, the drivers descended for about 80 to 100 yards before getting onto the brakes for a sharp corner. In the race, no sooner had things settled down than Jim noticed that brake lights were coming on as the cars in front of him were going over the top of the Leap. "Crikey", he thought, "They're braking early". With a certain amount of caution, he went over the top to see five or six cars all crashing into one another in a huge sheet of flame. He opted to try and scrub off some speed by swerving into and along the right-hand banking. This took off his front wheel on that side and threw his car across to the other side banking. This immediately took off the left front wheel and Jim sat helpless as he crashed into the back of Lance Macklin's car. His efforts had successfully taken off some speed and he was able to jump out, completely unhurt, to watch Macklin walk away across the field without so much as a backward glance. He had probably had enough with this so closely following his Le Mans involvement. Later, it was disclosed that two drivers had been killed in what was the largest accident in Irish motor racing to-date.

The crowd of them soon became bored in the hotel with no bar. Someone started the ridiculous idea of making the lounge into a large toilet Turning over the settee and making a toilet sign over the coal scuttle, they threw a toilet roll out of the window, letting it roll down.

Starting from the front row at Aintree's British Grand Prix meeting 1955.

John Cooper decided to climb up a pillar and had just reached the top and had struck a deliberately stupid pose when the owner walked in. There was a pregnant pause, then John slowly slid down the pillar. The owner looked around at their very sheepish smiles and, to their relief, said, "I realise that, with no drinks, you are all bored. Be good chaps and put it all back, please".

Having been involved in the accident, Jim was required to remain in Ireland for the inquest. As such, he had to report to the local police Station and Ivor, who had elected to keep him company, went along with him on the Sunday evening. After the formalities were finished, they asked the duty policeman if there was anywhere open for them to get a drink. He was sitting back in his chair, with his feet on the desk and started to give them directions to a barge on the river which had a bar open. Suddenly, the Inspector walked in. Quick as a flash, his feet were down on the floor and, at the same moment, he was saying, "Oh no, gentlemen, you'll not get a drink anywhere in Ireland tonight!"

They were pleased to get back home after that visit and it was back to FIII at Oulton Park where they each won their heats. Things looked good for the Cooper team, especially when they took it in turns to lead the final. However, a very on-form Lewis-Evans had other ideas and demoted them to minor places. The day was not a complete loss for Jim. He handsomely won the 1100cc sports car race later in the programme.

The Eastern Counties Motor Club's 100 mile event gave Jim a chance to race the 1100 Cooper sports car in front of his home crowd at Snetterton at the end of the month. With the

Crossing the finishing line in first place at Aintree's British Grand Prix meeting 1955.

big car class entry dominated by the likes of Roy Salvadori (Aston Martin DBS3) and Archie Scott-Brown (Lister Jaguar), his car was in the up to 1500cc class. The starting grid, for once, was decided by a draw for positions and this did him no favours at all. He was nearly at the back of the field of 23 starters. However, within a few laps, he had worked his way up to be 'dicing' for sixth place. This soon became fourth place on handicap and he had reached third place overall by the finish. He had been well and truly noticed by the media who universally described his drive and finishing position as fantastic in a little 1100cc car.

Even the famous Grand National Steeplechase crowds were surpassed when the 10th British Grand Prix was staged at the Aintree circuit in July. Entries for all the races were superb and with the North of England completely motor racing mad for the occasion, Liverpool experienced traffic jams as never before. It was reported that the police, used to handling large crowds for the Grand National horse race, couldn't cope with the largest invasion of vehicles they had ever seen. It was a very hot day and frequent car breakdowns in the Mersey Tunnel created chaos. Thousands were still trying to get in when racing started and the final attendance was over 150,000. For once, instead of winding up the programme, as so often they did at major meetings, the FIIIs were first on the grid. It was a packed field with 30 cars competing in the 17 lap race. Jim was on the front row, after a good practice, alongside Ivor Bueb, David Boshier-Jones and AFJ Fergusson. As the starting flag dropped, Ivor made a terrific start to lead away followed closely by Jim, Stuart Lewis-Evans, Boshier-Jones and Les Leston in a weaving bunch of Coopers. Before the end of the first 3 mile lap, Jim had passed Ivor for the lead. Lap 2 and

Stuart was in front. On the very next lap, Ivor was in the pits to retire as did George Wicken. This left a Lewis-Evans/Russell tussle for the lead. Seldom was there more than half a second between them as they fought for lap after lap. Just before half distance, Jim had taken the lead with Stuart right in his slip-stream. Fergusson was a distant third with Allison and Leston dicing for fourth place even further behind. Gradually, Jim edged away as he set several fastest laps including a new lap record and settled down some 5 seconds ahead of Stuart. Now all he had to do was concentrate on getting to the finish. This was achieved with no dramas and he came round in front of the packed grandstands to take the first win of the day. His lap of honour earned him a massive response from the enthusiastic crowd which, on reflection, was probably the largest of his entire career. His race set the trend for the day with Coopers filling the first four places ... Aston Martins, led by Salvadori, did the same in the sports car race and that was the year when the all-conquering Mercedes achieved the same in the Grand Prix Not only that, the first one home was driven by Stirling Moss, to make him the first British driver ever to win his home Grand Prix leading home, by inches, his team mate World Champion Juan Manuel Fangio. With so many foreign drivers entered, it had been a great day with British

Waiting for the off at the Palace.

drivers winning all three races.

August Bank Holiday provided a great weekend's racing for everyone. Unfortunately, Jim was not feeling at all like racing. For about a week, he had suffered from raging toothache and finally, on the Thursday before the racing weekend, he decided to visit the dentist. The outcome was that he had the offending tooth removed. The next morning, he attended the official practice at Crystal Palace with a very sore mouth. Feeling well under the weather, he wasn't at all surprised to see that he was well down the list when the times were announced. He couldn't have cared less about it but Steve Lancefield felt much differently. As always, he had been meticulously timing his man and was convinced that a mistake had been made by the official timekeepers. He was also very mindful that a position at the front of the grid was imperative on the tight little Palace circuit. Off he stormed to the timekeepers box and insisted that they rechecked their timing lists. Sure enough, after very carefully perusing their sheets, a serious error was discovered. They had completely missed the fastest lap time of all ... and it was set by Jim He had, therefore, qualified to start from pole position for the race.

However, before that they had to practise at Brands Hatch on Saturday morning in readiness for the meeting there on Bank Holiday Monday. This completed, they all trooped back to

46

Chasing Don Parker at Brands Hatch before passing him to go on to win the Daily Telegraph Trophy 1955.

On the Crystal Palace FIII grid 1955.

Ivor Bueb (left) congratulates Jim on his close win at Crystal Palace in 1955. Cliff Allison is behind them.

Winning the Daily Telegraph Trophy for the second time in 1955.

Crystal Palace for the afternoon's meeting. The FIII race around the tight little one mile circuit lived up to everyone's expectations. It was very much a Russell/Bueb affair. Lap after lap, they changed positions at the head of the field. Never more than a length or two apart, they kept the crowd on their toes as they pulled away from everyone else. When they went into the last lap, Ivor had just taken the lead. Down through the Glades and around Ramp Bend for the last time, it looked as if the race was his. Not so, a superhuman effort by Jim took him alongside Ivor as they went through the last corner. They headed for the flag side by side and somehow Jim managed to eke just a fraction more power from his overworked engine to edge ahead and win by mere inches Grinning broadly at each other, they completed their joint lap of honour and returned to the paddock. There they were greeted by Mike Hawthorn, who was competing in the main race of the day. "Congratulations on a super race", he said to them both. "I don't think there would ever be enough money available to get me to drive one of those things in a race like that".

As usual when they raced at Brands Hatch, the team were staying at the Hilltop which was a very friendly small hotel conveniently situated near the circuit. Jim was still suffering with a sore mouth and was unusually subdued. Feeling far from on top of the world, he arrived at Monday's big meeting where he was to compete again for the Daily Telegraph Trophy. The large entry was split into three heats and these were won by Les Leston, Ivor and Jim. Then came the final and Leston stole a march on them all to take the lead from the off. For the first three laps he held off everyone despite being under great pressure from Ivor and Jim. As they went into the fourth lap, Ivor slipped past to head them up to Druids. Jim was determined to take the Trophy again and, head down, he stormed past Leston to close on Ivor. Pushing all the time, he saw his chance a couple of laps later and swept into the lead. Now the roles were reversed and Jim again proved to Ivor that he was a very difficult man to pass in such circumstances. No way was he going to give Ivor a chance to reverse the positions as he tore to victory. He had again beaten the best in FIII and he took the famous Daily Telegraph Trophy for the second year running The excitement didn't end at the circuit presentation. The team quickly packed up and went back to the Hilltop for a proper celebration. They all piled into the small bar and proceeded to try, successfully eventually, to drink it dry. One of Jim's biggest fans from his home town was Tommy Grummet who drove a local brewer's dray for his living. He seldom missed a meeting where Jim was competing and he certainly hadn't missed this big one at Brands Hatch. As he walked into the bar, he was spotted by his local hero who immediately asked, "What are you going to have to drink, Tommy?" "I'll have a Guinness, please", was the reply. "OK", said Jim, turning to the barman to say, "Put a case of Guinness on my bill for him". So the evening went on with the Daily Telegraph Trophy being continually filled with champagne and passed around again and again. More people appeared, including a coach load of fans from Downham Market and the Trophy was getting emptied quicker than ever. Eventually, around about midnight, there was nothing left behind the bar and, to keep things going, those with anything in their glasses, poured the dregs into the Trophy and continued to pass it round.

The next afternoon driving back home, Jim felt great. He had won two International races over the weekend and, strangely enough, his mouth felt fine.

Just under two weeks later, he was back at his local Snetterton circuit for their big event of the year. The West Essex Car Club had 'pulled out all the stops' to promote their most ambitious programme to-date. It was a truly International meeting headed by a Formula I race and, it almost goes without saying, including a star-studded FIII race. The crowds poured in all morning but, unfortunately, the rain was pouring as well. It absolutely 'bucketed down' on the 30,000 or so people who waited for the first event to start. To make matters worse, it was the first rain for a long time and naturally, the track surface soon became extremely treacherous.

The programme opened with the 20 lapper for FIII cars. From the beginning, there was trouble. Jim made a complete hash of his start. Trying to make sure that he wasn't involved in any collisions as the cars slithered away cost him a lot of time. He was almost the last to leave the grid. As cars slid off in all directions, he proceeded to thrill the crowd with an exhibition of car control as he carved his way through the field. On the first lap alone, he passed more than a dozen cars and from then on made up time on the leaders. Stuart Lewis-Evans and Ivor Bueb were fighting out the lead with Keith Hall and Cliff Allison next up. Jim eventually got up to fifth and closing on Allison. The spray was making passing extremely difficult and now, of course, he was up with drivers in the same league as himself. While he was trying to work out which would be the best and safest place to try a passing manoeuvre, things changed dramatically in front of him. Bueb spun and collected Lewis-Evans, putting them both out. This left Hall with a

Out on his own. Brands Hatch 1955.

comfortable lead over the Allison/Russell scrap which was now, of course, for second place. The race running out and Jim deciding that, in the terrible conditions, discretion was the better part of valour, opted to stay behind Allison. Just half a second separated them as they crossed the line. It had been a hard race and the drivers who completed the race deserved the crowd's approval as they got out of their cars absolutely soaked to the skin. At the Aintree meeting early in September, a new driver entered the FIII scene. Welshman David Boshier-Jones immediately made his mark and, when Jim made a tardy start, the new man swept into the lead. His joy was to be short-lived as the Russell car soon made up the ground and very quickly demoted the cheeky young upstart. From then on, he saw the rear of Jim's Cooper getting smaller and smaller as it pulled away to lead him home by 11 seconds.

It was a long journey overnight to race at Brands the next day. Liverpool to Kent was far enough but not nearly as far as Ivor's journey to Sweden where he took in a race that weekend. Jim, meanwhile, was still in winning mode at Brands. He dominated his heat and then took on the very stiff opposition in the final where he beat Stuart Lewis-Evans, Don Parker and Henry Taylor for the Francis Beart Trophy. A nice one to win considering that Beart was a rival tuner to Lancefield who, with a rare smile on his face said of the win, "I think that calls for a shandy"

The following week at the West Country Castle Coombe International meeting, several of the leading drivers in F111 were caught out in a very fraught 25 miler. This one went to Ivor Bueb but to even things up, Jim made no mistake in the 15 miler. He led all the way for a very convincing victory.

Then it was back in the 'works' sports car for the 'Cooper Twins' when they were co-driving at the famous Tourist Trophy. Traditionally held at Goodwood in Sussex, it was one of the highlights of the British motor racing calendar. There was some sponsorship from Ribena which entailed having some crates of the drink against the pit counter for the sake of the cameras. From the start of practice, both drivers reported that the brakes

Friendly rivals. With Stuart Lewis-Evans in the Brands Hatch paddock 1955.

were 'grabbing' on and pulling to the left. The mechanics were working on the car in the pit lane. John Cooper was heavily embroiled in the problem when a newspaper man came up and asked, "Anything to report, John?" Exasperated, John looked around. To get rid of him, he pointed at the crates and said, "Oh, haven't you heard? We are having water pump trouble. Ribena has a higher boiling point than water and the rich fruit juices help to lubricate the pump" "Don't talk daft", said the reporter walking away. With that, John called him back. "You don't think we drink the bloody stuff, do you?".

Despite the problems, the race went very well and they proceeded to run away with their class leading home most of the bigger engined 2 litre class in the process.

Jim couldn't believe his eyes on Monday morning when he read in the National Press that Russell and Bueb had won their class in the Tourist Trophy driving a Vitamin C cooled Cooper Climax.

He needed to ring John Cooper to ascertain the timings for the following weekend's Oulton Park Gold Cup meeting. Cooper growled, "Have you seen the papers yet?" Jim thought it best to say no to that one. "Well, if you look at them, you'll see why I can't think about Oulton yet – I'm still trying to sort out the story about putting that stuff in the radiator at Goodwood". He certainly had a lot of explaining to do – especially to hospital staff who phoned to see what special properties were in Ribena The following weekend's race at Oulton Park was a single driver affair and there seemed to be even more press men about. No doubt looking for a follow-up to the Ribena story, they concentrated around the Cooper pit.

Ivor chasing Jim at Brands Hatch 1955.

Unfortunately, the car developed gearbox trouble and, while John was working on the troublesome box, one of the reporters looked over his shoulder. Still incensed by the previous weekend's affair, and in no mood for stupid questions, he looked up and barked, "If I told you we're putting Daz in the gearbox to get clean gears, would you go dashing off to phone that through to your paper?". The poor chap's mouth dropped open and, very red-faced, he walked quickly away It certainly cut out any further press involvement that day. The race turned out great and Jim won his class in the Gold Cup race.

With the Autumn final of the National 500cc Championship approaching, there was much speculation on the outcome. The Championship had 'gone down the wire' with Jim and Ivor separated by just one point at the top of the table. Obviously, the final would decide which one of these two good friends would be the 1955 British 500cc Champion. There was another subject causing much discussion as this important Brands Hatch meeting grew closer. It concerned the speed of the cars following the fact that John Surtees had just broken the motorcycle lap record for the circuit previously held by Geoff Duke. The popular question was, "Could a 500cc car beat this new time of exactly 60 seconds?" There were many supporters for both sides of the argument.

The day of the crucial meeting duly arrived and drew a huge crowd for the season's finale. The entry, as usual, was big enough for three heats and, sure enough, as expected, Jim and Ivor both won their respective heats. Reg Bicknell won the other one to join the duo on the front row of the grid for the final. Straight away, it was obviously going to be a straight Ivor -v- Jim fight as they quickly left the rest of the field to engage in yet another wheel-to-wheel struggle all the way. 'Swapping' places time and time again, it was Jim who took control near the end with Ivor trying all he knew to get the lead back. Out of the Druids hairpin on the very last lap, Ivor tried a desperate move which brought him alongside Jim but there was really not enough room for him. Jim had the line, to which he was perfectly entitled, and he was certainly not going to move over. Ivor kept up his effort down the hill into Bottom Bend, the left hander into the back straight where, still on the outside, he had nowhere else to go but onto the grass. Still he stayed, bumping along the rough until he managed to get back onto the tarmac behind his jubilant team mate In all this, he had over-revved his engine to 9,000 revs – some 2,000 above the limit.

An ecstatic Jim took the flag in first place, won the Sporting Record Trophy and became British 500cc Champion for the first time. Not only that, he had won the fastest race ever recorded at Brands Hatch with a race speed of 73.18 mph. And the bike versus car argument? That was settled in favour of a 500cc car by Ivor's fastest lap in the race of 59.85 seconds – quicker than the recent Surtees bike record and the first time anyone had lapped the circuit inside the 'magic minute' So the Cooper team had plenty to celebrate that night.

Suddenly, as Champion, Jim found himself in another world. He was being asked to make all kinds of personal appearances. He was approached by two businessmen enthusiasts from Jersey, jeweller Arthur Owen and motor trader Bill Knight. They had just purchased a brand new Cooper 1100cc sports car from the factory and had their eyes on breaking some of the existing Class G International land speed records. They needed a well-known 'works' driver in order to attract sponsorship for the attempt which was planned for mid-October. Montlhery, an ultra fast French circuit which had steep banking at each end, was to be used. The plan was for Jim to attack the first six records ... 50 kilometres, 50 miles, 100 kilometres, 100 miles, 200 kilometres, and the 1 hour. They planned to take over from him and co-drive the longer 3 hour and 6 hour records.

The arrangements all made, the party set off for France and on the 16th of October, Jim started to practise and learn the 1.58 mile circuit. He soon found, to his alarm, that a dip in the

Yet another trophy. Brands Hatch October 1955.

circuit just before the banking caused the car to move over towards the outside. The thought of going over the top and facing the big drop was far from inviting Back in the pits, he was met by long faces ... "You're only doing 45-46 seconds", said a despondent Cooper. "You'll need to be around 44 seconds per lap for a record attempt." Jim explained about the dip in the circuit where he was keeping on the white line but a circuit official said, "You'll only do any good if you stay right over where it's smooth and onto the very top of the banking". Jim thought, "Crikey, I'll be in deep trouble if I'm doing about 140 mph at the top edge of the banking and something goes wrong with the car". He had also experienced another problem. After 2 or 3 laps, the gear lever kept jumping out of top gear. As this gear was needed almost all the time, it really did need rectifying. To start with, everyone was mystified at it had never happened before. Then Jim reflected that they had never needed the car to stay in top gear for so long before. "After all", he said, "We only use it for half a mile or so on British circuits before we need to change down. It's never used continually as I have to here". John thought about it and agreed with Jim. "OK", he said, "I'll fix something for tomorrow".

Sure enough, by morning, without stripping the car down, he had found a remedy. Drilling a hole in a chassis member, he had attached a strong elastic (bungee) rope to it. The other end was firmly looped around the gear lever. It would obviously keep the lever in top gear, but Jim was concerned. He could see problems in getting into the lower gears ... to say the least, these changes could be quite difficult Cooper's advice wasn't exactly helpful ... "You'll just have to push harder for first and third", was his only comment.

It was about 7.30 am and the weather looked good. With extremely mixed feelings, Jim slid down into the car. He couldn't help thinking that he shouldn't be there at all ... as current British FIII Champion, he could be back home making the most of his status. "After all", he thought, "I could probably be getting some good sponsorship for next season. What the hell am I sticking my neck out here for?" However, pushing those ideas from his mind, he knew he had to concentrate on the job in hand. The circuit was not a forgiving one and any mistake could prove costly to him, apart from not taking the records. Having pushed against the bungee rope to get into first gear, he drove off, holding the steering wheel with his left hand while using all the strength of his right hand to keep the gear lever in place. As the revs peaked, with relief he let go for the lever to fly back into second gear. Now it was a case of building up the revs again before pushing with all his strength against the bungee to get into third gear. This wasn't all, of course. He had the added problem of steering the car with one hand, perilously close to the outside edge as he went up the banking. With no barrier to save him, he knew that the drop over the edge at the top was at least 40 feet Using the smoother part of the circuit, as he had been advised, took his outside wheels right to the moss on the very outside edge which had never been used by anyone. He was fighting to bring the car round and off the banking with one hand until he reached peak revs again and was able to let the lever fly back into top gear What a relief, and what joy when he started passing the pits, now constantly in top gear, to read the timing board ... not 45 seconds but 43.6, 43.5, 43.2 An ecstatic Cooper greeted him as he pulled into the pits. "Let's go for it", he shouted.

"Those French boys were right", replied Jim. "I do need to use the very outside to get the good times. However, I do have a problem with the sun ... it's so low at the moment that it's right in my eyes as I get to the top of the banking. It's like a wall of death I would like to see where I am when I'm so very close to the outside edge" So, it was decided to wait until the sun was further up into the sky and around 9 am, everyone agreed that things were right for the second record attempt.

Jim, knowing that it was vital for him to get through the gears cleanly, went through the same procedure as before ... holding it in first gear, getting the correct revs and letting it fly into second gear, up with the revs again and pushing like mad into third gear ... accelerating and fighting to bring the car round and off the banking as, with great relief, he got the revs up to 7,000 again and was able to let the lever fly back into top gear. Now he could concentrate on keeping the car on the right line for the rest of the run. He certainly had started well ... his first lap was timed at 56.4 seconds ... a new outright record for a standing lap of the circuit.

After what seemed an age of highly concentrated driving at maximum speed, out came the

After successfully setting six new world records, Jim waves out Bill Knight for his attack on the longer distances. Arthur Owen is on the left with Charles & John Cooper behind the car.

next timing board ... 50 kilometres ... a new world record So it went on ... 50 miles ... a new world record ... 100 kilometres, 100 miles, 200 kilometres and, finally, 1 hour ... all new world records.

He was certainly ready to come in but, in the excitement, Bill Knight, who was to take over for the longer distance attempts, wasn't ready. It was a further ten minutes before Jim was finally signalled in ... not a moment too soon ... the right hand front tyre was worn down to the canvas and just about ready to blow. Success could so very easily have turned to disaster.

Bill Knight and Arthur Owen carried on at a slower pace to set new records for both 3 hours and 6 hours before the very satisfied team packed up and returned to their hotel in Paris. Naturally, the champagne flowed liberally when they celebrated at a local club that night. Strangers and waiters alike were invited to join the party until the early hours. Unfortunately, John Cooper had to be at the circuit again at 7 am the next morning so that FIA Officials could check over the car as part of the procedure before confirming the records. He decided to awaken Jim and ask him to go along with him. Jim, nursing a thumping head, was not too happy when, on returning to Paris, John wanted to go shopping. He was looking to buy a new jacket and said he would value Jim's advice. When John tried on a very loud patterned black and white creation, Jim said, "That's it ... it's lovely", only wanting to get back to his hotel bed. It achieved the purpose and quickly ended the shopping expedition but, to his knowledge, the jacket was never seen again.

The International Class G Records set by Jim on 17th October 1955 at Montlhery in a Cooper sports car with rear mounted single ohc 1100cc Coventry Climax engine were:

KILOMETRES	MPH		MPH
50	128.27	50 Miles	127.63
100	127.36	100 Miles	125.86
200	125.33	1 Hour	125.34

A letter from John Cooper to Reg Tanner in 1956 formed the basis of Esso's advertising campaign at the start of the year. It was praising their oil which had been used to such good effect at Montlhery for the successful record breaking runs.

With his mother on his left at the reception when he was presented with an Illuminated Address by The Downham Market District Council.

His very successful 1955 racing season had also not gone unnoticed in Jim's home town. In fact, Downham Market was swept by motor racing 'fever'. The council had decided to honour him and collection boxes were distributed around the pubs and clubs so that everyone might subscribe to the event. Early in the New Year, a special function was arranged at the Town Hall. A packed gathering, including most of the local dignitaries, watched as he was presented with an illuminated address recording his 1955 successes. Among the speakers was Steve Lancefield who told the audience that they had every reason to be proud of their local hero who was an extremely good ambassador for the Norfolk town.

Before the season opened, Jim received a call from Lotus boss, Colin Chapman. He suggested that Jim might like to alternate with him in driving his Lotus sports car. Reg Tanner, the Esso motor sport manager, went with Jim to meet Chapman at the Steering Wheel Club, which was then the motor racing drivers' haunt in London's West End. However, they soon hit a snag when it was proposed that Jim would be responsible for any engine problems which occurred when Jim was driving. Both Jim and Reg realised that damage might well be caused during a previous race when the Lotus boss was driving. With thanks for the offer, they turned it down.

After that, they set up a meeting with Cooper cars for whom Jim was already contracted to drive in both Formula III and 1100 sports cars. Charles Cooper offered Jim the chance to drive alongside Roy Salvadori in a pair of Cooper 1500cc sports cars and this was agreed.

While the meeting was going on, there was a knock on the door and a staff member came in. "Mr Charles", he said, "There's someone here in answer to your advert". "Has he got a beard?" was the surprising reply. When the answer was in the affirmative, Charles said, "Well, tell him to p--- off".

They later learnt that a staff designer with a beard, and appropriately called 'Beardy' Owen, had upset him.

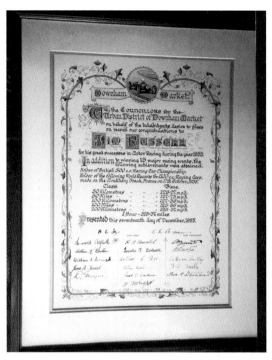

The Illuminated Address.

'Beardy', accompanied by Charles, had gone off to collect some gearboxes and on the way back to Surbiton, he had pulled off into a lay-by at about 12.30. He had taken out his lunchbox and serviette and, despite Charles pointing out that they were nearly back to the factory, insisted that it was lunchtime and carried on having his sandwiches. Hence the determination not to employ another beard-wearer.

Sometime later, Jim was racing at Aintree and nearly had a big accident when 'Beardy's' head suddenly appeared around one of the 50 gallon marker drums as Jim was taking the corner. It later transpired that 'Beardy' just wanted a closer look at the way the Cooper's suspension reacted through the bend.

Kirkistown was the venue for the first FIII event of the year. It was the annual one race Irish 500cc Championship and most of the drivers were taking the boat over on Saturday morning in time to go straight to the circuit for practice.

Jim decided to go over earlier and, together with his mechanic, he got to the Aerodrome circuit on Friday. It was a most uninteresting track, with no marker boards at all on the approach to the corners. They found some white stones and marked the braking distances for each of the corners. With all day at their disposal, they spent a lot of time testing and repositioning the stones until Jim felt they had them just right. As they went to leave the circuit late in the afternoon, he thought, "This is crazy – I've marked all the distances for everyone else tomorrow." So, before leaving, they moved the stones back about 30 or 40 yards.

The reigning Irish FIII Champion was Ivor Bueb and he was about the only well-known FIII driver not to make the journey to Ireland for this 1956 Championship. Jim took pole position after the official practice and led off the line from David Boshier-Jones followed by Cliff Allison and Stuart Lewis-Evans, all in Coopers. Don Parker's Keift was down in sixth place and no-one was making any impression on the leader. In fact, Jim started to put in some very quick laps, including one which equalled the lap record. He continued to dominate the proceedings, finally winning by a handsome margin of nearly half a minute from Boshier-Jones and Parker, who had moved up due to both Allison and Lewis-Evans striking trouble.

Jim proudly received the magnificent Trophy and became Irish FIII Champion for 1956 at his first race meeting of the season The typical local hospitality afterwards ensured that a very happy bunch of drivers boarded the boat for their return journey. In the bar on the way back, there was general discussion about the race. Lewis-Evans and Parker especially were uncomplimentary about the circuit. They thought it was particularly featureless. "Shocking place for a Championship", said someone. "It had nothing exciting about it", said another. "Well, at least there were some braking point markers, even if they were only little white stones". "Oh those", joined in Jim. "They were mine, only I made sure they were about 40 yards too early." He managed to save himself from getting lynched by buying the next round of drinks for everyone

On a high, he was next at the Snetterton season opener on Sunday 25th March. Many of his East Anglian supporters were out in force to see their new local Champion perform on his home circuit for the first time since taking the Crown. The spring-like dry and sunny weather provided the best possible conditions for fast and exciting racing. The crowd were not disappointed, well at least for the first half of the 15 lap FIII race. Jim shot off the front row to give a breathtaking display for his many fans around the circuit. Leaving Tommy Bridger and Stuart Lewis-Evans well behind as they fought for second place, he was soon recording fastest laps, one after another. Then came the reckoning ... he went by the pits at the end of lap 7, pointing towards his rear suspension and slowing dramatically. Sure enough, something was flapping about and he was forced to retire with a fractured off-side rear wishbone arm.

That left Bridger to beat Lewis-Evans and Jim to get the consolation of the fastest lap of 84.97 mph.

Jim's debut as one of the Cooper 'works' 1500 sports car drivers came at the Easter Monday International at Goodwood. When he arrived for practice, he was more than a little upset to find out that he had not been asked to attend the previous week's testing sessions. He found out that Roy Salvadori had been testing the car during the preceding week while he had to try and settle into the new car during the very short time allowed for practice on the morning of the race. So with just 8 laps in the car, he was some 4 seconds slower than Salvadori. This, naturally, put him well back on the grid for the race but he was incensed by the

Chasing Roy Salvadori home at Goodwood after very little Practise April 1956.

way he was being treated and very determined to make a big impression. He certainly did that ... making a superb start, while Salvadori shot off in the lead, he made up places as quickly as he could. In fact, his rapid move through the field brought him right up to the tail of Salvadori's car by the end of the second lap From then on, the two Coopers circulated as one with Jim matching every move by the leader and, resisting the temptation to try to pass him, he finished just four tenths of a second behind him. Just to emphasise his performance against the odds that day, he actually shared the fastest lap with Salvadori

A couple of weeks later on April 14th, Jim had his second date as a Cooper 'works' sports car driver. This was the occasion of the British Empire Trophy at Oulton Park. His heart sank into his boots when he arrived. Despite his Goodwood performance, he was still being treated as the poor relation ... in fact, his contract was for equal driver status, but Salvadori continued to get 'super-star' treatment On this occasion, Jim was forced to stand around while Salvadori tried out both cars to see which one he wanted to race. One had all drum brakes while the other had disc and drum brakes. By the time he had chosen, Jim had very little practice time left and was getting more and more disenchanted with the whole set-up.

The race was run in three heats, governed by engine size, and a final. The first heat for up to 1500cc engined cars contained mainly Coopers, including Ivor Bueb's privately entered one, racing against Jim for the first time. The main opposition was provided by Colin Chapman and

59

Leading Salvadori and Mike Hawthorn in the British Empire Trophy Sports Car Race at Oulton Park 1956.

Mike Hawthorn in Lotuses. It was Ivor who led the exalted entry away like a bullet. His success was very short-lived as he crashed on the first lap, badly damaging the car, but thankfully not himself. Chapman then took over and led a trio of Coopers all wanting to be second ... Moss, Salvadori and Jim. They were soon joined by Hawthorn's Lotus after he had passed Leston's Cooper. So it went on with Chapman edging further away and the rest all over each other every inch of the way to the flag. Without doubt, this proved to be the most exciting heat and, come the final, they were all on the front two rows of the grid.

From the off, it was a Moss/Hawthorn fight for the lead and, in fact, the former ended up as winner of the Trophy. Behind them, another great battle between Salvadori, Hawthorn, Leston and Jim went on for the minor places. Although he finished a very credible sixth in such a field, Jim still felt that he was not being given a fair deal.

Shaking off his depression, he concentrated on his next FIII race. This was at the Aintree International 200 meeting a week later. All went well in practice and Jim shot off from the front row for this 10 lap race. Not so quickly as young Colin Davis however, who snatched the lead initially. Putting on the pressure, Jim got past him on the fourth lap and romped away to what looked again like certain victory. Not so ... towards the end of the race, he was now leading by about 20 seconds and easing up a little with victory in sight. Then, as so often happens in such situations, he had a rare lapse of concentration and suddenly the car was sliding sideways as

60

he came towards the grandstand. In those days, at Aintree, the cars used to miss the corner of the grandstand by mere inches and that was Jim's undoing. His car hit the solid building and he sat helplessly watching as Davis eventually came through to win ahead of Lewis-Evans and Parker The event was not a complete loss however ... he had set a new FIII lap record for Aintree of 80.60 mph.

Back in the paddock, he was still kicking himself for making the mistake which had cost him a certain win when Stirling Moss walked up to him. Jim naturally thought he was about to offer some sympathy, but that wasn't the case at all. "Fancy you losing the race", said Stirling. "I was so confident that you would win it that I had a bet on the result – you cost me money".

In preparation for the Silverstone International Daily Express meeting, which was the next major event in the calendar, most drivers took advantage of a test day a week or so ahead. For once, Steve Lancefield didn't make the journey and that was probably why Robin Jackson, the rival engine tuner, approached Jim. He had his new twin plug engined car which was being driven by Henry Taylor. The problem was that Henry was some 4 seconds off Jim's lap times so Robin asked Jim to do him a favour and drive the car for a few laps. Jim obliged and within a very short time he was down to very competitive lap times, even equalling his own existing lap record Naturally, everyone was pleased. Well, not everyone ... Henry lost the drive to Don Parker for the forthcoming race and Jim made the mistake of mentioning it to Lancefield when he phoned him with the results of the testing For a moment, he thought Lancefield would have a heart attack "You bloody fool", he yelled down the phone. "Now he knows just how good his engine is ... no-one else could have told him that" "Steve, Steve", said Jim, who had only been allowed to call him by his christian name since becoming Champion, "Listen to me, please. I know where I'm getting the extra speed and it's not from the engine. Your engine is definitely superior ... it's because his car is last year's model, the 1954 all drum brake car. You know that Ivor and I have been continually complaining about this year's model with disc and drum brakes, but John Cooper insists we have to use them." Still disgruntled, Lancefield cooled down and reluctantly accepted the situation before putting the phone down.

Before this big meeting, however, there was another FIII event at Brands Hatch. It was on the Sunday preceding Silverstone and, as usual, attracted a very big entry which had to be split into three heats. Jim was in the first heat and soon stamped his authority by pulling out a massive 18 seconds lead within the first 5 laps. From then on, he romped home with the fastest lap also to his credit. Don Parker and George (the 'flying milkman') Wicken won the other two heats to join Jim on the front row of the grid for the final. The unlucky Stuart Lewis-Evans stalled on the line but Jim was out to continue his winning streak and didn't intend to hang about. Despite George Wicken sitting behind him for most of the race, until passed by Tommy Bridger, there was no way anyone was going to rob Jim of this second win of the day.

In a confident mood, Jim returned to Silverstone for the first official practice day and back to the aggravating situation of the Cooper sports car team. He couldn't believe that there was only one car present and, once again, Salvadori was getting exclusive use of it. Jim was told that his car would be there the next day for the Friday practice. The treatment he was getting was unbelievable. After his successes in Cooper cars ... the British FIII Championship, eight class wins and six world speed records ... he had no intention of being treated like a No 2 driver. When he voiced his feelings at the treatment he was getting, John Cooper snapped, "Don't get on at me, I'm ready for a nervous breakdown" At that, Jim blew this top and, telling him what he could do with his cars, he marched off without so much as a backward glance. That, of course, cancelled out his 1956 sports car drives and Jack Brabham took over the car for the meeting. For the record, a broken gearbox put him out long before the end of the race.

Meanwhile, Jim was still proving to be the man to beat in FIII. The race was last on the programme and, to everyone's surprise, he came round in fifth place at the end of the first lap. Lewis-Evans, Allison, Bueb and Davis were all ahead of him ... but not for long. Next time, he was up into third place behind Allison, who had taken the lead but, as they flew by to start the fourth lap, Jim had moved into first place. Despite much place changing behind him, he was never headed again. Unchallenged, he drove on to take the flag some six seconds ahead of second man, Davis. Proof that the racing had been hectic came with the announcement that no fewer than five other drivers had shared the fastest lap with him.

Whitsun weekend kept Jim's FIII team very busy with three meetings over the three days at Snetterton, Brands Hatch and Goodwood In front of his home crowd on the Saturday. he was initially upstaged by young Tommy Bridger, who cheekily led him for the first few laps. It didn't look too much of a problem for the local Champion however, and sure enough before half distance, he was in his customary first place where he stayed to notch up his first win of the weekend.

The next morning saw an early start for the team who drove down from Norfolk to Kent for the Brands Hatch Whit Sunday meeting. Again, the FIII entry was big enough to need three heats to 'whittle' down the numbers for the Sporting Record Trophy final. Jim was in the first heat and, when he made an unusual tardy start, Cliff Allison saw his chance and made the most of it. It took the Champion three laps to dislodge him and from then on steam away to take the win. The other heat winners were George Wicken and Tommy Bridger. None of the heat winners led the final however, as Stuart Lewis-Evans jumped into the lead from the off. He was in a winning mood and Jim was a constant threat until he managed to see a chance at Druids on the penultimate lap of the 15 lap race to scrape past and take his third win of the weekend. How those car horns were sounded on the south bank car park as Jim drove his lap of honour waving the Sporting Record Trophy above his head The finale to this extremely busy weekend was in Sussex. The tag, 'Glorious Goodwood' was never more true as the sun shone all day for this meeting. Tucked in a mainly sports car programme, the FIII race was highlighted by, you've guessed it ... J Russell esq. Racing at Snetterton on the Saturday had deprived him of the official Goodwood practice day so there he was on the very back row of the grid. Furthermore, it contained such nobilities as Don Parker, Cliff Allison and Colin Davis. This certainly did not deter the very on-form Champion. Scything his way through the field to such good effect, by the time they had reached Woodcote Corner on the first lap he was leading! Pulling steadily away, he looked supremely in control. Suddenly, no doubt losing concentration for a moment, he spun at Lavant Corner on the far side of the circuit. Before he could recover, Parker had gone by into the lead ... but not for long. The kind of form he was displaying that weekend ensured that, within a lap, Jim was back in front where he stayed until the line. It goes without saying that his fantastic driving also meant that he had recorded the fastest lap. Four wins from four races and three fastest laps ... not a bad weekend's work.

After that hectic schedule, there was a break of nearly three weeks before they all journeyed up to the Aintree circuit for what was titled, "The Aintree 100 Midsummer Meeting" on June 23rd. The main event was for Formula I cars, but with only eight starters, that turned into the inevitable procession on the long, fast, three mile circuit. The other support races offered little excitement on the very hot and sunny day but, once again, the programme came to life when the FIII cars came out for the final event Autosport's report said, "Trust the 500cc brigade to liven things up No matter what happens during the rest of the meeting, the FIII race invariably gives good value for money" This certainly was the case and Jim was in scintillating form. Setting the fastest time in practice, he tore off into the lead, taking Lewis-Evans with him and leaving the rest trailing. The two were so close for most of the race that they looked almost tied together. On the second lap, Stuart managed to snatch the lead but this was short-lived and within yards, the determined Jim had retaken him. So they went on in a race of their own, pulling away all the time from a squabbling quintet comprising of Bueb, Bridger, Allison, Boshier-Jones and Tommy Dickson, who were all trying to be third. While Jim went on to win by just 1.2 seconds from Lewis-Evans, it was nearly half a minute before Bridger came in third with the rest of the bunch still 'breathing down his neck'

The following weekend, the majority of the leading FIII drivers paid their first ever visit to the new Mallory Park circuit which had only opened a couple of months earlier. Near to Hinckley in Leicestershire, it was quite short. At 1.35 miles, it was almost the same length as Brands Hatch, and not dissimilar in layout with it's Shaw's hairpin something like Druids at Brands. Naturally, there was a very busy practice session with everyone striving to find the quickest 'lines' around the circuit.

The very full programme, in front of a large crowd basking in the sunshine, was opened with the first of two heats for FIII cars. Arguably, the top three drivers in the formula were pitted against each other in this one. Jim, thanks to his fastest lap in practice, was on pole position but alongside him were Don Parker and Stuart Lewis-Evans; both of them, incidentally, with a weight advantage over Jim. Parker was more like a jockey and Lewis-Evans, although taller, was also very slimly built. Parker made a terrific start and held the lead for the first three laps until Jim shot by him. Bu it was still anybody's race for the entire eight laps with, more often than not, all three abreast on the straights. Nevertheless, Jim held on and, after a magnificent display by all three of them, won by about a short nose from Parker with Lewis-Evans as close again. In fact, a mere 1.8 seconds covered all of them Not to be outdone, Ian (Puddle-Jumper) Raby, George Wicken and Tommy Bridger made it almost an instant replay in the second heat which was finally won by Raby. So to the final later in the programme and another crowd pleaser from the same trio. This 12 lapper, however, was led all the way by Jim with Parker and Lewis-Evans trying all they knew to get past. Into the very last lap, Stuart got past Parker and with a real super-human effort shot alongside Jim as they crossed the finishing line. The judges failed to separate them and pronounced it a very rare dead heat. Jim had held the lap record all afternoon, having set it at 58.4 seconds during the heat, but Stuart's efforts in the final gave him the new record of 58 seconds dead.

Jim, with his unbeaten run still intact, next met up with them all at the Silverstone British Grand Prix meeting in mid-July. As usual, the FIII drivers had to wait until the end of the afternoon for their 17 lap, 51 mile race which concluded the programme. Twenty-seven cars formed the grid and the only notable absentee was Don Parker who had damaged his shoulder in a practice accident. After a cloudy but dry day for the Grand Prix and other races, it started to rain in earnest before this race started. Sliding and splashing their way, the leaders avoided any incident, although there were plenty of spins behind them. As they crossed the line for the first time, it was Lewis-Evans who led from Jim with Bridger, Bueb and Dickson behind them. Stuart and Jim gradually eased away from the rest and Jim made his move on lap seven to take the lead. For the next eight laps, these two were tied together but Stuart could make no impression on Jim who didn't put a foot wrong in the wet. Then, Stuart joined the long list of spinners and George Wicken, who had steadily moved up the field, took over second position to finish eight seconds behind the very wet, but jubilant, Jim Russell ... still proving himself to be the top man whatever the conditions. He shared the fastest lap with Lewis-Evans.

The incessant rain carried on all through the week at such a pace that flooding occurred across the country. Not so, fortunately, in the Snetterton area of Norfolk. Bright sunshine greeted the competitors when they arrived at the circuit for the Vanwall Trophy meeting on Sunday 29th July. Once again, the programme opened with a FIII 500cc race, this time for the Eastern Daily Press Trophy. Young Tommy Bridger, alongside Jim and Ian Raby on the front row, stole a march on the local Champion. For two brief laps he held off Jim's passing efforts but then, going into Riches Corner, the local hero swept round the outside. As such, he was wide coming out and for a brief moment, Bridger retook the lead. A very determined Jim flung his car through the next few corners to put Tommy in his place and pull away from him. So, still holding onto his unbeaten record, Jim crossed the line to take the EDP Trophy and the fastest lap.

It was back to the rain, sometimes torrential and causing a partially flooded track, at the Brands Hatch August Bank Holiday meeting. Again, Jim was in the first race of the day and, in addition to coping with the extremely wet conditions, he had to hold off Tommy Bridger for the second race running. The youngster tried desperately to get past, setting the fastest lap in the process, but to no avail. Jim, as always going well in the wet, used all his skills to stay in front to the flag. Ivor Bueb won the second heat from Lewis-Evans and Wicken and it was Lewis-Evans who initially led the final later in the afternoon. Jim was third for the first two laps but after passing Wicken, he swept by Lewis-Evans just after halfway. From then on, another masterful display gave him yet another victory, again with the fastest lap and, more importantly, he had taken the Daily Telegraph Trophy for the third year running.

Oulton Park was the venue for the International Trophy meeting on Saturday 18th August. The main event was for sports cars but by far the biggest entry was for the John Bull Trophy where no less than 53 FIII cars were entered. This naturally enough, needed two heats and a final. This time it rained even harder than at Brands Hatch, with only the help of the local fire brigade's pumps making it possible to get racing going. Even then, the incessant downpour presented every driver with big problems. Jim's unbeaten record finally went this day and, to no-one's surprise, it was Stuart Lewis-Evans who did it. In the heat, Stuart drove like a man possessed to shoot past Jim and push him down to second place thus ending the Champion's almost season-long winning streak. In the other heat, Parker, Bueb and Henry Taylor also battled against the terrible weather conditions, as well as each other, to give another terrific display. In the end, it was Parker who won by a nosecone from Bueb. With everything and everyone soaking wet, firepumps and brooms were brought into use all round the circuit. As always, there was great determination by all to continue the meeting ... and so they did After the main event, out came the 500cc cars for the John Bull Trophy final. Jim, very determined to make amends for losing his heat, made a tremendous start ... too tremendous thought the judges and issued a 15 second penalty for what they termed a 'jump start'. Unaware of this, Jim pressed on and Lewis-Evans went with him. They had a real dog-fight in the terrible conditions, which took them further and further ahead of the following Bridger, Bueb, Parker and Boshier-Jones. Jim kept up the fantastic display of wet weather driving with Stuart staying close behind, hoping for a chance to get through the water spray. As many of the finalists slowed with spluttering engines caused by the severe rain, the Champion and his pursuer carried on relentlessly to take the flag almost side by side. In fact, without Jim's penalty, it could well have been their second dead heat of the season. As it was, the time penalty, naturally, placed Stuart first with Jim again second, but with the fastest lap to his credit, a full three seconds faster than any other lap time in the atrocious conditions.

It looked as if Snetterton was going to suffer the same terrible weather when Jim returned to his local track on the first Sunday in September. Sure enough it was wet for the morning's practice sessions but by the afternoon it had dried out and there was even a little sunshine to be seen. Jim was all set to make his saloon car debut until the modified Ford Anglia's gearbox called it a day during practice. So his only appearance was in the usual FIII event. Despite the presence of Parker, Bueb, Lewis-Evans and Raby, there was no sign of a real threat to his start to finish domination. Lewis-Evans spun out on the second lap but the others put up a spirited display in their vain chase. They probably pushed hard enough for Jim to pull out a little extra and break the Snetterton FIII lap record leaving it at 85.87 mph.

He was still in record breaking mood at Goodwood the following weekend. Colin Davis had equalled the existing lap record in practice and so started from the pole position. His joy was short-lived when both Don Parker (now driving the Robin Jackson tuned Cooper) and Jim shot off in front of him. By the end of lap one, the Champion was ahead and pulling away. His winning drive also included a new 500cc lap record of 84.87 mph. Lewis-Evans, Bueb and Bridger were among those completely outshone that day.

So to the Oulton Park Gold Cup meeting on Saturday 22nd September and the FIII entry of over 30 cars looking very much a 'Who's Who' of the formula. The popular question was could Jim Russell be beaten? The only man on current form who could possibly do it again looked to be Stuart Lewis-Evans. Sure enough, he certainly gave it his best shot. Derek Strange, normally a mid-field runner, had shocked everyone with a third fastest time in practice, behind Jim and Ivor, to line up on the front row. He was engulfed by the establishment as the flag fell and it was Stuart who took the lead. Ivor was second initially but was soon passed by Jim who was determined to catch Lewis-Evans. As if tied together, they continued to circulate while the squabbling pack fell further behind them. Then, around half distance, Jim made his move and was leading. Momentarily, Stuart got it back a lap later but Jim, as Autosport's report said, "looking his grimmest and how grim he can look when he's really racing", was soon back in front.

On he went, earning the name of 'King of his craft' as he took yet another superb win. Plaudits came thick and fast and it was generally acknowledged that he was now one of the most formidable drivers in FIII racing.

The Silverstone meeting on the last Saturday in September was mainly for these popular FIII cars and Jim, on his current form, was odds on favourite to take the main 100 mile event for the Commander Yorke Trophy. He easily led home a rather processional heat for a comfortable victory but it was a very on-form David Boshier-Jones who led the 63 lap final with Jim battling hard to get on terms with him. Just as he looked set to pounce and with only 12 laps to go, a drive shaft gave way leaving him to slow down and limp home.

Now nearing the end of the season, the aptly dubbed 'King of Snetterton' was back for his home circuit's final meeting. Obviously anxious to return to his winning ways, he found himself behind Parker on a very greasy and treacherous track. Trying just a little too hard for the conditions, on the third lap he slid off onto the grass. Before he could recover, he was down to fourth position. Proving that he was worthy of his popular title, a devastating couple of laps put him back in the lead where he stayed for yet another win.

The final meeting of the season at Brands Hatch on October 14th was notable for three things ... firstly, after so many wet meetings the lovely sunny Autumn day brought out a record crowd. Secondly, the programme contained the first race at the circuit for Formula I cars and, thirdly, Jim was beaten Little Archie Scott-Brown had the distinction of not only winning the first ever FI race at Brands, but also establishing a new outright circuit record in the Connaught. However, it was significant that his record of 59 seconds was a mere 8 tenths quicker than the 500cc record. It really put those little FIII cars into perspective Stuart was unbeatable that day and, after all, he had been Jim's only real challenger all season. Firstly, he won the heat from a hard-charging Russell who, it must be said, had needed most of the race to pass George Wicken before getting to grips with Stuart. The final was almost an 'instant replay' except that this time Wicken was behind Jim. As had happened several times before, Stuart and Jim outstripped the rest, but Jim was still a couple of seconds adrift at the flag. Nonetheless, he had taken his second consecutive British FIII Championship with no less than 14 wins, 3 second places and 11 fastest laps Autosport's annual review picked out both Jim and Stuart as two for the future saying that Jim was probably the greatest of all the FIII drivers and should make a brilliant FII driver.

Very shortly afterwards, the Middle East crisis brought petrol rationing and the curtailing of motor racing, which of course meant no meeting, as planned, at Brands Hatch on Boxing Day.

Petrol rationing was a big subject in motor racing circles during the closed season and there were doubts for a while about racing in 1957. However, a limited amount of fuel was made available and race meetings went ahead.

Jim's first event as double Champion was on his home ground on the very chilly last day of March. Despite speculation that drivers and fans would conserve their meagre petrol supply, there were good entries for the five races and the fans turned out in droves with duffle coats very much in evidence.

The uncrowned King of Snetterton was entered in two races. In addition to the 10 lap race for FIII cars, he had also cheekily entered the same car in a race for cars up to 1500cc engines However, a more in-depth look at the regulations put paid to that idea and left him in his usual race. Starting off the season again as the man to beat, he shot off from pole position to lead a very hard trying Tommy Bridger all the way. As they lapped back markers, Bridger got quite close occasionally, but there was no way he could do more and Jim took his first win of the new season together with the fastest lap.

67

In the Maserati 250F at Goodwood 1957.

The next meeting was the big Goodwood International over the Easter weekend which was almost a month later at the end of April. The FIII race was at the end of the programme but Jim was approached by Syd Greene to drive his Gilby Engineering FI Maserati in the Glover Trophy main event for Formula I cars. The car had been hastily prepared and was still giving the mechanics a headache, so much so that Jim had no official practice for a grid position. Despite this, he grabbed the opportunity to drive a FI car for the first time and lined up at the back of the grid. In front of him were the experienced FI drivers including Moss, Brabham, Ron Flockhart, Archie Scott-Brown and Stuart Lewis-Evans, who like Jim was driving in both the FI and FIII races. In fact it was Stuart who came through to win this race of attrition. As for Jim, he settled down to get used to his new mount and steadily increased his lap times throughout the race. It was very much a learning curve for him and he delighted the team by bringing the car home in one piece to claim fifth place.

Things weren't so good in the FIII race where, following only two laps of practice, he was again on the back row of the grid. While Stuart shot into the lead in the Francis Beart Cooper, Jim started to weave his way through the field catching the leader all the time. By half distance, he was with the leaders but a very rare engine problem suddenly developed and he was forced to retire to watch Stuart take his second win of the day.

Within a couple of weeks, petrol rationing came to an end and with restrictions ended, everyone headed for Silverstone in mid-May in high spirits. The weather failed to come up to expectations and torrential rain all morning saw a record number of spinners as practice was carried out. Luckily, the rain held off for the afternoon's races and Jim soon proved that he was still the master. There were two races on the programme for FIII cars and Jim won them both. In the first, a certain W G Harris in a Flather Special had a brief moment of glory leading Jim for just one lap before being engulfed by the Coopers with the Russell one ahead. From then on, Jim raced off into the distance with Derek Strange, who was becoming a front runner, in second place. The other race did provide a closer scrap with Trevor Taylor joining them for a crowd-pleasing tussle. Despite all their efforts, there was no way past Jim as he went on to record his second victory of the day.

Several of them journeyed across to Norfolk overnight to compete at Snetterton the next day. Tommy Bridger was all fired up and intent on beating the local star who initially led.

Bridger surprised Jim by passing him all round the outside of the long sweeping Coram Curve which led onto the pits straight. Naturally, Jim fought back and within half a lap had retaken the lead down the long Norwich Straight. Bridger never gave up trying to reverse the situation but to no avail. Having been caught 'napping' once during the race, there was no way Jim was going to drop his guard again. Setting the fastest lap, Jim stayed in front until the chequered flag with young Trevor Taylor taking a well-earned third place.

Trevor, some 15 years younger than Jim, has never forgotten those early days in his career which later took him into Formula One. He recalls that Jim was looked upon as the 'Grand Master' of FIII who always had time to talk to and advise the newer drivers. "I have a lot to thank Jim for", recalls Trevor. "But, I have to say that he was also the hardest man I knew to pass" He also remembers that Steve Lancefield was a different matter. Once, when Trevor's engine had a permanent misfire, his brother Mike, who was his mechanic, went up to the engine tuner and asked for help. "I heard your misfire", said Lancefield, "but, I went to my doctor last week and he charged me four guineas" Needless to say, that was the end of the conversation. There was another race for Jim that day at Snetterton. Syd Greene had asked him to drive the Formula I Maserati again and he jumped at the chance of a second race in the car. This time, it was in a Formula Libre race which actually allows any car to be entered although it normally means that the field consists of various single seaters and sports cars. This was the case that day. The other local hero, little Archie Scott-Brown, was in a big-engined Tojiero-Jaguar sports car. He shot off into the lead, closely followed by Jim who stuck to his tail all the way. They certainly didn't hang about as was proved by Archie improving on his existing lap record for large sports cars. Everyone was pleased with Jim's close second place, especially as he had handsomely beaten the very experienced sports car driver, Peter Whitehead, in an Aston Martin DB3S who finished a distant third.

In the middle of this hectic racing programme, Jim launched his racing school at Snetterton. Initially, he thought it would attract East Anglians and possibly some students from other parts of the country. Little did he even dream that it would grow to be the most renowned school anywhere and would attract would-be racing drivers from all over the world. Furthermore, he had no idea that there would be Jim Russell Schools in other countries and that forty years on they would all be going stronger than ever. Suffice to say that, at the time, he saw it as a low-key sideline operation run by his friend Wally Ward, with Jim instructing on weekends when he wasn't racing ... in fact the school's operational days were slotted into the free weekends in Jim's racing calendar. At the time, the most important thing was for Jim to win the British FIII Championship again.

There was one change in Jim's race team. Rudy Gates was moved to look after the school cars and Johnny Giles took his place. A local coal merchant, Les Gagen, who parked his lorry at Jim's garage, became Johnny's assistant.

At the Whit Sunday Brands Hatch meeting, the FIII cars were fighting for the Sporting Record Trophy over 15 laps and, although Bridger was present, this time Jim found both Gordon Jones and Don Parker ahead of him. It took him two laps to pass Parker and a further couple of laps to pass the on-form Jones. From then on they both saw the still unpainted Cooper going further into the distance. Despite a first few laps effort by Bridger, which saw him take the fastest lap, it was the Norfolk master who led at the finish to add another Trophy to his collection.

The Whit Monday Crystal Palace meeting was, as usual, well subscribed. In addition to the London Trophy for FII cars and several sports car races, the FIII event was for the prestigious Redex Trophy. Naturally, it attracted a first class entry and was run in two 7 lap heats with a 10 lap final. Jim looked all set to win his heat. Indeed, he led all but the last few yards. While he looked on course for victory, the ever-improving Derek Strange was getting closer and closer. On the final run to the finish, he managed to pull out just a little extra and, to Jim's surprise, came alongside him to win by a bonnet's length The excitement of winning must have gone to this head as in the final, he crashed out on the first lap This left the 'establishment' completely in control. Stuart Lewis-Evans, who had just signed to drive for Ferrari, had won the other heat from Don Parker, Tommy Bridger and Alan Cowley and this quartet, together with Jim, were the leaders of the final. Lewis-Evans was in top form and, try as he might, Jim couldn't find a way past him on the narrow Palace track. He had to be content with second place that day behind Stuart and ahead of Bridger.

Mallory Park, the newly opened pretty little Leicestershire circuit, hosted its first big meeting on the first weekend in July and attracted an exceptionally good entry for the FIII event, run in two heats and a final. Jim's heat was the first race of the afternoon and he made light work of winning this one. Pulling away all the time from second place man, Derek Strange, he had a full eight second lead by the finish with the fastest lap his as well. However, he seemed strangely off-form for the final. With the leading men from the second heat, Trevor Taylor, Don Parker and David Boshier-Jones plus Strange ahead of him from the start, he had to work hard to finish third.

This was to be his lowest finish of the season and he was quick to retrieve the situation. In fact, he won his next four races On the last weekend of July, he had meetings at Silverstone and Snetterton. The former's Saturday meeting had two heats and a 101 mile final for the Commander Yorke Trophy so, naturally, it had attracted a superb entry. In the first heat, Jim's main adversary was Tommy Bridger who clung to the tail of the Champion's Cooper through-out the entire race. His continued pressure failed to dislodge Jim who took the fastest lap as well as the win. Derek Strange won the second heat with a last minute dive past Don Parker, very similar to the way he had beaten Jim at Crystal Palace earlier. By the time the cars came out for the final, the rain, which had started mid-way through the afternoon, was absolutely 'pelting down'. Off they went and, again, it was Bridger who slotted into second spot behind him as several cars slid off the very greasy track. The gap between the leaders fluctuated as their main consideration was to control their cars in the now terrible conditions. With such a long race, most drivers had to make pit stops but, by the time Jim called into his pit, he had such a commanding lead that Bridger was still 22 seconds behind when the leader rejoined. Still it rained as hard as ever and, with lap times consequently some 15 seconds down on dry heat times, the race was taking much longer than expected. It was no less than 1 hour, 36 minutes and 12 seconds before the silver Russell Cooper shot over the line to win after one of his most masterful drives. Soaked to the skin, it was nevertheless an elated Jim Russell who collected the Commander Yorke Trophy that afternoon for the second time.

The next morning's weather at Snetterton didn't look too promising as they practised on a wet and slippery track for the circuit's biggest meeting of the season. However, the conditions improved so much that, with the track drying out all the time, several records were broken during the afternoon's racing. In fact, the FIII record changed hands that day. For the first time for many a day, it was not credited to Jim Russell. It went to Trevor Taylor during a very hard fought race. Despite this, the King of Snetterton lived up to his name and scored his third win of the weekend with Taylor second and Bridger third.

However, after a lot of checking, it was realised that Jim's lap record at Snetterton was still intact ... apologies all round when they found that Trevor's speed had been still 0.15 mph slower than Jim's record for the circuit.

Bank Holiday Brands in glorious sunshine and a packed programme was sure to bring out the crowds and they certainly arrived in their droves. The popular car park overlooking the circuit was packed from early morning and they were treated to a variety of events which included saloons, sports cars, vintage cars, FII and, of course, FIII. There was even a race for the little Berkeley 328cc sports cars.

After Jack Brabham had won the FII race, Jim set about keeping his current run of wins on course. He completely dominated the 20 lap race. The only driver looking like a threat was Stuart Lewis-Evans and he was delayed by a loose bonnet on his car. Towards the end, Jim was cruising to victory while Stuart was making up ground hand over fist. When Jim, on his last lap, was slowed by a couple of back markers, he was shocked to find Stuart right with him and almost alongside on the line It could have been a sensational reversal of fortunes and, not surprisingly, the fastest lap was set by Stuart.

Sunday 1st September presented completely opposite weather conditions. The Snetterton Motor Racing Club had put together a terrific programme of races for saloons, sports cars and a variety of single seaters. It had the promise of a superb day's motor racing but the forecast was wildly out as continuous rain and poor visibility together with a very cold wind took the edge off things for most of the spectators. In fact, the surface of the track became so bad that quite a few of the entries withdrew and went home The more hardy contestants who actually raced spent their time fighting against the 'skid-pan' like conditions and overtaking became rare that day. In fact, Jim had only one such move to make in the FIII race when Parker made the better start and Jim needed to take over the lead on the second lap. From then on it was a procession, except for Tommy Bridger demoting Parker. That was the way they stayed to the finish. Jim's fastest lap as he went on to win was indicative of the terrible conditions ... just 77.1 mph says it all.

The talented Lewis-Evans was again the opponent to pose the greatest threat at Goodwood's end of season meeting later in the month. After the experience of several FI drives, he was out to dislodge Jim from his now regular first place. In fact, he succeeded after Jim had taken up pole position with the fastest practice lap. Getting off the line like the proverbial 'scalded cat', he led all the way. Resisting Jim's every move to pass, Stuart was the main man that day as he took fastest lap and kept the lead to the finish.

Jim was now on his mettle, aware that the much younger and much lighter (by about two stone) Lewis-Evans was his only serious rival in FIII and he was determined to beat him at their final round of the season. This was on the first Saturday in October at the big International Gold Cup meeting at Oulton Park. Again, Brabham won the FII Gold Cup race for Cooper before the class field came out for the 15 lap FIII race. Lewis-Evans just 'pipped' Jim for pole position and they were quicker by far than anyone else in the field which included Bridger, Taylor, Parker, Bueb, Boshier-Jones and Strange. From the off, it was a two car race. Stuart led initially with Jim tucked in behind him. On the fourth lap, the Champion made his move, grabbing the lead and then concentrating on keeping the Kentish driver behind. Their titanic struggle took them further away from the rest as they raced around the undulating curves through the trees of the picturesque Cheshire circuit. By two thirds distance, they were over half a minute ahead of third man Bridger and still pulling away.

Suddenly, a completely unexpected factor came into the reckoning. Jim had always worn a support bandage on his right wrist and, until that day, it had never caused a problem. Trouble struck ... just as he was needing to use all his skills to keep Stuart at bay ... the bandage came undone Very quickly, it was flapping about and getting tangled up in the steering wheel. Jim was desperately trying to unwind it and, at the same time, keep the car on the road. This was inevitably causing his car to swerve from side to side and, naturally, Stuart thought Jim was deliberately baulking his efforts to pass Eventually, he managed to unravel and get rid of the troublesome bandage. Still keeping ahead of Stuart, they came into sight just inches apart for a nail-biting finish. Jim had managed to keep the lead but the gap was desperately close over the line ... a mere two tenths of a second. As soon as they had stopped, Jim got out of his car and went over to Stuart to explain about the problem. Somewhat reluctantly, Stuart accepted the story but Jim was never sure that he had been believed.

It was, nonetheless, a fantastic conclusion to another great season for him. He had won the British FIII Championship for the third successive time with eight wins, three seconds and a third place. Autosport concluded that, "It had certainly been a Russell and Cooper year again"

At the end of this season, Jim's extremely consistent mechanic, Johnny Giles, who had looked after the FIII car for three seasons, decided that he wanted to get back to the normal hours of the garage workshop. Fortunately, Mervyn Trundle, who was then in Jim's Downham Market garage workshop was happy to change places with Johnny and the arrangement suited everyone concerned.

Once again, the closed season had several occasions where he was prominent amongst the receivers of awards. In fact, at the BRSCC's Dinner Dance and prize giving evening in February, he need to make two journeys to the platform in order to collect all the Trophies he had won.

◁ *Another presentation.*

◁ *John Eason Gibson announces as Jim gets another trophy.*

◁ *Ist mine to keep! Jim gets the FIII British Championship Trophy which he won outright for three consecutive championship wins 1955, 1956 and 1957.*

▷ *Flanked by his mother and father, with brother Peter behind, Jim proudly holds the Dialy Telegraph Trophy after winning it outright.*

Ready for the 1958 FII Championship.

At the start of 1958, Jim felt it was time to move up to FII. He had won every major Trophy in FIII and had taken the FIII Championship three years running. He was now 38 years of age and for that reason alone, he was being passed by for the 'works' drives. He was receiving plenty of accolades but, as he watched his younger contemporaries getting signed up, he realised that the only way into FII for him was to run his own private team. He was well used to that in FIII, of course, and so he confidently ordered a new Cooper and sent his new mechanic, Mervyn Trundle, down to Surbiton to help build it.

In the meantime, he was approached by Robin Jackson to drive his Norton twin plug engined car in FIII. He gave the offer a considerable amount of thought. He was loathe to drive a car which was not prepared in his own workshop and, further-more, he had set his sights on moving up to FII. Jackson admitted that, with Jim as his driver, he could command more starting money. "Right", said Jim, "If I drive your car, I want a 50/50 split". Jackson said he was thinking more of 25% to the driver but Jim was adamant, pointing out that Jackson would be better off with 50% of the higher starting money. "Isn't half of £80 – £100 better than 75% of £40 – £50?" This was sufficient for Jim to get his way and, still somewhat reluctantly, he accepted the drive.

The opening event at Snetterton didn't help his confidence. Problems with the brakes in practice caused him to non-start What was worse, it was the day that his racing school entered some of their pupils in a public race for the very first time.

With the team's assurance that everything was OK, he went down to Goodwood the follow-ing week. A good start saw him in the lead ahead of Stuart Lewis-Evans and Trevor Taylor until the drive chain broke This was the first time in his entire racing career that he had ever suffered this problem. Always, with his own car, a new drive chain had been fitted for every race so that, after practice when, naturally, it had stretched, it was adjusted for the race. This had proved to be a completely reliable system. Imagine his amazement when he was told, "It shouldn't have broken ... it has only done three races".

74

The FII car was finally delivered and completed ready for Jim's first sojourn into the higher category. He certainly made sure he started at the top by entering the Aintree 200, one of the big events of the year. It was run for both FI and FII cars so that BRMs, Maseratis, Coopers and Connaughts were in the FI category with mainly Cooper and Lotus cars in the FII section. So on April 19th, he took his place on the grid. After only a brief test at Snetterton, he looked upon the race as a 'sorting out' session and set out for a finish. This he achieved, finishing eighth in the FII class in very exalted company.

Back in the FIII car at Silverstone in early May for the Daily Express International support race, he was up against all the 'big guns' in the Formula. Keeping his fingers crossed for a trouble free meeting, he had a good practice session, which saw him second on the grid to Stuart Lewis-Evans with Don Parker next to him. It was these three who fought for the lead most of the time. Stuart got away first but Parker headed them on the second lap. The third time they passed the pits, Jim was in front with Lewis-Evans pressuring him. These two began to pull away from Parker and for most of the remainder of the race they 'swapped' the lead. Suddenly, Jim found himself alone when Stuart stopped with an engine problem, leaving the Champion to cruise to victory in front of the huge crowd. On his lap of honour, he was waving to the crowd and thinking, "Thank goodness I had no trouble with the car", when a wishbone broke.

Saturday 5th July saw him arrive at Crystal Palace with fingers crossed that the car wouldn't let him down. All his usual rivals were present for this, the Redex Challenge Trophy race for FIII cars. In addition, he was competing in the Anerley Trophy for FII cars, so a busy day was ahead.

Setting off from the front row in fine style, he was mixing it with Don Parker and Trevor Taylor before taking over the lead and setting a new lap record. His joy was short-lived as trouble struck on the fifth lap when the carburettors became loose and started to fall off the engine. Steadily losing power, he sat helplessly driving his slowing down car as Taylor, Parker, Bridger, Raby and finally, Jack

Don Parker's wife admires the cartoon work of the Daily Mirror's Salon whose caracature of Jim was one of a set of all the top drivers at the time.

Newton all went by leaving him to slowly finish in sixth place. He was completely dejected with the situation and, on returning to the pits, had a long serious talk with the team about the future.

The day was far from a failure, however. Not only was the fastest lap outstanding as it had been set in drizzling rain, his FII races gave him a lot of satisfaction. There were two 10 lap

races that day and he made a storming start in the first one from the outside of the front row to lead pole man Ivor Bueb and the rest. That was the way it stayed as he warded off Ivor's every attempt to wrest the lead from him. He took the flag just over a second ahead of this long-time friend and rival. Things were somewhat different in the second 10 lap part of the Anerley Trophy. Sid Jenson shot into the lead with Bueb also getting the drop on Jim. Despite all efforts, the order remained unchanged to the finish but Jim had the satisfaction of setting his fastest lap of the day and, on aggregate, finished third in the Trophy results.

Next came the prestigious support race at the British Grand Prix meeting a week later. Jim wanted to race at Silverstone and, in fact, was entered, but the way Robin Jackson's car was letting him down made him very wary. Finally, he decided to withdraw his entry and give the team more time to prepare the car for the next event at Brands Hatch. It was a frustrated Russell who saw his arch-rival, Lewis-Evans, take the Silverstone win.

'Teething troubles' with the new FII car put him out on the second lap of the Vanwall Trophy race at Snetterton in late July which meant a busy time for his mechanics in readiness for the big August Monday meeting at Brands Hatch. He was in for a busy day with drives in both FIII and FII. He was particularly on his mettle in the FIII event for the World's Sports Trophy as he had won it every year since 1954, the year he beat Stirling Moss against the odds Starting as he meant to go on, he promptly saw off the efforts of Bridger, Lewis-Evans and Parker to win his heat adding the fastest lap for good value. He started so strongly in the final that he had posted the fastest lap again on only the second lap All kinds of dramas came on the following lap, culminating for Jim when he ran over Tommy Bridger's wheel which cut a brake pipe on his car and caused his immediate retirement from the race.

However, the main event was yet to come. This was the Kent Trophy for FII cars and he was competing with some of the top drivers who had been racing in this category for a long time. In fact, he stayed right with the two leaders, Jack Brabham and Stuart Lewis-Evans, who had been racing in FII since early 1957. He held onto third place just behind them for the entire 21 laps. Looking set to repeat this performance in the second heat, he was again in third place when his efforts were brought to a sudden halt with a broken crown wheel and pinion. Even so, he had proved himself to be more than competitive in the formula.

An even more important date was the next one, again at Brands Hatch, at the end of the month. This was the famous Kentish 100, the entry for which contained a number of Grand Prix drivers in addition to the regular FII brigade. This time the two heats were 42 laps long, in order to make the 100 miles. The first heat was led away by Jack Brabham with Stirling Moss and Stuart Lewis-Evans next. Jim was in a fantastic fourth place ahead of such notabilities as Graham Hill, Bruce McLaren, Harry Schell, Carroll Shelby and Cliff Allison to name just a few of the big field. Despite all attempts and much lapping of slower cars, Jim clung to fourth all the way to the finish.

◁ *Jim and Jack always good friends in the paddock.*

Both Moss and Jim made poor starts in the second heat. The former was down in fifth and Jim was a lowly twelfth at the end of the first lap. As Moss moved up the order to lead and finally win, Jim was having no regard for the big names as he passed Harry Schell, Bruce McLaren, Roy Salvadori, Ivor Bueb and George Wicken. In fact, he had lapped them all by the end of the race and, after passing Graham Hill for fifth position, he 'diced' for several laps with Cliff Allison, before taking him for fourth place. This was where he finished, again following home the same seasoned trio as in the first heat. Now, after racing with and beating many of the current Grand Prix brigade, he had definitely arrived in Formula II. It was after following

Jim joins Ivor for the lap of honour after their titanic 'David and Goaliath' race at Snetterton.

Graham Hill in this race that he went up to the future World Champion to tell him that he deserved a better car than the one he was driving that day. "Nice of you to say so, Jim", said Graham, obviously pleasantly surprised to get such a genuine comment from one of his fellow drivers.

Although he had practised with his new FII car at his local Snetterton circuit, it was Sunday 7th September before he actually raced it for the first time in front of his local fans. And what a race it turned out to be It was a 15 lap (about 40 miles) Formula Libre race, which meant that, although it was open to virtually anything, the main contenders were in big engined sports cars and FII cars. Jim put the 'cat amongst the pigeons' by setting the fastest lap in practice to claim pole position for the race, which was no mean achievement for a 1500cc car in such company. In fact, Ivor Bueb was next to

him in the 3442cc Lister Jaguar with Tommy Bridger and Bruce McLaren next up, also in FII Coopers. It augured well for the first ever Archie Scott-Brown Memorial Trophy for which Archie's mother was to present one of her son's trophies. They certainly did the memory of that brave little driver credit with a fantastic race. From the off, Ivor powered into the lead with Jim tucked in behind him. From then on, it was Ivor on the straights, using the brute force of his large engine to lead, while Jim's race craft and the nimbleness of the little Cooper gave him the advantage on the corners. For lap after lap, the large crowd were treated to motor racing at its best as the two great friends swapped places throughout the race. Their scrap took them further and further from the rest of the field ... in fact McLaren was over half a minute adrift in third place at the finish. On the last lap, Jim led onto the straight out of Coram but could do nothing as Ivor swept past to the line. A mere four tenths of a second separated them to round off what Autosport reported had been 'real motor racing'. Jim jumped out of his car to run to Ivor and congratulate him, while Brian Lister, manufacturer and owner of Ivor's car, was quick to praise them both. He insisted that Jim jump into the passenger side of the Lister-Jaguar for the lap of honour. As Ivor drove round, the huge crowd were so eager to show their appreciation of the 'David and Goliath' battle that, for the first time ever, they jumped over the banks to stand and applaud both drivers. It proved to be one of the slowest laps of honour at the Norfolk circuit as Ivor slowly moved through the mass of people It had been the fastest race ever at Snetterton and was almost a repeat of their fastest FIII 'epic' at Brands Hatch.

His first ever Continental FII race was at Avus. Designated the German Grand Prix, although it was for 1500cc Formula II cars, the organisers, for reasons best known to themselves, allowed Masten Gregory to start in a streamlined Porsche 2 litre sports car So in both parts of the race, Gregory went off to lead his own one car section, while the others got on with the race proper Avus was a very fast circuit comprising two miles of a dual carriageway with a first gear hairpin at one end and the infamous banking at the other. The straights were just about wide enough for two cars to race side by side but three cars abreast became very 'hairy'. On one occasion, Jim was braking hard for the hairpin when George Wicken and Cliff Allison came by him one each side and obviously going far too fast Suddenly realising their mistake, they both braked heavily and collided to fly off each side of the circuit Jim had to take some quick avoiding action and thankfully they were both unhurt.

For a long time, the first 100 mile race was a three car scrap with Brabham, Bruce McLaren and Jim 'swapping' places at over 150 mph on the straights. Suddenly, Bruce, who was just leading at the time, struck trouble when his engine threw a con-rod. As he slowed dramatically, Jim, who was side by side with Brabham, managed to swerve and avoid him.

Bruce then exemplified something Jim was later to stress at the school to the students ... after travelling for some time at high speeds, you lose all sense of how fast you are actually travelling. Bruce thought he had almost slowed to a walking pace and pulled onto the grass verge at about 80 mph He was very lucky as the car nearly rolled over.

Jim eventually beat Jack by about a length in the first race and when they lined up for the second part, several cars were missing. So, once again, it became a Russell/Brabham duel. Each lap they would streamline each other on the straights. In those days this took effect from about 60 yards behind the leading car. Both drivers were aware that they had to be second on the last lap to win the race and Jim started to plan his strategy, as no doubt Jack did Using four trees, which were spread out on the back straight as markers, he tried various manoeuvres. Trying the first tree caused Jack to move over and Jim knew if he took the lead, Jack would have room to repass him before the final fast corner. If that happened, Jim would have no time to retake the lead before the finish. After several more attempts, he realised that the third tree would be the one to use. All the time, Jack was trying to get him to lead but Jim was having none of that. Jack was furious and on the last lap slowed right down at the hairpin. Jim did likewise so Jack put up his hand and stopped completely. Jim immediately followed suit and, probably for the first time in any race, the leading two cars were stationary, with only a short distance to the finish. They sat looking across and waving at each other to continue. "After you, Sir" yelled Jim – almost a prediction of Jack's knighthood to come years later. They were so far ahead of the rest of the field that there was no danger of anyone else coming by to take the race. "Come on Jack, you bugger", shouted Jim. "You bastard", retorted Jack before reluctantly accepting the position and moving off. It all worked out as planned from then on, Jim using the third tree 'drafted' past Jack to win by about six lengths. This gave him the aggregate victory for the two races.

A couple of weeks later at Montlhery, it was the same story. Jack asked to borrow a set of 'scrubbed in' tyres. Jim needed a second gear so they did an exchange of favours. After a dry practice, it was wet for the race. Jim tried hard to get away cleanly from his pole position on the front row and succeeded. The circuit was rather like Avus with the dual carriageway and an even tighter hairpin. Again, there were no markers, so Jim looked to use trees, as before. During the dry practice, he had used the last of the five, so in the wet he decided to use the first one. Too late, he realised even that was not soon enough as he spun in front of the other front runners. Somehow, they all missed him and by the time he had recovered, he was back in sixth place He spent the rest of the 20 lap race fighting his way back to the front and ended up winning by some 19 seconds from Brabham. By so doing, he became the first Englishman to ever win the Coup de Salon ... and, furthermore, he had done so after only a season in Formula II Later, he had the honour of being awarded both the Benoit Musy Memorial Trophy and the Dunlop Trophy for this achievement.

Anti-climax was to come when, through a mix-up, he was not able to take part in the final round of the FII Championship at Casablanca in late October. Someone made a mistake and failed to apply for Jim's entry. Much to his disappointment, he had to miss the race, knowing full well that, if he had raced and won, he could have ended up as the FII Champion in his first year in the formula On the other hand, he was very saddened when his long-time protagonist, Stuart Lewis-Evans, died following a very bad accident while driving in the Formula I section of the race.

1958 had been a season of mixed fortunes, the downside had mainly been caused by car failures in FIII, which made him even more determined to revert to only driving cars prepared in his own workshops. Nevertheless, he was heartened by finishing third in FII after a shortened programme.

Intent on concentrating only on FII and sports car racing in 1959, the Cooper Climax FII car was updated with new disc brakes and other modifications. One of the first of the new Cooper Monaco sports cars was also purchased. Mervyn Trundle was entrusted with preparing and

△ *Leading Jack home to win the second part after their unique stop/start fight.*

▷ *Receiving the Daimler Benz Silver Salver for the Avus win.*

△ Jim (No8) starts from pole
position for the FII Coupe de Salon.

◁ The presentation of the
start/finish line...

maintaining the FII car while 'Pip' Preece, previously Ivor Bueb's mechanic, joined to look after the sports car.

The opening meeting of the season was at Snetterton on March 22nd and a couple of days before the meeting, Jim had his first run in the Monaco. It was mightily impressive. During this practice, he clocked a time of 1 minute 41.2 seconds which at 96.05 mph was faster than the outright circuit record of 95.6 mph held by Archie Scott-Brown in a Formula I Connaught So it was no wonder that Jim was eagerly looking forward to his first race in the new sports car. Sadly, it was not to be. The day turned out to be a very wet and miserable one and, as the Monaco had never been tested in the wet, it was withdrawn from the sports car race leaving Jim to concentrate on driving the FII car in the Formula Libre race.

The afternoon had started with the unveiling of the new scrutinising bay, erected and named in honour of the other hero of Snetterton, Archie Scott-Brown. He had overcome the problems of being disabled on his way to achieving many racing successes both at his home circuit and elsewhere. It was ironical that, having tried for years to be allowed to race on the continent, he was killed at Spa on his first visit to that circuit. His father was present for the ceremony and sometime later contacted the school as he wanted to drive a racing car. He explained that he had always wanted to get a better understanding of the sport which had been his son's all-consuming passion. Despite his advancing years, he duly came to the school and completed a trial lesson

The rain had stopped before the Formula Libre race got under way but the circuit was still extremely treacherous. This had no effect whatsoever on Jim that afternoon. Almost effortlessly, he pulled well away from the start, building up a huge lead over Ron Flockhart and John Bekaert, both very experienced drivers in the much bigger engined Lister-Jaguars. Any thoughts the

... *is repeated later at the reception.*

crowd might have had that day about a repeat of the Russell/Bueb tussle the previous Autumn were quickly dispelled by Jim's masterly display. The 10 laps quickly flew by as, not putting a foot wrong, he sped to victory. It came as no surprise for the crowd to hear that he had, once again, set the fastest lap. This, despite the adverse conditions, was just a touch under 90 mph. Not a bad start to the season.

Cliff Davis was a better than average sports car driver who was renowned for his off-track escapades and especially his annual 'staff dinner'. The large crowd invited to these highly popular nights belied the fact that his staff could actually be counted on one hand A real 'stag' night, it was one of the most popular off-season events for the motor racing fraternity. It was always attended by hosts of racing drivers, with many more trying to get an invitation. Cliff tried each year to make things more outrageous than before with such things, for instance, as bread rolls specially made to resemble male private parts Jim had received a telephone call from Cliff before the season started to ask him to take part in a special celebrity stock car race at West Ham Stadium on Good Friday. The stock car organisers were putting up a trophy and Cliff had been asked to get six well-known drivers to compete for it. Apart from himself and Count Steve Ouvaroff, who worked for him as a car salesman, he had Graham Hill, George Wicken, Dennis Taylor and Jim lined up for the event. As Easter grew nearer, Jim began to change his mind. He was more concerned with the big Goodwood meeting for which he was taking both the Monaco and the FII car. As he drove down the Good Friday evening, he decided not to risk things for the next day's very important practice at Goodwood. He left his racing overalls and helmet in his car and went to join the others They were all looking down at a race in progress and the more Jim saw the way the cars were colliding with the occasional one rolling over, the less he liked the idea. "Come on, Jim", the others said. "Get your gear on." "No way" was the reply. "There's Goodwood tomorrow and this looks too risky by far" However, the others were very persuasive, pointing out that people such as Daphne Arnott, for whom Jim had raced at Le Mans, and her designer, George Thornton, were present. Other celebrities there included the famous golfer, Harry Weetman and comedian Charlie Drake. Under pressure, Jim agreed to race and an old set of overalls with a helmet appeared from nowhere. The comments being made as they were changing

didn't help matters as the general idea was obviously going to be to chase the leader and hit his car as much as possible. Jim said, "I've never had a drink before racing but I'm going to have one tonight" One of the organisers heard this and within seconds arrived with a Scotch which was quickly disposed of before they were all taken down to the pits to get into the cars.

Doug Wardropper, who later formed the very successful Scholar engine concern, was a star stock car driver at the time. He jokingly said to Jim, "If I let you drive my car, will you let me drive your FII car at Snetterton?" This brought a quick, "You must be joking", before some of the differences were pointed out. "Firstly, the doors are welded ... you have to climb in and out through the windows. Furthermore, there are no brakes and the back axle is locked" Jim said, "Tell me how to start the thing before I climb out again".

There was no practice and the six of them were brought out to line up opposite the main grandstand. "Right, Gentlemen", said the starter. "I shall fire a rocket to start the race" As one, they all made for the first corner and Jim found himself in the lead. As he turned, he was feeling bump after bump at the back of his car as his pursuers did their best to punt him off There was only one thing for it. He had to get away and, with his foot to the floorboards, he did just that. For a while, he could see shadows out of the corner of his eye and thought he hadn't shaken them off. Then he realised that they were the shadows from his own car flashing past the stadium lights After a couple of laps, he could see the others coming up the other side of the

Jim gets the trophy at his only stock car race.

... and goes on the traditional lap of honour on the back of a pick-up truck!

oval so he knew that he had completely broken clear. All he had to do was to reel off the rest of the laps and win with ease some half a lap ahead of everyone else. The race had seemed much longer than 12 laps and he was glad to be helped out of the car's window before going up the steps for the presentation. Harry Weetman presented him with the Road Racers Trophy before joining him on the back of the Land Rover for a lap of honour complete with the Trophy and Chequered flag. It turned out to be quite a good evening, after all.

◁ *In action in the new Cooper Monaco sports car.*

After the light-hearted fun, they all journeyed down to Goodwood for the busy weekend which started with official practice on the Saturday and Jim caused quite a few eyebrows to lift as he proceeded to beat the 2 litre sports car record by over a second in his Cooper Monaco. On the Monday, however, the weather put paid to any record breaking. A cloudburst, combined with a hailstorm, dampened the proceedings well and truly. As Brabham led away in the FII Lavant Cup race, Jim and Bruce McLaren disputed second place. By the second lap, the Russell Cooper had disposed of McLaren and was right with Brabham but Salvadori was moving up and before the end, he had demoted Jim to third place with Graham Hill's Lotus in fourth.

It was still very wet for the 21 lap sports car race. From the Le Mans start, three big engine cars headed the field with Jim next up leading the 2 litre brigade. A couple of laps later and mechanical trouble struck causing him to retire for the day.

The weather was even worse for the British Empire Trophy at Oulton Park in April. Again, Jim had taken both cars as there was also an unlimited sports car race following the main event. The cars came out for the FII race; it started to drizzle. Soon, it was raining heavily. No-one was taking chances and for the first few laps, Jim was in fifth place. As the weather worsened, he began to attack. Moving past Tim Parnell, he began to pressure Tony Marsh for third place. Autosport reported that he had now acquired his well-known intent look. When Jack Brabham struck trouble, he inherited third place and was soon passing Tony Marsh for second, before hounding leader, Bruce Halford. It took only a couple more laps for him to take the lead and start to pull away ... by middle distance, he was some 18 seconds clear. Halford retired with gear box troubles and, with 10 laps to go, Jim was over 30 seconds clear of Marsh with Bueb, McLaren, Naylor and Salvadori in the minor places. Fastest lap was also his with an average speed of 78.76 mph. It wasn't until he had completed his cooling down lap, however, that he knew he had won In those days, of course, chalk was used to write messages on the lap boards held out for drivers and these were being obliterated by the rain before Jim could read them So he was completely unaware that Brabham had pulled out and he had been chasing a non-existent leader for most of the race.

With hardly any respite, most of them climbed into their sports cars for the next event ... the Unlimited Sports Car Race. Once again, it was a race with bigger engine cars against the 2 litre Cooper Monacos (Jim and Brabham) and the Graham Hill driven 'works' Lotus. Initially, Salvadori led with the 2.5 litre Cooper Maserati followed by the two Monacos. On the fourth lap, Jim took second from Brabham and proceeded to take the lead from Salvadori two laps later. With an average speed of over 80 mph, he continued to lead, pulling away all the time until he took the chequered flag some eleven seconds ahead of Salvadori with Brabham and Hill next up. His masterful driving in the wet had seen him beat his much more experienced opponents again and complete a brilliant double. No wonder he was dubbed 'Rain Master Russell' by most of the national press.

86

Roy Salvadori, Jim and Jack Brabham line up on the front row at Oulton Park for the British Empire Trophy in 1959 before Jim's win.

Because of his disagreement, and probably his age, he had been overlooked for a 'works' Cooper drive. He was now beginning to show the world that, with his own privately-owned Coopers prepared in his own workshops, he could take them all on and beat them, at 39 years of age After he had walked away from the Cooper team, it gave him great pleasure to have beaten the 'works' drivers in his own cars. He had certainly proved why he had not been prepared to be treated as a number 2 driver.

After his truly masterful display in the atrocious weather at Oulton Park, this point was further emphasised when he was called to the phone while instructing at Snetterton the very next day. It was Colin Chapman who offered Jim a very special deal. "You can have my 'works' Lotus FII and sports car which you can keep and prepare in your workshops", said the Lotus boss. Jim had never heard of him ever making such an offer before and felt very honoured. Just the same, he turned it down. "Thanks very much, Colin", he replied. "I really do appreciate the deal but I would rather stay as I am now with my own two Coopers." He often thought about the offer and wondered what might have been the outcome if he had accepted.

At the start of the season, the Dunlop Tyre Company offered Jim a deal to use their tyres. They would give him 50% off the price to race on their products. He wasn't too happy with this offer for his private team, considering that he had been getting 75% discount as a 'works' driver previously. He discussed the matter with his brother Peter who said, "Hold on for the moment, let me work on it". Sure enough, Peter's contacts in the trade paid off. He had a chat with Jack Thompson of CTS, the tyre distributors in Norwich, who in turn contacted their suppliers, Continental Tyres. The outcome was an offer from the German company to supply Jim with their products free of charge. Naturally, the offer was accepted and Jim raced on their tyres. One of the only drawbacks was that Jim didn't qualify for the £100 award given for an all British car winning the British Empire Trophy.

This was rectified when Jim was invited to bring his car and the British Empire Trophy to the Norwich Speedway Stadium one evening shortly after winning it. Jack Thompson was a Director of the Stadium and had arranged the event. There, he was presented to the crowd and he drove his FII Cooper round on a slow lap of honour waving the Trophy It didn't end there as the story of Jim missing out on the special award for an all British car had reached the ears of the Continental Tyres people. They had flown over a representative who presented him with a cheque for £100 saying, "Here's the amount you missed by using our tyres" No-one could understand why Jack Thompson hadn't turned up for the occasion he had arranged. It later transpired that, rushing to get ready, he had accidentally cut his ear so badly while shaving that, try as he might, he hadn't been able to stop the bleeding until it was too late to go.

Jim had also won the Siam Trophy for setting the fastest lap. It was a striking silver model of three elephants holding up a bowl with their trunks and was admired by everyone. It was already steeped in history as pre-war, it had been called the Bangkok Cup, made by Niello, silversmiths to His Siamese Majesty, and presented originally by the Thai Nakon Company of Bangkok. It had been won outright in the 30s by Prince B Bira, Siam's famous international driver who had been presented with no less than three Gold Stars, their highest award, by the British Racing Drivers Club. He had given the famous trophy to the club to present as one of their perpetual awards.

Obviously Jim was delighted to have such a special trophy in his home for the following twelve months. Brother Peter, looking closely at it, saw the maker's name and wrote to them asking if they could make a smaller replica for Jim to keep. To the brothers' delight, the answer was in the affirmative and Peter confirmed his order, pointing out that he would like it to be inscribed with Jim's name. They obviously didn't understand English as well as Peter had

Jim, Ivor and Tommy Sopwith on the front row for the 1100 c.c. Sports Car race at Crystal Palace.

expected so that when it arrived, 'P Russell' was engraved on it. Never changed, it has stayed in Jim's trophy room with that inscription ever since.

The following weekend's Aintree International 200 was run for both FI and FII cars. Naturally, FI cars filled the first three rows of the grid but Jim was next, heading the FII times. Masten Gregory's FI Cooper was on pole position (the only car to get under a 2 minute time for the circuit) with Jean Behra's Ferrari and Harry Schell's BRM alongside. Moss and Salvadori's FI Coopers were only on the row ahead of Jim. Amazingly, Roy's time in the FI Cooper was only 3 seconds faster than Jim's time in the FII Cooper He headed a star studded entry including Ivor Bueb, Bruce McLaren, Michael Taylor, Dennis Taylor, Jack Fairman, Maurice Trintignant, George Wicken and Graham Hill. The FI section went ahead with their own race which eventually went to the lone Ferrari. The FII race within a race soon became a Russell/Bueb squabble and, for 10 glorious laps, they kept the huge crowd enthralled. Suddenly, the clutch failed on Jim's car and he was out of the reckoning leaving Ivor to win the class.

It was definitely not Jim's day ... after beating the outright sports car circuit record in the Cooper Monaco during practice, his front row start in the race came to nought. On the very first lap he suffered his second clutch failure of the day and another immediate retirement. So a very disappointed team packed up and headed home. There was much work to do overnight as they were due at Snetterton the very next day. It was very important for Jim to be there, not only to race but the 'headmaster' needed to oversee the 18 school pupils who were also racing that day. All in all, it was quite an important date. It saw the very first appearance of the new Formula Junior cars – albeit in the end only two arrived and, instead of their own separate race, they were put into the Formula Libre event. Even then, only one, the Elva, was able to compete. The other one, the Moorland, was driven on one demonstration lap and the privileged driver was J B Alderslade, a Jim Russell School graduate.

The 'icing on the cake' was provided by Jim whose scintillating drive in the Formula Libre race created quite a stir. Not only did he win the first part of his two part race and, in doing so head home the mighty Lister-Jaguar of John Bekaert, he also broke the outright lap record for Snetterton. Considering that it had been previously held by the Formula I Connaught of Archie Scott-Brown, it was a tremendous feat and left the record at a staggering 96.05 mph.

After a couple of week's respite, giving the mechanics a chance to overhaul and prepare the cars, it was time for another big meeting. This was the Silverstone International Trophy, acknowledged as only second in importance to the British Grand Prix meeting. As usual, it spread over three days with practice on Thursday and Friday before a very full programme of races on Saturday May 2nd. The main event was again for both FI and FII cars. It had attracted a truly International field which included two Ferraris, for Tony Brooks and Phil Hill, Stirling Moss and Ron Flockhart in the BRMs and Jack Brabham, the eventual FI section winner, in the 'works'. 2.5 Cooper. It also saw the debut of the new FI Aston Martins in the hands of Carroll Shelby and Roy Salvadori.

The FII section was also well supported with Jim's Cooper lined up against Bruce McLaren, Ivor Bueb, Tony Marsh and Bill Moss amongst others in Coopers and Innes Ireland in the Lotus. Jim proved to be fastest in practice on both days. On Thursday, he was only 0.2 seconds behind Hill's Ferrari However, the gap was a little more the next day but Jim still headed the FII brigade on the grid for the race.

Five times World Champion, Juan

Overtaking Horace Gould in the FII car at Silverstone 1959.

Manuel Fangio, was given a great ovation by the enormous crowd as he helicoptered in and was driven around the circuit in an open Land Rover before dropping the flag to start the main event. As Brabham and Moss disputed the FI section, Jim headed McLaren and Ireland in the FII class. The order remained the same for most of the first half of the race but Jim was pulling further away all the time. McLaren's 'works' Cooper came to a halt with 10 laps to go and Ivor Bueb had passed Ireland to be second in class. With a couple of laps to the finish, Shelby's engine expired and the Aston Martin rolled to a stop at Stowe Corner. This moved Hill up to fourth, Jack Fairman's Cooper to fifth and Jim, who was next up became a crowd-pleasing sixth overall He had, of course, handsomely won the FII class, some half a minute ahead of Bueb and had set the fastest FII lap time which equalled the outright lap record for the class On his cooling down lap, he stopped at Stowe to collect Shelby, giving him a shoulder-lift back to the pits. This was a popular way of bringing back a fellow stranded driver in those days when the uncluttered design of the cars allowed one driver to sit on the shoulders of the other in 'piggy-back' style.

It looked as if the Russell Cooper Monaco would make a big impression in the up-to-3 litre sports car race when it came round at the end of the first lap in the leading bunch. Considering that his engine was only about half the size of the other leaders, he was causing quite a few raised eyebrows Confounding the sceptics, he stayed right them for several laps until, suddenly, something broke and he had to retire. So it was with mixed feelings that the team packed up and went home.

Crystal Palace meetings always seemed to generate a special excitement. Probably it was the fact that the very narrow circuit meant that overtaking was mostly difficult and, when it was successfully carried out, gave the driver a special satisfaction. The foreboding outer walls, lined with their unforgiving railway sleepers kept everybody sharp. No wonder practise was so important as a good grid position was essential. The almost rectangular 1 mile circuit was also unique for spectators. It was the only one in the country which was set in a city park so public transport was readily available right outside the gates. Furthermore, there were normally only four meetings held each year making each one a little more special.

Just about all the current leading drivers descended on the little London circuit for the Whitsun meeting and Jim had both cars present. Practising for the sports car race, his Monaco was one of four cars to post times under the existing lap record.

He did even better in the FII car to claim pole position for the 36 lap London Trophy race. Salvadori, Bueb and Bristow were next up and shared the front row of the grid with him. It was Bueb who made a storming start with Salvadori also getting away ahead of Jim. At the end of the second lap, he had managed to squeeze past Salvadori and start to close on Ivor. After several laps, he was right on Ivor's tail but Roy was also making up ground and, in one desperate move, he got past them both. A lap later, Jim had taken Ivor. Now he was back in second place and started to relentlessly hound Roy for lap after lap. Finally, on lap 16, he saw his chance and swept into the lead. His joy, however, was short-lived as he went missing on the very last lap ... the clutch, which had suddenly failed to disengage, took him out just when he looked all set to stay ahead to the finish.

The unlimited sports car race was next and many of the drivers just had time to change over cars for this one. The 2.5 litre cars of Salvadori (Cooper Maserati) and Hill (Lotus) had Jim and Bristow alongside (both in 2 litre Monacos). Jim slotted into second place behind Salvadori and ahead of Hill. The three of them were absolutely tied together as they raced around the narrow circuit. Halfway, Hill slithered his way past Jim whose third place meant that he was again the leading 2 litre car as they finished in close formation.

Back at Snetterton for a West Essex CC meeting a couple of weeks later, he was entered in the Formula Libre race. Before the race, he was presented with a special trophy by the Snetterton Motor Club for his amazing record of holding no less than 5 lap records at the circuit. This unique list included FIII, FII, 2 litre sports cars, unlimited sports cars and the outright lap record It was obvious why he had been dubbed 'King of Snetterton' and proof, if needed, to all the pupils of the school that they had the right chief instructor.

He was on pole for this race, despite the presence of several 3.8 litre engine cars. In fact, it was the 3.8 Lister-Jaguar of John Bekaert which shot into the lead while Jim made a tardy start for once, leaving him way back. He was soon 'on song' however, and making up time 'hand over fist'. By the third lap, he was breathing down Bekaert's exhaust and had swept past him as they started the fourth lap. From then on, he steadily increased his lead until the flag. A fastest lap of 95.11 mph completed his satisfactory day.

He now concentrated all his and the team's efforts on the impending Le Mans 24 hour race. He was once again on speaking terms with John Cooper. He had surprised John by telling him that he thought the Monaco was the best Cooper he had ever driven and willingly agreed to John's request that he enter his car as a 'Cooper entry' at Le Mans. The entry was accepted and Jack Brabham had arranged to co-drive with him. When Jack had to cry off due to another commitment, he approached Bruce McLaren who gladly accepted the opportunity. There was plenty of work for the team to do as, in addition to preparing the Cooper Monaco for the long distance 24 hour race, they had to prepare the FII car as well. The plan was to go straight on from Le Mans to Clermont Ferrand in Southern France for the next round of the FII Championship. This was to take place a week later and, if Jim could win that one, he was almost certain to become the 1959 FII Champion.

Jim was still a frequent visitor to the Doric in Attleborough and regularly met a trio of friends from the locality. Jokingly known as the 'Three Musketeers', Bill Richardson, Malcolm (Harry) Broom and Tony Mullins had become three of Jim's big fans. So when one evening he asked if they would like to go to Le Mans, they jumped at the chance. They joined the Monaco and FII car on the transporter and headed for France in mid-June.

92

Tony was a commercial artist and had made them all Tyrolean type hats out of trilbys with the brims cut off, which were adorned with bright ribbons. They wore these all the time and, naturally, attracted a lot of attention. This led to quite a few French people mistaking them for drivers ... Jim and Bruce thought this was great and 'egged' them on to sign autographs.

They became part of the signalling crew and on one occasion during practice, knowing that Jim was in the pits, hung out his board with some outrageously fast times. Before long, the commentators were reporting this and really getting to the other teams until the hoax was realised.

Bruce McLaren and Jim relax in the Le Mans paddock 1959.

Although they had run out of money at Le Mans, Jim had already offered to take them on to the FII meeting which, of course, was not to be.

However, despite the fun, the Russell/McLaren Cooper was making everyone sit up and take notice. Going quicker and quicker, Jim set a phenomenally fast time of 4m 13.6 seconds to give the 'works' Ferrari team, who were the 2 litre class favourites, a severe shock.

Unfortunately, the advantage gained came to nought in the race as Jim's worst fears were realised. The Cooper engine could never be relied upon to 'fire' up at the first attempt. It was always a gamble and he quietly prayed that it was going to be all right as he ran across the road for the traditional Le Mans start ... for many years this method was used where the cars were in one 'echeloned' line and the drivers stood across from them, running to their cockpits after the flag had dropped. There were no seat belts in those days He leapt in and tried to start the car but to his utter dismay, it wouldn't start. All the other cars were getting away as he tried again and again. Still he sat in the stationary Cooper until all the other 52 cars had gone. Then, suddenly, first one, then two, and finally all the cylinders sprang into life He had lost a valuable 50 seconds and was the very last car By now, he was seething over the set-back and set off, driving like a man inspired, to make up for lost time. He was the sensation of the opening laps, passing no less than 24 cars on the very first tour He made up another four places on the next lap as he chased after the leader of the class. The advantage gained by his fastest practice lap in class had been lost through no fault of his own and he was relentlessly making up time. By 9 pm, continued progress had brought the car into third place in class and it was looking all set for a sensational result. It had certainly caught the imagination of the commentators and one of them, John Bolster of the BBC, was actually forecasting that this little private team could even win the race.

With the Monaco before the
Le Mans 1959 start.

... Not long to go now.

Drivers and mechanics
have their last minute
discussions.

Jim waits (on left) for the
flag to drop for the dash to
the cars ...

... jumping into the cockpit.

... when success turned
sour...the debacle at the
White House ...

... the remains of the
Monaco after the circuit
had been cleared.

Then, just before 10 pm, disaster struck as Jim rounded the infamous White House corner. As already recorded, the accident, not of Jim's making, effectively brought his brilliant racing career to an end. Furthermore, it prevented him from continuing in the FII Championship, which he was looking a very good bet to win, and going into FI Grand Prix racing the following year. At that very time, Cooper-Climax were building up a new FI engine for Jim to fit into his Cooper chassis for this purpose at the end of the season.

That would certainly have broken new ground on two counts ... they had never done that for a privateer before and Jim would have started Grand Prix racing at the age of 40.

One wall of Jim's trophy room. 1959.

Ivor Bueb had become a very good friend of Jim's by now, despite their hard fought races. They had already formulated plans for 1960. With Jim's aim to go into Formula I, they planned to share the Monaco in some long distance sports car races. In addition, they had discussed plans for Ivor to join the school as a Director/Instructor. He had agreed to move to Norfolk during the closed season but it was not to be.

Ironically, he was killed at the very Clermont Ferrand FII race which Jim had been forced to miss due to his Le Mans accident.

During the year, Jim had been offered a drive in the Coronation Safari Rally. Because of his commitments to Esso, he had turned down the chance of the Mercedes drive. When he was in the hospital bed after the accident, he watched a film of the rally which showed the Mercedes winning.

Between 1953 and 1959, Jim was British FIII Champion three times and won 64 FIII races, 11 FII races and 6 Sports Car races. He also took 22 second places and 19 third places resulting in his finishing in the top three no less than 121 times out of a total of 135 races He also set over 50 fastest laps and over 20 lap records during this time.

▷ *How it all began ... a well wisher, Jim Wally Ward and Johnny Giles with the school's first 'fleet' of cars.*

Chapter 5 *A School Is Born*

Claude Martin, a farmer from Downham Market, was indirectly responsible for the start of the Jim Russell Racing Drivers School. He was having a drink in the town's Castle Hotel late in 1956 and had asked Jim, "How do you get into motor racing?" "Well", replied Jim, "You buy a racing car ... say a 500cc FIII car that will cost you about £700 – £800, then you're lucky because you've got me around to help you". "Hold on a minute", said Claude. "I haven't got that kind of money" "So sell your TR2 and buy a cheap ex-Army utility pick-up – then you can put down the deposit on a racing car". Claude didn't like the idea of taking his girlfriend out in a pick-up and soon dropped the subject.

However, it got Jim thinking about the many people who wanted to get into a racing car but didn't have the money to buy one. After many discussions with friend, Wally Ward, it was decided to start a racing school. As Jim was already committed to his racing, Wally agreed to run the school and Jim would instruct when he wasn't racing. They contacted Oliver Sear, who was running Snetterton circuit, and arranged a meeting at his house. Jim, Wally and Jim's brother-in-law, Dick Dack, went along armed with a quantity of beer Oliver was happy with the idea of a racing school and agreed that they could run at weekends when there were no race meetings. Rent was discussed and agreed at £2.10.0 (old money) or £5 for the whole weekend "Fine", said Jim, "Now everything looks good ... how much are we each going to put in to start

it off?" Oliver and Dick were aghast. They hadn't thought that way, figuring that student's joining fees would give them the necessary cashflow. Jim had to point out that money was needed to pay for cars and advertising before they could get any customers. He estimated that they would need about £5,000 Everything went quiet and the meeting soon 'fizzled out'. Finishing off their drinks, they all went home.

Wally Ward, much to his credit, hadn't dismissed the idea. The very next day, he went to Jim with a proposition. "I haven't got any money but if I put my road car on hire purchase, I could invest the proceeds into the new school", he said. This was agreed and he was able to put £600 in which, together with Jim's initial £2,000, started them off. The world's first ever racing drivers school was launched in May 1957.

Rudy Gates became the school's mechanic to look after the odd trio of cars which were assembled for the first trial day ... Jim bought an 1100cc Cooper Climax and a Triumph TR2. Jim used to drive for London enthusiast Daphne Arnott and she, hearing of Jim's plans, donated one of her old FIII 500cc cars.

With the cars in place, an advertising campaign was started aimed mainly at motor clubs, RAF camps and farmers. To their delight, about 40 people turned up for the first trial day. Everyone was given two drives – one in the morning and one in the afternoon. Very few of them realised that the racing cars had no speedometer and, consequently, the rev counter was all important. When some were driving, Jim talked to the others. As there was no way he would let them loose on the full circuit, he had devised a trial lesson to be run on the Norwich Straight. This entailed them driving down one side of the straight where different coloured flags showed brake, change gear, brake, change gear before turning round a cone and driving back the other side to carry out the same procedure. This trial was meant to get students used to handling the car and its non-syncromesh gear box in the simplest way. Jim didn't want anything to distract them from the important rev counter. It was deliberately kept simple but the students still had the thrill of driving a racing car. Once they could comfortably carry out that procedure, they would be ready to tackle corners on the circuit. Amazingly, the system was to prove so successful that it has continued to be used, virtually unchanged, by the school ever since.

After the trial, Jim would ask them to continue with further training – some only wanted the taste of course, but many others joined to continue with the next step. From the very beginning, the policy was step-by-step progress with safety uppermost and, although some pupils were impatient to get lapping, the majority then, and ever since, have appreciated this method.

The next stage was the all important corner learning and each corner was a lesson in itself. Riches, Sear, the old Hairpin, the Esses and the Coram Curve each took a lesson. With the trial, this took six lessons at £5 each or £30 for what was called

98

Stage 1. This was on the old 3 mile circuit and before there was a Russell Bend. Putting it all together and starting to lap the whole circuit was designated

Stage 2. The continuing 'slow but sure' policy meant that they were started with a limit of 4,000 revs moving up by 500 each session until they reached a maximum of 5,500 The price for each lap was £1 and pupils bought the number of laps they could afford. Many came for just 5 laps each visit but some went for as many as possible, sometimes buying over 30 laps in a day.

Of the three cars, the only failure was the TR2. Many students arrived in TR2s, MGs and Healeys. Consequently, no-one wanted to use it so before the second trial day, it was sold and another Cooper Climax sports car replaced it.

They found that the trial days continued to draw new pupils and the numbers who wanted to carry on increased all the time. Jim soon realised that he had gauged his training methods correctly and stuck with Stages 1 and 2 unchanged. In fact, they were so correct that they have lasted, with only slight changes, ever since.

Peter Plummer, a lay preacher from Stanton near Bury St Edmunds, was one of the early pupils. He used to arrive on his bicycle, riding up the lane on the far side of the circuit. He would then dismount and push his cycle across the circuit near the start line. After leaning it against the pit counter, he would proceed to take off his cycle clips and change into soft shoes before starting his lesson. This went on throughout his early training and when he had progressed to lapping. If he was attending on a Sunday, it had to be after he had given the morning sermon at his local chapel.

One of the local TV companies were told about this unusual student and his cycle. They arranged to come along one Sunday and film the unique sequence. With cars at the ready and TV cameras in place, they waited. Anxious to hold their interest, Jim kept talking to the TV producer. "He'll come into sight over there any minute now", he said every few minutes. Suddenly, to Jim's horror, not a cycle but a car appeared out of the lane "What the hell's happened", exclaimed Jim as Peter, blissfully unaware that he was about to become a TV star, got out of the Austin A35 and walked across the circuit. "Where's the bike?" demanded Jim to a bewildered Peter. "Well", stammered the preacher, still not realising why his appearance had caused such interest, "I finally managed to afford to buy that little car, so it's no more cycling for me" "Well, all right", Jim replied. "You weren't to know how important the bike was today. Just hang on everyone, please", he implored to the TV crew. "I'm sure we can find a bike around here somewhere." But, no. A thorough search failed to come up with one anywhere on the circuit. Finally, he went to the service station on the main road just outside the gates. Success at last. He found one there and the owner was persuaded to loan it for a short while. Back came the triumphant Jim to hand the bike over to Peter. The ecclesiastical student duly retraced his steps down the lane, reappearing on the bike to go through his usual sequence for the benefit of the TV crew who finally got the film they wanted.

The school's first promotional unit!

On another occasion, a local TV station came along to film some training. In view of the TV exposure the filming would bring, it was decided to run a trial lesson on the main finish straight in front of the pits. In addition, a concrete apron on the opposite side of the straight was set up as the school's very first skid pan. This was swept and liberally coated with old engine oil. An old 'banger' car was used for skid control training.

The flags and cones were placed in position on the circuit and the cars lined up ready for the start of a training session. This was timed to suit the TV station so that a telecast could go out live in a 6 pm programme. The TV crew arrived and set up their cameras in position. Everything was ready for the countdown. Suddenly, to everyone's astonishment, a mobile fish and chips van appeared coming towards them from Coram Curve Everybody rushed forward to stop him but it was no use ... the van driver was adamant. Circuit owner, Oliver Sear, had given him permission to use the circuit as a short-cut and nothing, not even TV cameras, was going to stop him. They pleaded to no avail so the only thing to do was move the TV cables and other equipment and let him through. The minutes were ticking away as they worked in a panic to clear a path for the van and then frantically replace everything just in time to start the broadcast.

Another pupil, David Cuff from Norwich, puzzled Jim as he always walked into the circuit for his training. "Surely you don't walk here from Norwich", said Jim. "Oh no", was the reply, "I've only got an old £10 van and I'm ashamed to bring it in. So I leave it outside the gates"

Jim couldn't have cared less and was very much aware that his students were often willing to put up with old vehicles and other discomforts just to be able to start motor racing. David was better than most as witness his selection to work on the film 'Grand Prix' in 1966 and to be one of just three students chosen to drive a Yeoman Credit Formula One car when, keeping a long-standing promise, Reg Parnell brought it to Snetterton later on. He was very impressed with the way all three students had handled the FI car from the way they settled into the cockpit and carried out a thorough check before leaving the pits. He was equally happy with their handling of the car on the circuit, feeling it unnecessary to even leave the pits area as they lapped his precious equipment At the end of the test, he stressed that the way all three had handled the afternoon only went to reflect the thorough training methods of the school.

With the number of students increasing all the time, it was necessary to build up the school's fleet of cars and Jim sought out and bought more of the Cooper Climax sports cars. One day, as the cars pulled into the pits from a lapping session, one was missing. Thinking he had broken down on the circuit, an instructor went to find him but, having been all the way round, he came back shaking his head. Completely mystified, the majority of the staff went off around the circuit. As they slowly drove around the hair-pin, a muffled cry for help was heard. It was coming from the deep sandpit on the inside of the corner which sup-plied all the sand used on the circuit. A look into the sandpit confirmed their fears. There was the missing car and pupil completely out of sight from the track. He had braked too late, lost control and had slid off the circuit and down into the pit Eventually, the car was hauled out with, thankfully, very little damage to either car or driver.

With one of the first lady pupils.

At the end of 1957, Jim decided that one of his first batch of students, Mike McKee , was ready to have a pub-lic race. He secured an Elva-Climax sports car and Mike delighted everyone with a third place finish at the tradi-tional Brands Hatch Boxing Day meeting which was the one 'oasis' in the long winter's break of those days. In fact, it was March 1958 before another opportunity came along with the Snetterton season opening meeting.

A Mrs Kay Gibson from Watton made history as the first lady student to race at that meet-ing in one of the school's FIII 500cc cars. Through the 1958 season, more students qualified to race and by the Scott-Brown meeting in September, there were eight entries from the school in the programme. Graham Scotton, P Graham and A Longfield were in the 500s while M Kaye, G Smith and J York were entrusted with the 1100cc Cooper sports. Another couple of students were in their own cars, entered by the Jim Russell School. The students also had the bonus of watching their 'headmaster' at work and, at that Scott-Brown meeting, they saw one of the best races ever at the circuit. Fully described in Jim's race career chapters, suffice to say no-one who saw his titanic scrap with his friend, Ivor Bueb, ever forgot it. His students revered him even more after that race.

As the school's student list grew, so did the staff. Rudy was joined by a couple of mechanics, Tom Morley and Roger Bailey.

Then Australian, Frank Gardner, came on the scene. He was a lanky laconic character who had come over to try his luck in England after several seasons of racing sports cars in his home country. Jim met him at a race meeting and, realising that Frank was also a skilled mechanic, offered him a deal. Frank would work on the school cars and Jim would help him with his race career. It didn't take long for Frank to become a very established member of the staff.

When lapping sessions began to produce damaged cars, Jim realised that he would have to take some positive steps and called a meeting of all the students who had progressed enough to take part in lapping sessions on the full circuit. The 'lappers', as they were called, were told about Jim's new idea. There would be a school 'crash fund', which meant that everyone who wanted to take part in a lapping session would pay a deposit of £10 before starting. If they returned their car undamaged, the £10 was returned. If there was damage, they forfeited the deposit. The system proved so successful that it has continued ever since, with inflation

The Ruskat.

causing the amount to be steadily increased over the years and the name changed slightly to a more accurate 'accident deposit'.

From the time they started at Snetterton, it became the practice to visit the Doric restaurant in Attleborough for lunch and, very often, return for a drink after training had finished. Colin Campbell, who was later to join the school as the Jim Russell Club Secretary, and his wife Sheila were running the Doric. They welcomed the business which the school brought them and made everyone, both the school staff and students, extremely comfortable.

Jim took over an old crisp factory near the railway line at Downham Market to use as the workshop for his ever-increasing fleet of school racing cars. When the new go-kart craze began to take hold, it was decided to get involved. The other half of the crisp factory was available and was given over to the production of the aptly-named 'Ruskat'. School student, Freddy Dack, and a few other enthusiasts were encouraged to form a local club and Downham and District Go-Kart Club came into existence. Jim gave them one of his new Ruskats to get them started and suggested that a 24 hour kart run at Snetterton would give both the club and the Ruskat some good publicity.

As suggested, the run was organised but not long after the start, the weather suddenly changed and it began to rain quite heavily. The poor drivers, resolutely carrying on and sitting just inches from the tarmac, were getting soaked to the skin. Standing shivering in the pit lane, they were loath to give up, but worse was to come. As darkness fell, they realised that they had no lighting on the kart. Just as they were about to abandon the run, with the lighting problem on top of the wet weather, one of them suddenly came up with an idea. "Why don't we follow the kart round in one of our road cars so that our headlamps will provide the lighting?" he asked. Everyone thought it was a brilliant idea which they immediately put into effect. Through-out the night, they took turns to follow the kart. Everything worked fine until George Shipp took over the kart and Terry Farnham followed him in his Austin A35. Going down to the hair-pin, Terry inadvertently knocked his light switch and, for a few seconds, poor George was in complete darkness. As Terry switched the lights on again, he was just in time to see George's head disappearing under the railway sleeper barrier which lined that part of the circuit. Very luckily, the kart was so low that George escaped unscathed, Suddenly bathed in light, he realised where he was and swung the kart round back onto the circuit. A very relieved Terry watched him continue the run and kept his hand very much clear of the light switch for the rest of his session.

There were no more dramas during darkness and, when dawn broke, they all felt much better. Things settled down to a steady pattern and they began to relax when, suddenly the kart was overdue. "Quiet, everybody", someone shouted. They all strained to hear the sound of the kart engine. For what seemed an age, but in fact was only a couple of minutes, they listened in dead silence. Then a couple of them jumped into a car and quickly toured the circuit, coming into the pits shaking their heads. "No sign of it", they reported. A couple of minutes later, they heard it in the distance and, very shortly afterwards, it passed the pits with the driver giving them the 'thumbs-up' signal. They could hardly wait for him to finish his session and come in to report. The explanation was quite simple. Knowing that it was getting towards time to top up the petrol tank and that the petrol cans in the pits were getting low, he had turned into the slip road which existed then just before the hairpin. This led him onto the forecourt of the Snetterton Service Station. Having topped up the tank, he simply turned round and drove back onto the circuit to continue the run.

With no more dramas, the 24 hour run was successfully completed and, although it gained quite a lot of newspaper coverage, it failed to create much more interest in the Ruskat. Very reluctantly, after producing some 300 of them, Jim decided to discontinue production. It really bothered him that it hadn't taken off properly and he wondered whether, even at just £55, it had been priced too high in the late 1950s. Then again, in retrospect, maybe he was just too early as, of course, karting really took off later and has flourished ever since.

With student applications growing, Jim started to search around for more sports cars until he had built the numbers up to a strength of 9 plus, of course, the FIII 500cc car which was still very much in use.

By looking for race programmes with both a sports car race and a Formula Libre race (which allowed entry for just about any racing car), the school could enter 9 students in each race using the same cars. When one of the sports cars was badly bent, Rudy set about rebuilding it as a single seater Monoposto. It was a fat, ugly-looking thing but, when it appeared at the school, everybody queued to use it. Jim started to think about that situation and it made him realise that it would be easier to teach people in an open wheeler car where they could actually point the wheel at the apex of a corner Coupled with the fact that they were actually having to persuade the students to use the sports cars and not wait for the single seater, he made the decision that was to influence the very future of the school. He would go for a fleet of single seater racing cars.

Straight away, he approached Colin Chapman about a car with removable bodywork. This was a feature of the Coopers but, by then, John Cooper had almost ceased production. Up until then, the Lotus Formula cars had featured all riveted bodywork. After their discussion, Chapman came up with the very versatile Lotus 18 and the school purchased 25 of them which was almost a quarter of the total made in the first year.

John Paine, a major force at the school much later, attended for training in 1959 and soon joined the ever-increasing bank of student racers. Some were still driving the Cooper Climax sports cars but most were now in the new Lotus 18 Formula Junior single seaters. The school continued to increase its number of race entries and seldom was there a Formula Junior race anywhere without the majority of cars being entered by the Jim Russell Racing Drivers School.

Multi-Championship winner, Syd Fox, recalls his training days in early 1959 and the time he

The popular converted monoposto.

Lotus 18's alongside the school early van.

incurred Jim's wrath by driving too fast on the trial straight. Nonetheless, he was forever mindful of Jim's help. Free lapping and free racing in the old Elva-Climax he shared with fellow school graduate, Peter Postlethwaite, were never forgotten. Syd has vivid memories of the day when a couple of Triumph TR2s were on the circuit during the school's lunch break. One of the drivers lost control and crashed into one of the school's Coopers. A moment later, Jim turned up and demanded to know what the TR2 driver was going to do about the damage. The reply was an amused, "Nothing, we're not on a public road" Jim wasn't at all amused and the next moment the truculent driver was on his back before Jim confiscated the TR2 and left him with the parting shot, "When you've paid for the damage, you can have your car back" Fair minded Jim might have been, but he certainly didn't suffer fools gladly.

There was no petrol supply on the circuit in those days and it became the practice for the students to drive the racing cars off the trial straight down the slip road and into the Snetterton Service Station. This invariably led to looks of complete disbelief and bewilderment as the road users filling up suddenly saw a queue of racing cars forming up behind them.

With much fewer cars on the road, the embryonic racers made a habit of continuing their high speed driving into Attleborough for lunch at the Doric. History doesn't record anyone getting caught for speeding although it was quite likely that the local Police were a touch more tolerant in those days.

About that time, the latest cinema craze was Circlerama which had the audience in the middle and the screens virtually all around them. As such, fast, exciting films were the order of the day. When the students arrived one morning, they found Jim waiting for them with a camera crew ready to film for Circlerama.

An E-type Jaguar had a bank of cameras already mounted on it and Jim was set to drive it with the students primed to 'mock up' a race. Apart from the fact that the extra weight of the cameras made the E-type a handful for Jim, there was no way the film could be speeded up. So, everything had to be done at full speed. Surprisingly, no-one crashed and the end result made exciting cinema. Naturally, the students only got the glory but, no doubt, the E-type driver got paid. At least the students had a chance to see themselves on screen, that is, of course, if they visited the only Circlerama cinema in London's Leicester Square.

Colin Stokes was one of those early pupils who had cause to remember and appreciate Jim's instruction methods, despite his very strict controls. He was one of the unfortunates to feel very small when Jim suddenly stepped out somewhere on the circuit to wave them in. They knew they were in for a JR 'tongue-lashing' for doing something wrong. Very often, it was for over-revving and they would frantically try to zero the tell-tale needle as they were braking. As a rule, they were unsuccessful as it meant being able to reach right under the instrument panel to find it and try to steer off the circuit under the 'guvnor's' eagle eyes Despite these happenings, they all respected him, knowing full well that he was a very successful racer as well as instructor. The overwhelming reaction to Jim's training was that, as well as helping them to become racing drivers, it also dramatically improved their road driving. This was to continue over the years as his successors religiously followed his methods.

Suddenly, there came a change to the regular pattern when Jim's accident at the 1959 Le Mans 24 hour race brought a swift halt to his instructing. Everyone rallied round and the school continued with senior student and racer, Mike McKee taking over as chief instructor. By a strange coincidence, it was Mike's father, a surgeon at the Norwich Hospital, who sorted out Jim's badly broken leg. During this time, he also allowed Mike to race his Formula II car which had been brought back from France. One day, Mr McKee came into the ward and said, "Come on Jim, I'm taking you to Snetterton to watch Mike race your car". A rather shaky patient was taken to the circuit only to see Mike make a mistake and go off in a big way at Riches corner Jim wasn't really sorry to get back to his hospital bed that day.

Around the same time, he received news that the school had suffered its first, and only, fatality. Captain Musker, a local man who was a cousin of the Duke of Grafton, was killed while lapping. Ironically, it was his final lapping session before his first race, due the following day.

Luckily, Jim had something to counteract these depressing occurrences. He had just met Jennifer Firman at the hospital and a friendship was developing which was to lead to Jennifer becoming Mrs Jim Russell.

Chapter 6   Different Horse Power

After his accident, Jim was living in the little bungalow at his garage. Still using walking sticks, he was being driven around the circuits to watch Mike McKee race in his FII car. Going off to Oulton Park in 1960, he asked brother Jack to look for some properties with a view to buying and moving away from the business. Like anyone who has lived at a garage, he was getting tired of being 'knocked-up' for petrol out of hours. He rather liked Suffolk, so Jack found about half a dozen properties around the Bury St Edmunds area. One of them was Bardwell Manor and this was the place Jack insisted that his brother saw first. Down they drove and as soon as Jim saw it, he fell for its charm and setting – a far cry from his two bedroomed bungalow, Although it was empty, the owners lived nearby and were soon on hand. Jim made an offer They hesitated, but when they realised that he was determined to buy a house that very day, the deal was struck. It nearly came unstuck the next day when the Russell brothers returned; they found trees being cut and loaded on a trailer However, another hasty phone call had the vendor back to change his orders and the trees stacked ready for Jim's fire requirements.

With over 60 acres of fenced grassland, he was keen to put it to use and one of the garage customers, Peter Poston, provided the solution. He had a wholesale meat business and the garage serviced his lorries. He was also a part-time National Hunt horse trainer and was looking for somewhere to rest the horses in the summer. "Fine", said Jim, "But there are some barbed wire fences". "No problem", was the reply. "They are not youngsters – they'll be all right". So they came to Bardwell and were soon part of the family.

Towards the end of the season, Peter said he was taking one of them called Whitehall Bloom to a Yarmouth flat meeting. He stressed that it was just for an outing before the start of the jumping season. With Peter's warning not to waste money on a bet ringing in his ears, Jim went off to watch. However, he did have a £1 bet and the horse won at 10-1 Peter rushed up and apologised – "You'll never want me back after telling you not to bet" He was very relieved when he realised that Jim had not taken his advice and it was decided that the rich park grass had given Whitehall Bloom the edge around this time. With interest increasing in horses, it was suggested that a stud would do well at Bardwell Manor. Very quickly, ten boxes were erected and a small yard laid down. The barbed wire was replaced with wooden fences and Bardwell Manor Stud was ready for business.

The idea for this project had come about a few months earlier when Wally Ward and Jim had gone to Yarmouth races. With the selling plate very much in mind, Jim promised himself

▷ *Doratella, ridden with Willie Carson,*
winning for proud owner Russell ...

that he would have a bet and, if the horse won, he would put in a bid. Sure enough, it all happened and his choice for the race and the tote treble, "Zip goes a million" won at 10-1. His bid of 175 guineas topped anyone else and before he could take it all in, another Newmarket trainer, Mr Sidebottom, offered to train it. "OK", said Jim, "You're my trainer", and went off to the owner's bar for a drink with him. However, it suddenly dawned on Jim that he had to exchange his treble tickets at the tote window. It was here that he was met by a distraught Mr Howes (the owner) and trainer, O'Gorman. Both had thought the other was bidding to retain "Zip goes a million" Howes told Jim that he couldn't face going home to his wife with no horse. "No problem", said Jim. "Give me £25 profit and you can buy it back" So the deal was done and poor Sidebottom was told that his job as trainer was over before it had started. The story hit the press and one 'daily' worked it out that Jim had made more money in half an hour than the Aga Khan It did, however, fire his imagination and resolve to breed a winner himself.

Off he went to the Newmarket sales and bought his first brood mare, "Voltella". She was already in foal so very soon the stud had its first filly, which was named "Doratella". Considering that it had been bred with an unknown 100 guinea stallion, it showed a lot of promise as a 2 year old and was sent to trainer 'Fiddler' Goodwill's yard – the nickname came from violin playing, not for any other reason.

Jim chose his very appropriate colours – black and white chequered body and cap with British racing green sleeves. She started to race and after about 3 or 4 races, Fiddler entered her at Yarmouth. Almost brought down at the start, before they had starting stalls, she finished a promising fourth. Fiddler then announced that he wanted to enter her for the last day of the meeting – just two days later Jim was alarmed. "What about your usual three week gap between races?" "Well, she went very well today and she's ready, so I'm sure she'll do well", replied Fiddler, who also agreed to hire a jockey, not the usual apprentice. He booked Greville Starkey. It was a very wet day and Doratella led from start to finish.

The next race was at Newmarket and with an apprentice in the saddle, she was using stalls for the first time. The PA announcer informed the crowd that she was late out of the stalls and, sure enough, she trailed home a furlong in arrears. The jockey explained in the unsaddling enclosure, "She was standing with her legs all wrong in the stalls, guvnor". Jim replied, "I wouldn't expect to start a race with the car wheels pointing sideways" It was obvious that an experienced jockey could get the best out of Doratella and for York, Willie Carson was engaged to ride. Sure enough, she won at 100-8 to finish the season.

Back at the stud, she was rested until it was decided to send her to Alf Dalton's yard to train as a three year old. Willie Carson was booked again to ride her in the Fred Darling stakes at Newmarket. It was a 30 horse field with lots of top bred entries. No-one had any hope of success for Doratella and Jim suggested to a friend that he should bet on her finishing at the back of the field. To the delight of the Russell entourage, she finished a remarkable third at 33-1 As she was being unsaddled, Carson told Alf that he'd done a remarkable job with the horse over the winter – "She now runs straight providing she's not boxed in on the rails", he added.

At the Queen's Sandringham Stud with his new foal produced out of his visiting mare with the Queen's stallion.

An evening meeting at Wolverhampton was her next outing and Frankie Durr was the jockey. She ran in second place and was 7 lengths behind with 3 furlongs to go. Durr urged her on and she hauled in the leader but going between the other horse and the rails proved her undoing. Her dislike at such a situation was apparent when she reared up and Durr was forced to use the whip. Completely unsettled, she lost a certain victory by half a length. She never raced again and she was sold at the next Newmarket sales. When she turned up at the next year's Doncaster sales, she looked sad and neglected with an old rope collar. Jim bought her back for a race and for breeding.

Around this time, Jim bought a 2 year old gelding. With Emerson's permission, he christened it "Fittipaldi" and even arranged for yellow and green colours in the Brazilian's honour. Fred Armstrong came to look at the horse and suggested that his son, Robert, took it on for training. Sadly, Fittipaldi never lived up to his name.

Jim had a beautiful breed mare called "Snap" who had just foaled a super filly from a stallion called "River Chanter". He managed to get a nomination for Snap to go to the Queen's stallion which stood at Sandringham House stud. While she was there waiting to be covered, Jim was busy with the film,

'Grand Prix'. He told special effects man, Milt Rice, that he planned to visit Snap and her filly at Sandringham. Milt asked to accompany him and it was arranged. An ecstatic Milt exclaimed, "Goddammit – are we going to the Queen's house? Boy, that's really neat" To commemorate the occasion, he brought his camera and, among other things, took a photo of Jim with the foal.

Through his visits to Newmarket, Jim got to know ex-jockey, Peter Robinson, who had become a trainer for the stable owner, Jack Fisher. Jack bought the occasional yearling from Bardwell Manor Stud. On one of their visits, Jack suggested that if more boxes were erected, he would be willing to stand a stallion there. True to his word, the moment the boxes were added, he bought "David Jack" from Ireland to become Bardwell's first stallion. Although the horse had been a winner on the flat, he sired natural jumpers and became so well known that the Queen Mother sent a couple of mares to him David Jack was eventually sold to the West Country and other stallions took his place.

By now, Jim was flying his own plane, a Cessna 172, from an airstrip behind the stud. One day, Peter Robinson asked him for a lift to Yarmouth races. Before returning, Peter asked if they could bring back two others. Jim pointed out that three people on board would be the maximum for take-off on the short Yarmouth airstrip. With a smile Peter replied, "Both of them will only weigh as much as one because they are both jockeys" So Pat Eddery and an apprentice climbed in and they took off safely. Talking about the racing school on the flight, it was decided to drop in at Snetterton. Naturally, the jockeys were interested in sitting in the racing cars but it was obvious that they would never reach the pedals Jim was quick to point out that seat height and pedal length could soon be altered if they would like to join the school The offer was politely turned down.

Other horse racing personalities came along from time to time, all of whom were impressed with he set-up. Henry Cecil's future wife had a horse in livery at the stud and one Sunday, they came up to see it. As he looked around, the trainer exclaimed, "What a lovely place you've got here, Jim". In view of the fantastic Cecil training facility, Jim thought this was quite a compliment.

Lester Piggott was another visitor. He arrived in his wife's car and Jim asked what car he drove. He was delighted to hear that Lester had a Mercedes. "They're very expensive", said the Champion jockey, "But then I suppose you only get what you pay for in this world".

Gradually, the various syndicates sold off their stallions which had been standing at the stud – one of them, "Bold and Free", sold to Japan – and Jim realised that the stud needed its own stallion. At the next Newmarket sales, he bought a well bred 5 year old called "Tudor Rhythm", and for the next few years, he was the stud's only stallion. Eventually, commitments at both the racing school and the garage caused Jim to have a rethink and decide that he couldn't give it the time it needed. So, with a certain amount of regret, he leased off the stud.

Chapter 7 The School Grows Up

Late in 1959, Jim had returned to the school, at least part-time. He was instructing on crutches and, as he couldn't really use his left leg, he devised a method of driving himself round the circuit to keep in touch with the training. He used his walking stick, pushing it down with his chest to depress the clutch By then, the trial lesson had been moved to the straight between the old Hairpin and the Esses and the school had taken delivery of the new Lotus 18 Formula Junior cars which the staff were keen to keep in pristine condition. When the students were driving the cars back to the Hairpin, a very loud bang was heard. Everybody jumped into their road cars to investigate. When Jim arrived, he found one of the cars stuffed into the barrier with a badly damaged nose cone The guilty student was standing looking forlornly at the damage. He had a small cut on his forehead and Jim, exasperated by the stupidity of the unnecessary accident yelled, "Stand back man ... you're bleeding on my car".

Early the following year, it was necessary to increase the workshop staff as it was rapidly becoming too much for Rudy on his own. They persuaded David Clarke to leave his apprentice-ship at a local garage. The offer of double his current wages did the trick. Frank Gardner was, of course, working with them when he wasn't training and racing with the school. Soon after-wards, an American from Indianapolis, Charles Kelsey Jnr, arrived. Somehow he managed to get himself a job as a 'go-for' but everything he touched seemed to go wrong. Nevertheless, despite this and the mayhem he created, Jim's patience with him lasted. At the time, Frank was staying at the local Temperance Hotel but after Charles joined him there, things started to go seriously wrong. Charles was a 'three baths a day' man and the hotel's ancient heating system just couldn't keep up with the constant demand for hot water One day, the system burst, flooding out the place. The damage caused was so extensive that the hotel had to close down and it never opened again Luckily for Frank and Charles, who was never blamed for the havoc he had wreaked, they found out about Mary's Cafe. She had available rooms and they moved into the cosy atmosphere. She was a motherly lady who prided herself on good com-fortable accommodation and giving 'her boys' plenty of home-cooked food. With his natural charm, Frank soon had her eating out of his hand.

The school had a small transporter and trailer to take racing cars to and from the Snetter-ton circuit. Each journey could take three cars and had to be repeated in order to get enough cars there for the training sessions. Driving the transporter was one of the jobs allocated to Charles. This went on without any dramas for a while. Then one day, after Wally had sent him

112

off to collect three cars from the circuit, things took a definite turn for the worse As Charles arrived back, Wally was watching and, seeing the transporter virtually roofless, yelled, "What the hell has happened to the transporter?" "Well", replied Charles, "After we loaded up the cars, I thought I would just do one steady lap of the circuit, but the Dunlop Bridge was lower than I thought" "The cars are all right, I hope?" said Wally, but worse was to come. When he walked around to the rear, there was no trailer Shortly afterwards, a telephone call from the Stoke Ferry Police provided the answer. "We have a racing car and trailer in someone's front garden near here. Is it yours?" This time Jim's patience did run out and Charles was rapidly dismissed, never to be heard of again.

One of the early students who became very successful, especially in big sports cars, was Mike D'Udy. He was a bit of a 'loner' but he had a charming personality. Jim found him to be very receptive during training and marked him down as having a natural ability with loads of potential. He rapidly became one of the stars of the school. He was getting his turn racing the school cars but obviously was 'champing at the bit' to do more. Jim talked to him at length about motor racing and told him that the real answer was for Mike to have his own racing car. Jim added that it would probably cost about £2,000 to buy one, not realising that Mike had a fortune in trust Within days, Jim received a phone call from the trustees in London. They wanted to come up to have a meeting. Very shortly afterwards, they met Jim for lunch in Bury St Edmunds. When he told them that Mike listened and followed every word of advice he was given, they were amazed. "This is wonderful news", they said. "We've never known him to get so interested in anything before. We'll arrange for the money straight away" They were anxious to know where Mike would be staying during his racing season. Jim said, "There are no Hilton Hotels in Downham, but I expect he can have a room at Mary's Cafe with Frank and the others" Sure enough, the money came through and Mike got his own car to start his successful racing career.

Jim teamed Mike with John Mastin in a couple of Formula Juniors and after they had both done a lot of laps around Snetterton, they discussed their times with Jim. His average time around the full circuit in an FJ car was 1 minute 42 seconds but neither could get under 1 minute 44 seconds. "I'll tell you what", said Jim one day, "I'll drive Mike's car and you can follow me, John". This was agreed and off they drove. As Jim warmed up, he began to get down into some competitive times and, going through Sears Corner, he looked into his mirrors just in time to see John bouncing across the field towards the main road. Stopping just in time, he turned and drove back to the pits where he stammered to Jim, "I think I'll stick to my own times".

Later, Jim took them down to race in the Formula Junior race at Monaco. That meeting proved to be disastrous and they left there short of money. On the way back, Jim had entered John in a race at Magny Cours and in practice, John wasn't to do too well. He kept coming into the pits and complaining as he so often did. Finally, Jim lost his patience with him and, in frustration, brought down his clipboard on John's helmet. "Now get out there and do the job properly", he yelled. Sure enough, John responded to this approach and qualified on the front row. Before the race, he complained of the heat so Jim took off his racing boots and socks before plunging his feet into a bowl of cold water. When he was back in the car, Jim gave him another lecture. "We desperately need some prize money to pay our hotel bill", he warned, before despatching him from the pits. After a very well driven race, John took second place, much to everyone's relief. Up he stepped to get the trophy and the envelope containing the prize money. He hardly felt the envelope as Jim's hand was already there to snatch it away Luckily, it contained just enough to pay the hotel bill and get them back home.

Despite Jim's harsh treatment, John still wanted to be around and soon afterwards, he was appointed a Director of the school. John Spurgeon was another student who was also to reach school Director status, but after a couple of years, he was bought out.

Belgian driver, Andre Pillette phoned Jim to arrange for this 18 year old son to come over to the school. It was agreed that Teddy would not only do the training course but would join the staff as an apprentice mechanic to work on the cars. When he arrived at Downham, he had an old bus which he used to sleep in. Jim let him park it on the forecourt of the garage but, after a month or two, Frank Gardner and Jim decided that he really ought to move indoors somewhere. Luckily, there was room for him at Mary's Cafe.

In the workshop at the old crisp factory, Rudy kept Teddy cleaning cars day in, day out. Finally, Frank persuaded Rudy to let Teddy start helping with simple mechanical work. Gradually, the young Belgian learnt more about car preparation alongside his race training ... both of which were forming a solid basis for his future years. When he arrived, he had great difficulty in getting himself understood. He couldn't speak a word of English but he learnt fast and, as usual, the swear words came first Frank really took him under his wing, including him in everything. To help him learn, he even took him along to the Holbay factory where he worked on their engines in the evenings earning some extra money for his racing career.

Teddy had a little autocycle which was his pride and joy. When he arranged for a long weekend off to go to Belgium and visit his family, he bought a chain and padlock for the cycle. On the morning of his departure, he secured it to a post with the chain and lock. The station was nearby and the train would be passing alongside the workshop so he told everyone that he would wave to them. "OK, have a nice time", they all choroused. The moment he had left the yard, Frank grabbed a hacksaw and rapidly cut through the chain. He warmed up the little engine and took the cycle to the side of the yard next to the railway line. As the train went by, Frank was riding around on the cycle, everybody else was waving furiously, and Teddy was almost having a fit on the train.

During this time, another racing driver, Horace Gould from Bristol, decided to send his son Martin to the school and also arranged for him to work on the cars. Martin arrived in a little three-wheeler which his Dad had bought him. At his age, he was only allowed to drive something without a reverse gear Unfortunately, he had an attitude problem and consequently wasn't too popular with the rest of the staff. When he went off on the train for a weekend with his folks at Bristol, Frank and Teddy got busy. They stripped down the gear box and changed the gears around. Martin returned on Monday morning and jumped into his car. Putting it into first gear, he accelerated and the car shot backwards, straight through the rather weak fencing and onto the railway lines Everyone had been standing around watching the fun and they fell about laughing. Martin jumped out of the car, tried unsuccessfully to push it off the line and yelled in panic, "Come and help me before a train comes" Winding him up further, they all protested that they were too busy and eventually, when he was almost in tears, they went across and heaved it across the line. When he had calmed down and carefully tried the car again, he rang his father. "Dad, you know I'm not supposed to drive anything with a reverse gear. Well now I've got three reverse gears" Horace said, "Are you absolutely sure? OK, I'll come up tomorrow and take a look". Naturally, Frank made sure to listen to the conversation and that evening, after Martin had gone, he and Teddy put everything back the right way.

The next day, Horace arrived, walked over to the car and tried it. To his amazement, it was perfectly all right He got out of the car and said to a perplexed Martin, "What sort of game are you playing, son ... have you started drinking?" Everyone else kept a low profile and eventually Horace calmed down and went back to Bristol. It continued to remain a mystery and no-one ever told either father or son the truth.

Martin went well with his training and, when he got to lapping, Horace came back to watch. He tried to keep his visit a secret from Martin and arranged to meet Jim outside the circuit. Unfortunately, he couldn't keep out of things and, marching up to Martin, he said, "Come on son, I'll show you the way to lap this circuit". They got into his road car and Horace soon got it all wrong, so much so that he rolled the car.It was a very deflated father who drove off in his badly damaged road car that day. When he returned for a later lapping session, he made no attempt to interfere and, as they watched Martin lap his race car in pouring rain, Jim said to Horace, "He drives better than you ever did, so stop worrying". Nevertheless, even after such a good display, Martin gave up, possibly due to pressure from his worrying father.

By now, Henry Morragh was instructing and one evening a discussion took place in the Doric bar about a Jim Russell School get-together. After talking to Colin, they set the price at 10 shillings (50p) per ticket. Henry suggested that as Jim, Wally and he would be selling the tickets, they should have a three way bet on who would sell the most. The two losers would have to pay the winner £5 each.

Jim drove home thinking about the bet and the next day started to sell his tickets. They were going like 'hot cakes' as Jim told everyone that they two big names in pop music, Adam Faith and Alma Cogan, would be doing the cabaret Very soon, Jim's tickets were all gone and he was borrowing more from the other two Naturally, he won the bet and collected his winnings from the others. Then, on the night, he coolly announced that apologies had been received from the stars and called for volunteers to sing Amazingly, this not only proved very successful, it also seemed to make them all forget the fact that they had been 'hoodwinked'. As the evening wore on, Jim was persuaded to take his turn at the microphone. He chose to sing, "South of the Border" and, unwittingly, started a great tradition. It has become Jim's special song which he invariably sings at the school's annual Dinner Dance every year.

With the school's operations becoming known worldwide, they were not only getting students from all over the place, they were also getting asked for help and advice from other countries. A good example of this was the request they received from Holland. The Dutch Motor Club asked Jim to bring out some cars to Zandvoort so that he could test some young Dutch enthusiasts with a view to them racing. Jim negotiated over the final details which eventually meant taking six cars. The deal was finalised for Jim coming back with a total of six cars, three of which would be driven by Dutch students and three by British students chosen by Jim.

Off went Jim, Wally and Frank to Zandvoort and carried out the initial trials as requested. In the evenings, they visited the local bars. Wally, who was only about 5'6" foot tall, got very aggressive after a few drinks. He suddenly decided that he didn't like the look of two very large Dutch Marines standing further along the bar. "Come on". he said to Jim and Frank, "We'll take them on" The more they tried to shut him up, the more he wanted to fight them "Come on", he said. "Backs against the bar and we'll take them on." It took a long time and all the persuasive charms of both Jim and Frank to restrain him from doing something completely suicidal.

One of the Dutch drivers who took part was Rob Slotemaker, who operated a skid pan at the circuit. Jim and Frank thought that he would be well worth watching but it was not the case. He might have known about skid control but he was desperately in need of some circuit training. In fact, after his first lapping session, Frank said, "that's a bit of a record ... we've seen at least 20 different lines through that corner so far" The fact was, Rob used all his skid control skills and seemed to be able to control the car no matter which line he took through the corner.

Nevertheless, it turned out to be a very successful operation and some time later, they made the return journey with the cars and to watch the British and Dutch competition winners compete in a public race. Also at the meeting were the Ken Tyrrell team and later, when Ken was safely back in his hotel, Paul Hawkins, Frank Gardner and a couple of others decided that it would be a good idea to take Ken's Mini to the fairground. Not only that, they decided to drive it with the dodgems Naturally, this created utter chaos and the fairground attendants were tearing their hair out. Soon , the Police arrived and Ken Tyrrell had been alerted as well.

Luckily no real damage had been done to anything and plenty of rapid talking saw them all get away with it.

Back home, Roger Bailey joined as a mechanic, working with Frank Gardner. He was to go far. After he left the school to join the Tyrrell Racing team, he moved to McLaren and eventually on to run a team in the American Indy Lights series.like most of the staff at the time, he stayed at Mary's Cafe. She had a cat and, in order to give it easy access to and from the garden, some-one had removed a piece of glass from the glazed door. When it got to winter, the wind really howled through the opening. Frank decided to do something about it. He measured the aperture and bought a piece of glass which he brought in one evening. Having puttied the glass into place, he settled down in a chair near the fire. Presently, the cat came out from under one of the chairs and ran straight into the new glass, knocking himself out After a short while. he came round, did a lap of the kitchen and promptly repeated the process He took longer to come round that time but a lesson had been learned the hard way ... from then on, he waited for someone to open the door to be let out.

Another Australian, Neville McKee had joined the band at Mary's place by then. He had come over with John Layton, who kept destroying his own racing cars. So much so that he gave up. Neville bought all the pieces off him, took them back to Australia and put together a com-plete Lotus 20 which he successfully raced.

Chapter 8 The Comeback

The 1961 season saw a host of Jim Russell graduates racing, mostly in Formula Junior. Frank and Teddy were joined by John Paine, Graham Scotton, Ed April, Ed Harris, Peter Postlethwaite and many more. There were quite a few American Servicemen from the local air bases attending the school and some of their wives. One was called Sandy and it was obvious that she and her husband were not getting on too well. One day, she came up to Jim and asked him to 'fix the brakes' on the car her husband was using Naturally, Jim laughed it off but wasn't quite sure whether she was serious or not.

Ironically, it was she who had a big accident, turning her racing car over in the process. She was unhurt and to commemorate the incident, she had a gold brooch made showing the car upside down When this was admired by Jenny, Sandy had another made as a gift for her with the car the right way up Sandy had plenty to say for herself and was always in animated discussions with the instructors and fellow students. On one occasion, she seriously suggested setting up a male brothel in Newmarket, pointing out that there were plenty of rich bored women in the district who would welcome such a place "Well", said Jim, trying to keep a straight face, "We've got Wally Ward and Rudy Gates, but I think they're getting a little too old for the job", which put paid to that particular conversation.

The opening meeting of the 1961 season had two Formula Junior races and school graduates shone in both of them. In the A race, Mike McKee set the pace and ran out a comfortable winner after Frank Gardner had given him a hard time, setting the fastest lap before a broken clutch cable caused his retirement. Also looking good in a school car was motorcycle racer Bob Anderson, whose promising debut saw him scrapping with Brian Hart, whose engines bearing his name, were later to become so well known in the Grand Prix world. The B race field was dominated by Jim Russell graduates and John Horrex, Ed Harris and Ed April finished in that order giving the Jim Russell school all three top places.

Frank said to Jim one day, "Why don't you race again?" to which Jim retorted "Don't be daft ... I'm 41 and I've only just thrown away my crutches". Frank wouldn't let the subject go and kept pointing out that Jim could prove to the students that he could race the kind of car in which they were being taught. Eventually, Jim started to give it serious thought. He rang Reg Tanner at Esso and told him he was thinking of making a comeback. Reg said, "You're crazy ... you were in Formula II and about to move into Formula I ... in any case, Formula Junior is full of young, hungry drivers" "Well", replied Jim, "I still want to ... after all, the Le Mans accident was not my fault ... if it had been I wouldn't try again ... so I feel I must give it another try. Let's talk sponsorship ... I'll tell you what ... rather than paying a lump sum for the season, how about £500 a race?" Reg thought that was fair and a deal was agreed. Jim then contacted Colin Chapman who supplied a new Formula Junior Lotus 20 and practice sessions began. It was at the Snetterton International Lombank Trophy Meeting at the end of March that Jim made his return to racing. While he could only watch some of his contemporaries race in the main Formula I event, he drove his Lotus 20 in the supporting Formula Junior race. He did, however, renew his rivalry with Trevor Taylor, who had now advanced to 'works driver' status with Lotus. He also had a whole bunch of young talented drivers to contend with in this, his first race for nearly two years. Apart from Taylor and his team mate, Peter Arundell, Tony Maggs and Bill McCowen (who was on pole position), the school's star graduate, Mike McKee and the redoubtable Frank Gardner were also entered. Trevor shot off into a lead he was never to lose and Jim, showing all his old flair, was in a constant fight for the minor places. Although in the end Tony Maggs was second, Jim held off Peter Arundell to score a very commendable third place. "Well", he thought, as he was being congratulated by all and sundry, "I can still mix it with these youngsters at my age", and he decided to carry on with his comeback.

The next meeting was another major event ... the traditional Easter Monday Goodwood International. Revelling in his return, Jim had an excellent practice session which put him on the front row alongside Peter Arundell and Tony Maggs. As the flag fell, all hell broke loose. Arundell's car, probably hit from behind, swung across and hit Jim's so hard that his right-hand rear wheel flew off and his car was turned completely around. He was facing the rest of the field. He had the horrifying experience of sitting helplessly in the three-wheeled car as the other fast starting drivers tried to avoid him Mike McKee failed to do so glancing off the side of Jim's car before driving off. It was far from over. Suddenly, someone else came straight at him, launching himself over the nose of Jim's car, smashing the windscreen and grazing his shoulder as he threw his head sideways to avoid being decapitated "Yes", he thought to himself, "Reg Tanner was right ... I shouldn't be here at my age".

Ironically, Peter Arundell, who had been very much the centre of the incident which put four cars out altogether, went on to record the very first dead-heat at Goodwood. Not only that, the other driver in the dead-heat finish was Tony Maggs, whose well-battered Cooper had also survived the startline melee.

By the time of the next meeting at Oulton Park later in the month, Jim had put his unsettling experience behind him. Once again, there was a formidable Formula Junior entry. It was to prove to be a day plagued by brake problems on Jim's car and he was an early retirement in the race which was won by Trevor Taylor.

Back at Downham, they worked on the car ready for the next weekend's Aintree International. The day started off raining and, in practice, Jim revelled in the wet conditions which always suited him. He set the fastest time and took pole position for the race. Tony Maggs was next up but the Lotus pair, Arundell and Taylor, were several seconds slower. Unfortunately for Jim, the weather dried up late morning and the race started in brilliant sunshine. Despite rocketing away into the lead, Jim soon realised that he was, once again, losing out in the braking department. He was driving on the limit but it was not good enough to make up for the better braking of the 'works' cars. After three laps, he was passed by Arundell and a couple of laps later, Taylor came past them both John Love and Bob Anderson had closed up to make it a five car scrap after Maggs had retired. Throughout the race, Jim kept realising that he was a match for the Lotus drivers but could do nothing about their superior brakes. They had the latest 9" brake drums while he still had the 8" drums. Fighting all the way, he had to be content with the minor placing but he was determined to do something about it before the next big race which was the Silverstone Daily Express meeting in May.

Back in his office, he phoned Colin Chapman. "Colin, I must have those bigger brake drums for Silverstone". "I'm sorry, Jim – I'm afraid there's no chance of that happening" he replied. "OK", said Jim, "But I'll have to cancel my order for six more school cars." Immediately, the reply came back, "You can have your new drums tomorrow"

The new drums were duly collected and fitted to the car before leaving for Silverstone. What a difference He wasn't being out-braked by Taylor and Arundell any more and he ended up sitting next to them on the front row of the grid. Arundell made the best start with Taylor next to him and Jim just behind him. Mike McKee was following in his teacher's wheel tracks with Tony Maggs and John Love holding the next two places. Jim started to thoroughly enjoy the race and sat watching the Lotus pair swapping the lead. He felt on equal terms with them and even let McKee past for a few moments of glory. Then, at about half distance, he decided to step up his efforts. He had long re-passed McKee and reeling in Taylor and Arundell, he swept past them into the lead. Arundell called into the pits, and when they started to lap the back markers, Jim showed that he had lost none of his race craft. By the time they had cleared these slower cars, he had opened up a sizeable gap from Taylor, Love and Maggs. From then on, he commanded the race from the front, eventually winning by over 5 seconds from the second man He had proved that he was still able to meet and beat the best up and coming drivers in the country.

Back at the school, there were many congratulations and even more respect for the head teacher, especially from Frank Gardner. "Well", thought Jim to himself, "That's a good way to finish" and did just that.

Wally kept a very tight reign on the school's finances all the time and there was a constant 'war' between him and Rudy Gates. Rudy was always trying to get various new pieces of equipment and Wally would not authorise the purchases. Frank Gardner reckoned that amber traffic lights were invented for Wally because he only started up his engine when the lights went to amber.

When Rudy wanted a steam cleaner and Wally had refused to buy one, Rudy arranged to get one on a free trial for the day. After trying it out, he wanted Wally to see how much it helped and speeded up the cleaning of the engines. Wally was in the office with his rather straight-laced secretary called Lavinia, and came out to see the steam cleaner in action. Before long, another typical argument had started between them and Wally, unaware that Lavinia had come out of the office to tell him that he was wanted on the telephone, was giving Rudy a torrent of strongly-worded abuse Probably hearing obscenities that she had never heard before, she turned and ran back into the office much to the amusement of Frank Gardner who was revelling in the row between the two men. Wally continued his highly colourful diatribe against the purchase of a steam cleaner, blissfully unaware of the drama which went on behind him Lavinia never said a word about it and no-one told Wally until he left the job.

Little did anyone realise at the time that 1962 was going to be a very special year for the school. It would be the year that the school trained its first World Champion. Of course, no-one is ever aware at that stage in anyone's career. New students were arriving all the time and some were outstanding. Nevertheless, it would have been impossible to forecast that every now and then one student would go all the way. Motor racing has always been like that. Many drivers who have been very special have failed to reach the top through lack of money or lack of opportunity. That year, a man who caught Jim's eye was Derek Bell. Destined to become a Sports Car World Champion, he was a starry-eyed youngster who was determined to succeed in the motor racing world. He has never forgotten his days at the school. "Jim was like a father figure to us", remembers Derek. "We hung onto his every word with great respect. There was one occasion when Jim packed about five of us into his road-going Vauxhall and took us around the circuit. He kept using the wrong lines and falling off on every corner. Then he did another lap using the correct lines ... it was very much a case of the hand of the master. He certainly showed me the way to go". Derek has followed much of Jim's advice throughout his illustrious career, remembering to always walk a new circuit before attempting to drive it.

Jim would never tolerate idiots on the circuit especially those who drove in a crazy fashion and looked likely to have an accident any moment. So when Jim strode purposefully towards a group of students, which included Derek, one day they all started to quake. Which one was in the wrong, they all thought, and they tried to think back over the last lapping session. Jim asked who had been driving a certain car and, with great trepidation, Derek owned up. To his relief, Jim said, "Well done, you drove a really good session. You've obviously been taking notice and you should do well when you get to public races. In fact, providing you can get a sponsor, you ought to go right to the top" Jim very often recalled that day as Derek went on to win Le Mans no less than five times and became double World Sports Car Champion. For his part, Derek was always willing to put something back into the school, acting as a judge at the World Scholarship and being Guest of Honour at several of the Annual Dinners. Many years later, he sent his son Justin to the school.

Jim was almost fanatical about keeping his students safe and was ready to jump hard on anyone who ignored the rules. One day an American got carried away by the fact that his girl-friend was watching from near the bridge. Trying to impress her, he forgot his cornering instruction and lost the car completely. It ended with a frightening looking somersault. Almost instantaneously, Jim's road going Vauxhall Cresta appeared from the pit lane going the wrong way around the circuit at a high rate of knots The driver had just extricated himself from the car, with very little personal damage, when Jim arrived at the scene. Grabbing the student by the overalls, he proceeded to shake him violently whilst giving him a very loud lecture on his stupidity, laced with a generous input of insulting invectives Needless to say, the American kept well within the safety limits for the rest of his stay. Like just about everyone who incurred Jim's wrath during training, he made a point of thanking him at the end for his excellent instruction.

Bill Knight, who had been associated with Jim's successful World Record attempt in 1955, arranged for his son, Mike, to take a training course and to stay on during the winter months. He worked as a mechanic and generally helped out. Then Bill approached Jim to open a Jim Russell School in France. Jim liked the idea and mutual friend, Jabby Crombac, was asked to find a suitable location. He came up with the future Grand Prix circuit at Magny Cours.

Wally and Jim went down to help set up the school and, on the way, Jim decided to fit in a long-standing commitment to give a talk at the Wandsworth Prison Motor Club. They were met by the club secretary who said, "We haven't got any cars, of course, but everyone's keen to meet you". He was right and after Jim had shown a motor racing film, he gave a talk followed by a question and answer session.

The Great Train Robbery had not long taken place and, on the way down, Wally had said, "I wonder if you will get asked about The Weasel?" Sure enough, the very first question was about this up and coming racing driver, Roy James, whose nickname The Weasel, had achieved national notoriety through his part as a get-away driver for the train robbers. He had become a front-runner in Formula Junior, which was probably the reason why the robbers had wanted him to join them Jim told them that he had only met him a couple of times at Snetterton when he had rebuked him for not signalling before entering the pit lane. The Weasel's retort was unprintable but to his credit, the next time he saw Jim a couple of weeks later, he had apologised. He admitted that he had been very wrong and couldn't thank Jim enough for his advice.

They asked if he was any good and Jim said, "Well, he was reasonably good at club level, and he might well have been very good with another couple of season's experience, but instead of that, he joined you lot in here".

As they were walking out with the warder and the club secretary to the main gate, the secretary held back a little with Jim. In a guarded voice, he said, "I'm getting out in a few weeks and, when I find something I've got hidden under a tree, I'm coming to your school". Jim was never sure whether he had done so.

At the Magny Cours circuit, the 'Ecole de Pilotage Jim Russell' was successfully opened with Henry Morragh, who had jumped at the chance, taking over as Chief Instructor. Bill Knight had bought six of the school's Lotus 18s and approached Shell for sponsorship. This came in the form of a Scholarship for one pupil to win a car for public racing the following year. His son, Mike, was entrusted with towing the prize Cooper car down to Magny Cours. He was very nervous as he had vivid memories of incurring Jim's wrath at Snetterton after colliding with a trailer carrying Teddy Pillette's racing car. No problem with this trip, however, and the prize car safely arrived. When the Scholarship finals were to take place, a panel of six judges were formed and Jim was asked to return as Chairman.

Back at Snetterton, a Frenchman had been going through the school course and when it came to the race at the end, he had refused to take part. No-one could understand why until it became clear when he went back home to attend the course at Magny Cours and take part in the Scholarship finals. He had been astute enough to know that if he had competed in one race, the rules would have excluded him from the Scholarship It all worked out for the talented and shrewd competitor. He was unanimously voted the winner. His name? Jean Pierre Jassaud and, of course, he went on to become one of the most successful of all French racing drivers.

On this occasion, Jennifer had accompanied Jim on the trip. After the Scholarship finals, the owner of the circuit, who was also a bullock farmer, invited everyone back to his farmhouse for dinner. The hosts served the starter and then asked Jim and Jennifer if they had enjoyed it. "It was certainly different", was Jim's cautious reply. "Well, they were actually bullock's testicles" the farmer said. That certainly made Jim's eyes water!

The French school continued to operate in Jim's name for a couple of years until Bill Knight and his two sons, Mike and Richard, negotiated with Jim to take over completely. With this done, the name was changed to 'Ecole de Pilotage Winfield' (the maiden name of Bill Knight's mother) and has continued to flourish ever since, producing many top drivers such as the aforementioned Jassaud, Francoise Cevert, Alain Prost and Damon Hill.

Jim meets his first Japanese pupils in 1963. Tetsu Ikuzawa is fourth from left.

Chapter 9 A Truly International School

When a letter arrived from Japan in 1963 asking about training a group of Japanese, no-one realised the major change it was to bring to the school's training programmes. They had been advised by the RAC to contact Jim Russell. The very nature of their visit meant that, for the first time ever, Jim had to devise a concentrated course instead of the spread over training he had offered students up until then. As the Japanese students wanted to include some sight-seeing, a 14 day course was designed, giving them days off for other activities.

The five students arrived with their interpreter and it wasn't very long before it became obvious that two of them were much the best of the group. Jim had been asked to select the best pupil whose prize would be a return visit to race in England in 1964. The two star pupils were Tetsu Ikusawa, who was to successfully race for several seasons afterwards, and Tojiro Ukiya, who soon became known as 'Oh boy' because of his constant use of the phrase He had been educated in America and spoke English very well. Everything which impressed him brought those words, "Oh boy" There was very little to choose between Tetsu and Tojiro and Jim and the other instructors found it difficult to separate them. Eventually, Tojiro was chosen by a very small margin. While Tetsu went on to prove his ability for many seasons, the unfortunate Tojiro didn't get the chance. Just a few weeks after he had returned home came the distressing news that he had been killed. Apparently, he had been practising in his race saloon when someone walked across the circuit causing him to take avoiding action. He had swerved into a post at racing speed and hadn't stood a chance. It was a sad end which cut short a promising racing career. He had left his camera behind and had asked Jim to look after it until he returned to race the following year. After his untimely death, the family got in touch with Jim and suggested that he kept the camera in memory of their son. Many years later, in the 70s, John Paine and Jim visited Japan to investigate the possibility of opening a Japanese Jim Russell School. They visited the family and were made very welcome. Jim proudly showed them photographs of his family taken with their son's camera. They were invited to stay for a meal and after they had eaten, their Japanese hosts asked their visitors to follow them into another room. To their astonishment, they found that the room had been converted into a shrine in memory of Tojiro. The walls were adorned with motor racing memorabilia from their son's brief career and most of the floor area was taken up by his racing saloon. They had even fitted an extension to the exhaust system which went out through the wall so that the engine could be regularly started up. The whole set-up made a lasting impression on them.

Back in 1963, however, the Japanese 14 day course had set Jim thinking. If he could run a course for a Japanese group, why couldn't he do the same for students from America, or Europe, or anywhere else in the world? It didn't take long for the idea to be developed and the Overseas Training Course came into being. With it came an advertising campaign in other countries and soon, the Snetterton area was getting used by visitors from all over the world. Interpreters were present, more often as not, helping to get the instructions across to non-English speaking students. Over the years, the full Overseas Training Course became the very backbone of the school. Contrary to its name, British students were also welcome and many worldwide friendships developed as they spent most of their free time together.

Chris Alford was one of the many young students who had to spread their lessons over many months due to lack of money. He was an apprentice at Saab UK and it took him most of 1963 to go through from the trial lesson, followed by the corners and eventually to the lapping circuit. He, like so many others, saved up for weeks to return and eventually he got his first race at the end of the year.

Chris has never forgotten one lesson. Jim was teaching Coram Curve and time was getting short. "Instead of walking through this one", he said to the four students, "Get into my car". With them all in his Vauxhall VX/490, he drove through the corner twice at walking pace, explaining the line. Then he drove it at full speed and finally saying, "Now this is the wrong way to do it", he got all crossed up with the tail hanging out. They were all convinced that they would crash but Jim's fantastic car control straightened it out while, at the same time, he was calmly saying, "See what happens when you don't do it right?" As Chris recalls many years later, "He was right; I never did forget that lesson".

After setting fastest time in practice to claim pole position, Chris spun the car and finished second. Geddes Yeates, later to become a firm friend, won his race and together they attended the prize giving in the Club House. Apparently, Ralph Firman, who had not been with the school long, had changed a gear box during the meeting in record time and Jim, instead of congratulating him, caused a cheer by telling him that all gear box changes in future would need to be as quick.

One Sunday, while about thirty students were enjoying the Doric's lunch, a local horse trader called Fred Lowther came up to Jim in the bar. He started to sing the praises of a donkey he had for sale. He had obviously decided that he should sell it to Jim so, to get rid of him, Jim asked the price. "£30", was the reply. "OK" said Jim. "Bring her into the bar here tonight for a drink with Wally and I". Fred departed and Jim thought, "That's that", as everyone finished their lunch and returned to the circuit. Little did they know that Fred had been talking to Colin and had decided to call Jim's bluff.

That evening, Wally, Jim and Frank Gardner were all having a drink in the bar when their eyes nearly popped out of their heads. To their astonishment, Fred appeared through the back door and proceeded to calmly lead the donkey across the ballroom floor. Into the bar area they came and Jim was so taken aback that he meekly paid up the asking price The well-prepared Colin produced a straw hat for the donkey and his camera to record the unique event. While he

126

was busy taking photographs from various angles, other people were coming into the bar. Their looks of astonishment were met by Jim's announcement – "We always take our donkey for a drink in the evenings". When things had quietened down, it was decided that Fred should take the donkey out and deliver her to Bardwell the following Wednesday. Well – what a game It may have been possible to bring her across the polished dance floor the first time but there was no way she was going to return by the same route All the pushing and pulling achieved nothing ... she just refused one step onto the shiny floor. A hurried discussion brought the decision to try the front door. This was fine except for the size of the lobby. There was only room for two people and the donkey so Wally and Jim went outside to pull on the lead rope. Colin and Fred were wedged in behind her, pushing, and still she refused to move. Sheila then mounted the donkey, trying to ride her out. Suddenly, digging her front feet in, the donkey half-bucked, sending Sheila sailing over her head. Luckily for her, when the donkey had bucked, the lead rope had slackened causing Wally and Jim to collapse in a heap on the pavement. So they were there to cushion her fall Meanwhile, Colin wasn't so lucky. He was dancing around the room because the donkey had come down on his foot Except for the hapless Colin, they were all rolling around completely helpless with laughter. Jim finally controlled his mirth and stood up. As he walked towards the door, the others chorused, "Are you going to leave us to it Jim?" "No", he replied. "I'm just going for a bale of hay and a bucket of water" After that, they all decided to take a breather and consider their options. It was generally agreed that the front door exit was no good, so they had better try her across the dance floor and out through the back door again.

Suddenly, Frank Gardner, who until then had done nothing to help, announced that he would take care of things. "Which door do you want me to use?" he said with great confidence and proceeded to grab the donkey's mane in one hand and her tail in the other. It was obviously the wrong approach and the next moment, Frank was sent sprawling across the floor into Jim who was still trying to get his breath back. Without a word, Fred stood up, took off his jacket, put it over the donkey's head and led it straight across the floor. Ignoring Jim's offer of another drink, he just kept going out through the door without so much as a backwards glance.

She was duly delivered to Bardwell and given the name, Jenny. She was a feature of Bardwell Manor for many years and was frequently loaned out for local events. On one Easter Weekend, she was picked up in a horsebox and taken to a hospital fete in Bury St Edmunds. Some time later, the horsebox driver met Jim and asked him how the donkey was keeping now that she was in foal. "She's not", was the instant reply. "Oh yes she is", said the driver. "I had Lady Fisher's jack donkey on board and I saw it happen" Sure enough, right on time as donkeys take 12 months to produce, the following Easter Sunday the foal was born. Amanda, Jim's little daughter, rushed in that morning to shout excitedly, "Jenny's got a baby".

Jim reflected on the difference between the simplicity of that and the costly and involved system needed in his stud to produce foals.

Chapter 10   *Film Maker Russell*

Around 3 am one morning in January 1966, the telephone rang at Bardwell Manor and as Jim, still half asleep answered, a voice said, "Hi Jim, it's Carol Shelby – I haven't seen you since you gave me that shoulder lift at Silverstone in '59" Before Jim could answer, he continued, "There's a big motor racing film coming off and you're just the guy to help put it together. Can I come over to see you?" "Of course", said Jim, only too happy to put the phone down and get back to sleep.

The next morning he began to wonder whether it had been a dream – or maybe Wally Ward, renowned for his practical jokes, had phoned from some club in America after an evening's drinking Jennifer confirmed that there had been a phone call but Jim still thought it had been some sort of leg pull. Then, a couple of weeks later, Shelby rang again and this time he was at Heathrow Within a few hours, he was at Downham Market explaining that about 20 'mocked-up' Ferraris, BRMs, Lotus, Eagles etc were needed for a film to be called 'Grand Prix'. Jim was the only one with such a fleet which could be converted and the expertise to train the actors for the film. On top of that, Shelby announced that they had just 9 weeks to get things ready for the film "To do that", replied Jim, "I would have to close down the school tomorrow – sell the cars to MGM, if you like, and start straight away". "I was hoping you'd say that", said Shelby, immediately shaking hands on the deal. Within a few days, a cheque for £10,000 deposit arrived from MGM and everybody got busy. The first priority, in order to 'mock-up' the new season's Grand Prix cars, was to see the designs. The script was written around Lotus and off went Jim to see Chapman. Despite receiving an order for 18 new school cars, to replace the fleet which was about to be cut about for the film, Chapman would not reveal his new models.

Jim came away and phoned John Frankenheimer, the film's director. "OK", came the reply. "If that's the case, why not try BRM?" Jim took a trip to Bourne where they were happy to show him around. Using his small pocket camera he shot pictures of the partially assembled new models. One of the staff even held up the exhaust against the body for one picture. Amazingly, the end result was almost exactly right. When Jim reported this to Frankenheimer, his prompt reaction was, "Fine – we'll change the script and stars James Garner and Brian Bedford will have to drive BRMs".

Meanwhile, MGM had bought all the school's cars for the price of new ones. The regular students were kept happy by being given the chance to 'run-in' the new cars for nothing in readiness for the school re-opening.

◁ *Mock up Grand Prix cars being prepared at Downham Market.*   **129**

Body builders William and Pritchard in London were approached to make the 'mock-up' bodies and were aghast at the lack of drawings. They were persuaded to work from suitably altered pictures of the previous season's cars together with Jim's recent BRM photos. Fortunately, with no wings or spoilers, design changes were not too dramatic from year to year. While the bodies were being made, the staff at Downham Market were busy preparing the wheels. In order to make them look like the real thing, school wheels were split in half and widened. Carved out wood and locally-made plastic discs completed them.

Transport was the next problem to overcome. The school only had one transporter and Jim estimated that 6 two-tier transporters plus a mobile workshop were necessary. The 'hot-line' to Frankenheimer brought the go-ahead and Jim approached Hertz with 5 weeks to go. They were quoting 6 months delivery It took lengthy negotiations and agreement that their name would be prominent on the bodies for the film to get the required chassis cabs released. The coach builders in Norwich, when asked to build the bodies in 5 weeks were adamant – no way was it possible with Easter coming up and a queue of work waiting. Again, fast talking by Jim and the offer to pay for overtime at double rate made the difference. They would build 6 with 2 car ramps and one as a mobile workshop in time. "Put that in writing", said Jim, "And you'll get 50% deposit by return of post". A similar story applied with the 6 trailers required. Don Parker, Jim's old sparring partner from their Formula III 500cc days was too busy, but another double priced deal with a different company ensured that the two-tier trailers were ready to link up with the transporters.

While this was going on, James Garner, Yves Montand, Brian Bedford and Tony Sabato, the stars of the film, arrived at Snetterton to be trained. Although like true professionals they took to the training very well, Garner's size proved to be a problem. A car had to be cut and lengthened for his 6'2" frame before he could start. Drivers were recruited to double in the film

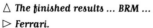

△ *The finished results ... BRM ...*
▷ *Ferrari.*

including Belgian father and son, Andre and Teddy Pillette, Jo Schlessor, Paul Frere, Bob Bondurant, Tony Lanfranchi, Ken Costello and several of the school's senior student racers.

Everything had to be at the MGM studios in Nice by May 2nd as the filming was to start around the Monaco GP. In those hectic last few weeks, Downham Market became the focal point. The mock cars were being assembled – mechanics and helpers were being engaged but finally everything was assembled and loaded. The impressive caravan of transporters and trailers rolled out of the Norfolk market town on its way to the South of France.

When everything was settled at Nice, Jim announced that he was returning home to look after his other investments – the garage, the school with the new Lotus cars arriving, and school race meetings. Frankenheimer said, "I need you in my pocket while we're making this film. My pipe is in this pocket and I want you in the other – and by the way, I've got another job for you. I've got 9 Japanese students with their professor and I want you to train them to look like mechanics in the film" So after concluding a satisfactory monetary agreement and arranging for regular flights back home, Jim took on the extra training job. He found it one of the most difficult tasks of the film However, MGM, true to their word, made sure he was on a plane back for race meetings involving the school while John Maston and Colin Campbell looked after things at Snetterton. Getting payment through from the States began causing a few problems so Jim decided to have a word with his Solicitor, Jack Jeffries. He suggested that Jack should travel down to Nice with the crew. Jack got his passport and travellers cheques quickly organised ready to leave the following day. In addition to proving invaluable during negotiations, he was given a job with mechanics for 3 weeks and greased up to the elbows

It was in Nice that Jim made his first acquaintance with 'Beady Eyes', who sidled up to him to introduce himself. A

„Not so much room as in my road car back home" says James Garner.

Co-star Yves Montand seems engrossed in the rear suspension.

131

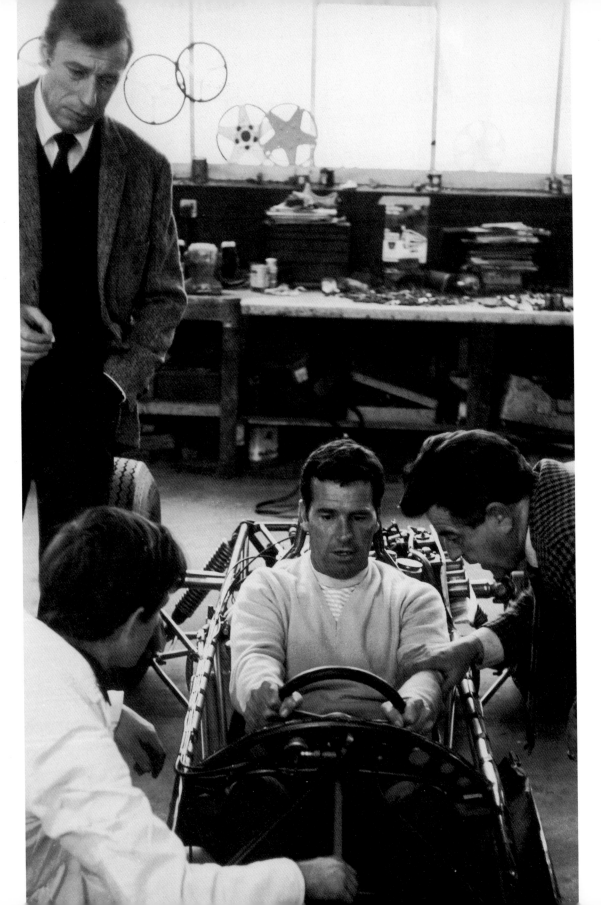

Ralph Firman watches Garner's attempt to get into a racing car!

Looks like we'll have to lenghten the car for you ...

... yes we will.

Montand „I suppose I'll have to give up smoking if I want to be a racing driver!"

◁ *James Garner gets the JR instruction while Montand looks on.*

„Take care", says Jim.   *Wagons roll ... the journey to Monaco starts.*

larger-than-life Bronx individual, 'Beady Eyes' explained that he was the props man on the film. "What's a props man?" asked Jim. "Well, you know if it's a cowboy film I look after the horses and if there's a stable, I put the horse s--t down – that sort of thing. But I'm the most worried man in the whole unit; I've never worked with racing cars before. Whatever you do, don't leave me". So Jim had another task – showing 'Beady Eyes' everything in the lorries and explaining about stop watches, pit signalling boards, cans, funnels, jacks and everything else regularly around motor racing. 'Beady Eyes' was a real character – always getting 'bawled out' by Frankenheimer, running around all day long. In those days, GP cars didn't have a permanent number allocated for the season, so at each venue stick-on numbers were used and, naturally, the 'mock-up' cars had to be the same. 'Beady Eyes' had to check and make sure that he had all the numbers right each day. On one occasion, watching a play-back, John Frankenheimer said, "'Beady Eyes', you've got those numbers on wrong again – what happened?" To which the props man replied, "I've gone through 300 sets of numbers already". "What are you doing – playing Bingo? How can the best props man in the business get through all those numbers in such a short time?" said the Director. "Oh that's easy, John. All you have to do is keep putting them on and pulling them off" was the reply.

One of the most dramatic scenes at Monaco was the re-enactment of two cars touching and one of the going straight over the harbour wall into the sea with the other one hitting the cliff face. For this, a special gun – known as the 'Big Blow' – had been designed by the special effects team and built at Downham Market in advance. In fact, it had been successfully tested at Snetterton to the great delight of Frankenheimer who also persuaded the local press to keep their photos under wraps until after the film had premiered. 'Big Blow' was a sort of cannon

134

with about 600lb pressure provided from a large tank attached. It was fitted into a engine-less car with a steel tube to slide over the power nozzle. It worked a treat to fire one BRM into the sea, so the next day, cameras were readied with an automatic one placed on a straw bale about 30 yards ahead. The BRM was expected to hit the wall but the force was much greater than expected. The car rode the cliff face like a 'wall of death', ending up on top of the automatic camera. John, despite the damage, was delighted shouting, "OK, that's it – cut and print it" He knew it was a once only chance to get such a spectacular scene.

Price Rainier, Princess Grace and family were in attendance while these scenes were being shot – and so were the TV crew from Whickers World who filmed MGM filming with the Royals watching.

It was in the pits at Monaco that Frankenheimer noticed a shortage of stop watches. "Beady Eyes", he yelled, "We need some stop watches by tomorrow at the latest" The next day the watches were there ... a whole gross of them Everyone down to the lowest assistant had one

They were filming Yves Montand driving through a section of the circuit ... just after Casino Square ... he suddenly lost it and veered off right into the wall. Jim went running down and before he could get there, Montand was out of the car. He grinned at Jim and said, "Jim I don't die at Monaco ... I die at Monza" "Well, just make sure you stick to the script from now on", replied Jim, very concerned for the Frenchman's safety.

At this time, Frankenheimer was most concerned about an opposition film, 'The Day of The Champion'. It was being put together by Warner Brothers starring Steve McQueen. Stirling Moss was doing a similar job to Jim for them. The main worry was timing – if 'The Day of The Champion' was released first, it would affect the sales of 'Grand Prix'. So it was

△ *'Big Blow' is tried out at Snetterton.*
▷ *„Looks O.K." say Peter, special effects man Bobbie Ronning and Jim!*

'Big Blow' has done its job
and the BRM nears the
Monaco harbour ...

... goes over the edge ...

... nose dives into sea ...

... and splash!!

becoming a race to complete. Then, as the unit left Monaco for Spa, Frankenheimer said, "Jim, you are staying in the best hotel in Belgium and we're going out to the best restaurant for dinner". "What's this all about?" said Jim. "Well", came the reply, "They've scrubbed 'The Day of The Champion' – in fact we're buying lots of their equipment" A very jubilant crew arrived to film the Belgium Grand Prix.

It turned out to be a wet race so naturally the actual race footage showed this. Subsequently, the sun was shining for the film scenes and a Belgian fire engine had to be hired to spray the circuit The story called for Yves Montand's Ferrari to lose a wheel, go off course and kill two children. The car was fitted with a split pin in the hub which was pulled out by the driver with a lever on the dashboard. Jim did the driving – the pin came out, the wheel dropped off and the car spun. Then 'Big Blow' was brought into use to fire the car through the corner of a building to 'kill' the two boys. Because 'Big Blow' hadn't been shot at an angle before, they wedged it against a small bridge across the road. The two dummies were put in place, three cameras and crews lined up and Frankenheimer did his usual countdown. The gun moved around missing the building and the dummies. More importantly, it very nearly shot the car into the pack of cameramen "Goddammit Jim", said the Director. "What went wrong?" "We need a lot more sandbags to hold the gun steady",

Princess Grace and Prince Rainer get the details from John Frankenheimer during the filming. Jo Bonnier (centre back) seems disinterested but Jim looks very pleased.

Jim replied, adding that it would take a further two hours to prepare the gun and another Ferrari 'mock-up' for the stunt. "You've got one and a half hours only", was the Director's retort. But despite this, when the equipment was ready with a new Ferrari body in place, he yelled, "We haven't got any badges on it Where the hell are they?" "In my briefcase in the pits", was the reply and despite more time lost, the meticulous Director waited for them to be placed in position although he knew they wouldn't even be seen in the shot With the sequence completed everyone returned to base at Downham Market to refettle for the British GP at Brands.

Before they could get things going, they had problems with the RAC who, to say the least, were unco-operative.. Jim set up a meeting with Basil Tye, who at first was adamant there could be no film crew and actors all around just before the Grand Prix. Jim said, "But Basil, we're trying to make the first serious motor racing film – we need to be authentic – crowd scenes – our actor drivers in the pits with the real drivers etc – it's got to be good for motor racing" So Basil relented and they had the circuit for 30 minutes prior to the event after Jim

'Big Blow' is readied for the
accident scene at Spa.

The 'mock up' Ferrari at Spa. Rudy
Gates greases the tyres. Jim is
engrossed in discussion with
'Beady Eyes' while Frankenheimer
urges him to hurry!

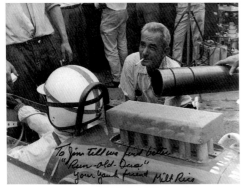

Special effects man, Milt Rice,
with 'Big Blow'.

had met him at Snetterton to finally get the details sorted out. There was even a helicopter on stand-by in case Montand broke down on the circuit so that he could quickly be brought back to the pits where they needed the stars to be filmed mingling with the real Grand Prix drivers. Jim drove the lead car and they set off around the circuit with cameras on the cars to film the crowds. All went well and the Grand Prix timetable stayed as planned.

Later, the fire sequence was filmed. Rudy and the special effects crew fixed a gas jet on the back of Garner's car. He had to hit a special switch to ignite it. Frankenheimer wanted to increase the drama and asked the crew to fit another jet outside the cockpit for Garner to hit as he was getting out. They set off for a lap of the circuit with Jim, doubling as Montand, leading. Garner decided to overtake him just before the pits straight where he was to ignite the jets in front of the cameramen. Things nearly went wrong in the biggest possible way when Garner's knee caught the switch which was fitted in the American way of up for on, as he went to clamber out. The car was ablaze before he could stop in front of the camera crew. As these cameramen hauled him to safety, Jim had memories of his own Le Mans inferno and backed off very quickly. It could so easily have been a disaster and, as Garner was getting over his miraculous escape, he was very relieved to hear Frankenheimer yell, "OK, cut and print ... we don't want to go through that again".

Back at Downham Market, all the cars were stripped down in preparation for the Dutch Grand Prix at Zandvoort when the phone rang. It was Frankenheimer who said to Jim, "We have an American TV crew coming to film us filming. So, I need three cars for Montand, Garner and you at Brands Hatch this Wednesday. You will have to lead them for as long as you think necessary for them to be ready to drive one fast lap of the circuit". All the stops were pulled out to prepare the cars and get them down to Brands Hatch. When Jim gave them the instructions, Garner said he didn't think he needed to be led round but Montand said, "Jim, I'll follow you all day" So

Jim led Montand round the circuit for some laps and then arranged the dummy race. He put Garner on pole position with Montand alongside and the camera car behind them.

On the grid, Garner said, "Tell Montand that I'll lead into the paddock bend and he can tuck in behind". Jim told this to Montand who gave him his famous wink and grinned. Knowing what was likely to happen, Jim dropped the flag and disappeared. Sure enough, the Frenchman made a storming start and Garner had to be content with 'second fiddle'. He was most annoyed at being upstaged in front of the TV cameras and had to be placated with promises that such a thing wouldn't happen again.

The next call was for them to all go to a pub in Kent where, allegedly, the drivers were celebrating after the British Grand Prix. This, incidentally, was where Graham Hill had his line to speak. The pub was taken over and all the drinks were free. 'Beady Eyes' had his most unusual job – he was sent off to London to find an attractive French prostitute for what was called the 'tit scene'. Needless to say, – the evening became rather blurred in everyone's memory.

After an almost uneventful filming at Zandvoort, the caravan rolled onto Clermont Ferrand and 'mocked-up' the French Grand Prix which was being held at another circuit. Next it was the Italian Grand Prix at Monza where the script called for them to 'kill off' Montand. Back in England before the British Grand Prix, Jim had devised a way of filming a close-up of Montand's face at the very moment of his spin. A turntable was built over the suspension of one of the school's old cars. The car could be driven by someone else while the turntable, 'mocked-up' as the front of a Ferrari, gave this effect of a spin To try it out, someone else drove the car at Snetterton while Jim sat in the 'Ferrari' cockpit with his cine camera. The resultant film proved that it worked and Jim told Frankenheimer, adding that Montand would look too high from the ground. "Since when have you been a director, Jim Russell?" he growled. "Your idea is great, now just leave the rest to us".

Montand and Garner lead the rest to form the grid at Brands Hatch.

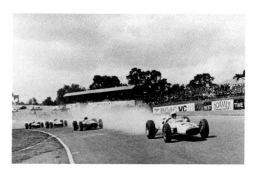

James Garner out in front at Brands Hatch followed by Jim 'doubling' for Montand.

Phil Hill in discussion with Montand while Jim seems distracted by something else.

It was at Monza that Frankenheimer asked Jim to take out the restrictive rotor arm from Montand's car so that they could film it showing 7,000 revs on the clock. By using these cheap rotor arms, costing only about 37 pence, they could successfully keep the engine revs down to below 6,000 revs and save a lot of expensive engine rebuilds. Sure enough, not used to having to watch his rev counter, Montand promptly took it up to 8,000 revs with the inevitable cloud of expensive smoke as the engine exploded.

"Goddammit Jim – I'm sorry", said Frankenheimer. "You can shake hands through the engine block ... you were so right ... let's make sure we always keep those rotor arms in".

When they got to filming the sequence where Montand was 'killed', they used the old banking which had been in disuse for a couple of years. The scene entailed Montand's car hitting an exhaust system which had fallen off another car before spinning up and over the top of the banking. This was filmed in three stages. Firstly, the normal car coming upon the loose exhaust. The second stage was Jim using the special turntable car with Montand in the 'Ferrari' cockpit. Because the camera was on the side of the car and the banking on his left, it worked out well and Montand didn't look too high despite his elevated position. After the spin had been performed, the third stage was to bring in 'Big Blow' to launch a car, and the dummy of Montand which ended up in a tree at the top of the banking.

This was probably the major scene of the film and Jim missed the final part after going to the aid of one of the mechanics. A car fell off a jack and landed on the unfortunate worker. Jim immediately rushed forward and physically lifted the car up for the man to roll clear, only to end up himself in hospital with back trouble. It was brother-in-law, Ralph Firman, who flew out to Italy to oversee the last of the filming.

Frankenheimer had devised a scheme to get crowds on all the non-race meeting days around Europe. Apart from paying everyone £5 as extras, he made sure to have some half a

Mock up Ferrari on display.

dozen cars and caravans which were raffled off each day. When he wanted the crowd to stand up and cheer for the cameras, he simply had someone announce a winner's name.

Flying back with the MGM executives, Jim was given a form to sign. In return, he was handed a cheque for £100. "What's this for?" he asked. "Well, you remember being filmed at Monaco for Whickers World? You were in the shot so you get paid" Not bad, thought Jim, at 25,000 feet With the film finished, they

With Frankenheimer at the film's premiere.

were asked to build a special BRM for the London cinema foyer when the film was premiered. The big night arrived and everyone was standing around waiting for Frankenheimer. He stepped out of a taxi on his own and was immediately asked who he was with. "Goddammit – I'm with Jim Russell", he said, walking over to shake Jim's hand. After the premiere, everyone moved over to a local hotel for a celebration dinner and one of the film's stars, Francoise Hardy, was appearing in cabaret. Over the meal, Frankenheimer asked Jim if he would make another motor racing film. "You mean like 'Son of Grand Prix'?" said Jim. "Well yes, with what I've learned over the past months – no problem as long as I've got twice as long to do it".

Naturally, the school had suffered through the closure. To help put it back on its feet, a leaflet was quickly prepared about the school which had trained the stars for the film. These were used on boards in cinema foyers to great effect. The commissionaires were paid to keep the stands topped up with the leaflets and a steady stream of new students headed for the school again.

John Mastin, who had looked after the school while Jim had been mostly away for the film, decided to move on and Jim bought him out. So for some time, Jim was the sole director of the school.

Some time later on, an American journalist came to interview Jim about the film Before doing so, he played him parts of a recorded interview he had done with John Frankenheimer. Asking the director about the costs, Frankenheimer had said, "To weight it all up, the stars cost thousands of dollars and the cars cost thousands of cents, but the cars were the stars" The interviewer said, "I thought that would make your day". "It certainly has", was Jim's reply.

Jim with staff and pupils and the Lotus 51's under the long gone Esso footbridge.

Chapter 11
Back to Reality and Formula Ford

Sometime late in December 1966, John Webb and Geoff Clarke came up with an idea for a new 'junior' racing formula which was to sweep the world. Rumour has it that the concept came during a rather extended drinking session after the pair had slipped away from the Racing Car Show 'setting-up' day at Olympia. Clarke, who was then running Motor Racing Stables discussed the high costs of running his school cars with the boss of Brands Hatch Circuits. He remembered enough of the conversation to continue talking it through further with Jim over the next few days. Jim was very enthusiastic and together with John Webb, the two school owners 'knocked' the idea into shape. While they saw the idea of a cheap school single seater using standard Ford Cortina engines and road wheels, Webb saw a new 'starter' racing formula. When Ford's Competitions Manager, Henry Taylor, agreed to supply Cortina engines at £50 each, it was agreed to call the new concept 'Formula Ford' With the much lower costs of the engine and road-going wheels and tyres, they were able to make the controlled ceiling price of the car under £1,000. Apart from anything else, this was only about a third of the cost of a FIII car which was also very expensive to maintain. Naturally, this took the motor racing scene by storm. Colin Chapman was keen to build the cars using the Ford engines and, at a Snetterton meeting the following March, wanted Jim to

order 50 cars. "No way", was the reply. "I'll order and pay for 10 straight away. Then I'll order and pay for more as I want them". They agreed to disagree and, while Chapman did a deal with MRS, Jim approached Jack Brabham to build an initial batch of 10 cars. It was several weeks before Jack phoned to say that his other commitments were too great to allow him to build Formula Fords. Another manufacturer to also turn down the idea was McLaren who was very busy building Formula B cars for the States. No doubt both were to regret their decision later as the formula really took off. It wasn't long before Jim had met and talked to Allan Taylor, who was producing Alexis cars on a small scale in Birmingham.

Lotus 51's ready to go.

Russell Alexis in the Snetterton pitlane.

A deal was struck for Allan to produce Formula Fords which were to be financed and sold by Jim. The new Russell-Alexis car was soon designed and being produced. Not in time for the first ever Formula Ford race at Brands Hatch, however. This was held on 2nd July 1967 and, in order to enter his students, Jim converted some of the school Lotus 51 cars to the new specification for this first race. History was made by Ray Allen when he won that very first Formula Ford race in an MRS car but the Jim Russell cars filled the next three places driven by Malcolm Paine, Claude Bourgoignie and Malcolm Fletcher.

By using the tried and tested Hewland gearbox, the Russell-Alexis was soon proving to be a much better option than the Lotus FF which was using a Renault gearbox. This was constantly giving problems, especially for MRS. The Hewland box also scored because, unlike the Renault box, ratios could be changed for the different circuit requirements. The Russell-Alexis sales started to take off, especially with Claude Bourgoignie winning race after race in the JRRDS car. Claude not only won the next four races on the trot, he also set lap records every time. Jim was selling racing cars so well that the Russell-Alexis factory was working flat out to keep up with the demand. By the end of the year, they had sold 54 of them, including one to a novice driver named James Hunt. Geoff Clarke who, unlike Jim, had given Colin Chapman his required order for 50 cars in two batches of 25, was regretting his decision. He had raised money to buy the first 25 cars and due to the fragility of the Renault gearbox and the successes of the Russell-Alexis, he was stuck with most of them. He cancelled his order for the second batch and Chapman immediately came to Jim to ask him to become a Lotus agent It gave Jim a lot of satisfaction to be able to remind the Lotus boss of their earlier conversation and follow it up by telling him how well the Russell-Alexis operation was going. "I'm very much a rival manufacturer now, Colin", he said with some relish. "Anyway, I thought you would only deal with orders of 50 or more cars at a time" For once, Chapman had no answer.

It wasn't long before Lotus were fitting Hewland gearboxes to their Formula Ford cars but they had lost a lot of ground to both the Russell-Alexis and Merlyn, another newly designed and competitive car.

Dave Walker originally came to England from his native Australia in 1963. Working as a car salesman at the renowned Chequered Flag Garage in Chiswick, he was able to get some money together to help start a racing career. With fellow countryman John Layton, he enrolled in the JRRDS, visiting Snetterton as often as time and money would allow. At the end of the year, he returned home. For the next three years, he raced everything he could before returning to England in 1966. Like so many other impoverished racing drivers at the time, he joined the infamous travelling Continental FIII 'circus'. The principle was simple. On the continent, it was possible to get 'starting' money, which was a small amount paid to each driver who turned up and actually started a race. This pittance, sometimes augmented by prize money for a good finish, just about kept the drivers going. Like a nomadic tribe, they would tour the continent, going from one race meeting to another. Most of them were towing their race cars behind ancient vans in which they also lived Eventually, like many others, Dave found his money wouldn't even support his frugal needs and returned to England. A chance meeting with Allan Taylor led to a three way deal for Dave to have a Russell-Alexis and keep it in the Jim Russell workshop. Also sharing the space and facilities was the JRRDS car which was being looked after by Ralph Firman and driven by Claude Bourgoignie. Ralph Firman was working as a mechanic in an Ipswich garage when his sister, Jennifer, became Mrs Russell in the early sixties. When a vacancy came up in the JRRDS workshop, Jim offered the job to his brother-in-law. It wasn't long before Ralph caught the motor racing bug and was moved to the racing team. Then Claude had a big accident and the remains of his car were stuck in the corner of the workshop. After some time with nothing happening to it, Dave and Claude went to Jim to suggest that the car be repaired. Jim had more or less written off the idea of repairing it, but there was another way. "Tell you what", he said to them, "You repair it and I'll pay the running costs. Any prize money will be yours". They didn't need more than that to start them rebuilding. They worked day and night to quickly get it back into racing trim. Claude finished up the season by not only winning the 1966 Ford Cup but also becoming the world's first Formula Ford Champion.

Sales of the Russell-Alexis were still buoyant and Claude continued to shine in the FF Championships. Henry Morragh was now School Manager and he was joined that year by David Waring, who had completed a full course and had impressed Jim as a potential instructor. As was so often the case, Jim was absolutely right and within a year, he had appointed David as a director of the school.

1967 was the year they moved onto the Snetterton circuit. The move only came after long drawn-out talks with John Webb of Brands Hatch Circuits who had, by then, bought Snetterton from Oliver Sear and Fred Riches, still remembered by the corners named after them. John Webb would only offer Jim a year-by-year agreement but Jim naturally wanted more security than that before he would move in. While they were at loggerheads over this, Jim started thinking about building a circuit of his own. He looked around the area and found a suitable site at Shepherds Grove, near to Stanton, between Bury St Edmunds and Diss. As the 'crow flies', it was only a couple of miles from Jim's Bardwell home He had plans drawn up and applied for planning permission. This was actually granted and furthermore, he was able to get agreement to run meetings up to National status When John Webb heard about this, he immediately rang Jim and arranged for an urgent meeting. He and fellow director, Chris Lowe, met Jim for lunch and they were obviously anxious to prevent the new circuit going ahead. John relaxed his demands and said to Jim, "What do you want to go to all that trouble and expense for when you've got the use of Snetterton?" This time, the terms were much different and a renewable seven year lease was agreed. The paperwork was soon finalised by the school's solicitors, Wright Hassall & Co who, despite their name, efficiently acted for the school for many years. With hindsight, and the various changes at Snetterton over the years, Jim often thought back to the Shepherds Grove project. As time went by, he felt that he had made a mistake and regretted not going ahead with those plans.

Apart from using a Nissen hut just outside the circuit to store a few cars, for 10 years they had moved most of the cars to and from Downham Market every time the school operated. They also only had a small caravan which acted as both office and classroom. Woe betide the students if it was wet as most of them stood outside for instruction lessons The meeting put an end to that situation. John Webb and Chris Lowe offered Jim a deal. He could move the school onto the circuit and pay them a rent, provided that Jim paid for the buildings and everything else. Having agreed to this, he was soon off to Stoke Ferry, about mid-way between Snetterton and Downham, where he knew they sold ex-Army Nissen huts. He purchased three and they were dismantled, taken to Snetterton and erected at the back of the paddock. Two of them were for workshops and the other one was the office and classroom building. They fully expected to use a generator, like everyone else, for electricity but their luck was in. The move coincided with mains electricity being brought onto the circuit.

Ted Lusted, who was then the track's regular fire marshal, had a friend, Brian Feltham, who was a GPO engineer. Together, they wired up the buildings. Brian already looked after the circuit's PA system at the weekends and a solid friendship grew between Brian and Jim.

The school staff luxuriated in the new arrangements and Colin Campbell, who had left the Doric restaurant to join the school a few months earlier, set up the offices. Despite the fact that, in some places, the ground could be seen through large gaps in the floor, it was a lot better than the previous involved arrangements.

The race car was not moved from the Jim Russell Garage at Downham. It had to be towed back and fro when needed. Henry Morragh was asked to do the towing one weekend. After practice at Snetterton on the Saturday evening, Henry hitched up the race car on the trailer and left for the workshop. When he drove back in on the Sunday morning, Jim's eagle eyes spotted some new-looking repair work on the race car. He didn't take long to find out the facts and

146

The fleet of Merlyns outside the Snetterton HO.

Henry had to own up. He had gone to a party on the Saturday night and, instead of parking the trailer and race car in the garage, he had left it behind his road car outside. Coming out of the party in the early hours, he had been horrified to find that someone had crashed into the trailer, damaging the race car With some friends, he had tried to carry out hasty repairs in the limited time available before leaving for the circuit. Unfortunately for him, the repairs had failed to fool Jim. The outcome, putting it mildly, was that Henry was asked to leave forthwith.

Operating the school without a Manager was not in Jim's plans. He suddenly thought of John Paine who, after attending the school a few years earlier and coming back to race, had applied for the Manager's job. At the time, John was unaware that the position was taken by Henry. However, when Jim told him of the vacancy, he was still very interested. A meeting led to a mutual agreement and their long association started on January 1st 1968.

John didn't find it too easy to settle in at the school. There was a certain amount of resentment at the change and he found some resistance to his efforts to take control. He was never quite sure that Colin Campbell was on his side in those early days. Colin had been looking after things while the school was without a Manager and it seemed that he was reluctant to give up the chair. Fortunately, after some initial problems, things settled down.

On one occasion, just after Jimmy Clark had been killed, John received a phone call from Lotus. They were anxious to give Jimmy's replacement driver, Jackie Oliver, some circuit driving time before going off to the Monaco Grand Prix. They had been unable to book the circuit as the school was using it for training and so they asked whether they could come down for part of the day. "Fine", said John. "It will be no problem to let Jackie drive in between our lapping sessions. Please check before going out on the circuit so that we can make sure that our students have stopped lapping".

Later on, John was down at Sear Corner watching over the lapping when suddenly the Lotus FI car appeared As it flew around the outside of the school cars, the petrified student drivers didn't know which way to go John hastily waved them off the circuit before the Lotus could come by again and went back to the pits to find out what had gone wrong. The Lotus crew insisted that 'the office' had given them clearance to start lapping but didn't know which person. John decided that, as no real harm had been done, he would let the matter rest but he had his private suspicions for a long time.

Wally Ward.

Wally Ward was no longer with the school. He had come to an agreement with Jim a couple of years earlier that he would like to go it alone in America. Taking a few cars as his pay-out, he had gone to the Willow Springs Circuit to open his school. This was, of course, the very first Jim Russell school in the States. Whether after a year or two he tired of the country or, as was rumoured, he lost the school in a card game, it passed into the hands of the Kastner family. Father Chet and son John continued to run the 'Jim Russell School' although they had never asked for, or had been given, permission from Jim.

Jim was still very embroiled in the daily running of the Snetterton operation. John Paine was taking care of a lot of the administration and was rapidly becoming a regular instructor alongside Jim. As he had from the very beginning, Jim strove hard for student safety above all else and encouraged his staff to do likewise.

Although there had been several lady students at the school ever since it opened, it was 1968 before a young lady from Birmingham, Sheila Islip, had the honour of becoming the first lady graduate to get her International racing licence. Like other female racing drivers before and after her, the media took a lot of interest and, naturally, they liked glamour photographs around the racing cars. In their case, Sheila and her boyfriend, Mike Underwood, bought one of the Russell-Alexis cars which they shared in public races for the next few seasons.

Not long after John had joined, a suggestion was made that the school ought to have a get-together. Apart from the Doric dinner a few years earlier, they hadn't organised a social event. It was decided to keep the costs low, so it was held in the circuit's cafeteria complete with plastic knives and forks About 30 students, guests and staff attended the meal which was priced at 6 shillings (30p). The unexpected guest was Miss India, who had just been voted Miss World a few days before. Needless to say, her escort was the proudest student present. The evening did, in fact, set a precedent. Although no plans were made at the time for another one, the school's Annual Dinner Dance and Prize Giving had been launched.

There have always been under-financed

Claude Bourgoignie receives his awards from Miss India. Colin Campbell (with mike) and John Paine (centre).

embryo racing drivers will to make any sacrifice to get into a racing car. Naturally, a lot of them converged on to the Jim Russell School and, saving as much money as possible for vital lessons, many of them forsook even the cheapest local bed and breakfast establishments. It was quite common to see tents pitched and cars, vans or caravans parked around the school which served as living quarters during their owner's stay. One such pupil in 1968 was Rod Pithers, who has vivid memories of sleeping in a tent in the pits area. He looks back thankfully at his training, stressing that the basics learnt applied equally to the driving school he has run for many years.

Although the new F100 sports car series, launched to use the new Firestone tyre of that designation, failed to make a lasting impression, it did introduce the Firestone family to the school. Brooks Firestone, son of the Chairman, initially arranged to bring a very prestigious small group of important business associates to the school for a driving day. They included a couple of financiers, Richard Hambro and a Mr Weinberg, the boss of Rothschild Finance. The day was a success and Brooks had been hooked on motor racing. So much so that shortly afterwards, he came back to do a full course His father, Harvey Firestone, flew over at the weekend specially to watch him race with the school. Brooks carried on through the season and even did a couple of public races but the family and business colleagues began to get nervous about the risks involved. By the end of the season, the promising career of Brooks Firestone had come to a premature end.

When Lincolnshire lad, Mo Harness, finished his training course, he wanted to stay around. Like so many others, he was loathe to leave the special atmosphere of the school. He badgered

John for a job and, although there was no obvious vacancy, he was taken on as an odd-job man. He would collect spares and move cars around. One day, he was driving the school van back down the very wide road which had originally been a runway, when he saw one of the mechanics coming towards him in his car. Messing about, they both started to swerve one way and the other. Before they knew it, they were upon each other and, misjudging things, they collided Jim soon heard about this and the needless damage to his van. "What are you going to do about it?" he demanded of Mo. "It's all right", was the reply. "Your garage is going to loan us another one" No-one knew how, but the event blew over and Mo was still around If the truth was known, it was probably that his rare turn of speed in a racing car was Jim's reason for keeping him. In fact, he was beginning to get chances in a third race team car augmenting Dave Walker and Claude Bourgoignie from time to time.

Up until then, of course, student racers had been entered in public races using the school's cars. It was decided that, with some 70 to 80 racing members, they should form the Jim Russell Racing Drivers Club. With Colin Campbell as Secretary, they approached the RAC for a licence to run their own meetings. At first, the reaction was unfavourable. The RAC pointed out that there were plenty of public races where the students could compete. However, Jim argued that the number of racing students were now far too many for a couple of races to accommodate them. Only

Race day officials ... Bert Mitchum, Brian Feltham, John Clifford, Harry Driver and Colin Campbell.

about a quarter of their number would get to race at each meeting. It really needed a full programme to allow all of them to race. After some deliberation, the RAC relented and issued the licence. Straight away, the JRRDC race programme was organised and became a very popular feature of the school. In order to run their own meetings, they needed to recruit people to fill the necessary positions of Clerk of The Course, Scrutineer, Stewards and Marshals etc. Fortunately, Jim had a circle of friends acquired mainly from his racing days and once they had started, they nearly all stayed on year after year. Phil Hessletine was a regular Steward, Harry Driver was Clerk of The Course, Henry Rylett and Dallas Smith were regular Scrutineers and John and Oona Clifford were nearly always involved in the race organisation. They and many others who marshalled became staunch supporters and the backbone of the school's race meetings over many years. The meetings attracted large entries, sometimes well over a hundred graduates took part, many of them returning again and again. In fact, there are always some who have never raced in anything but school races, just enjoying their racing as a hobby and having no aspirations to make a racing career. These

A typical Snetterton race day scene.

school race meetings attracted some students to come back from all over the world just to enjoy the special atmosphere of the unique 'closed to school' events.

Jim's important 'rev' limit, which was such an integral part of the training programme, continued with the race meetings. Jim insisted that rev limits were the best way to make a driver disciplined and very few could argue with that. It meant that, very often, the first man to pass the flag was not always the winner. As the cars came into the pits at the end of a race, the instructors ran forward to check the rev counter. It had a 'tell-tale' needle which went up with the revs but did not return A time penalty was applied to drivers according to the amount they had exceeded the limit by and the results were amended accordingly. Most graduates accepted this as part of the school's rule book but it didn't take long for some of them to try to 'buck the system'. Those who did quickly found out that, by putting a hand up behind the rev counter as they entered the pit lane, they could push the button which sent the 'tell-tale' needle back to zero. Admittedly, that took some explaining but they figured they would dodge a time penalty The school soon realised that this was happening and devised a system which eliminated the opportunity for the driver. They fitted tubes down through the body cowling so that only an instructor with a length of wire could reset the needle.

Over the years, the excuses for 'over-revving' could have filled a book ... "Missed a gear" or

"My foot slipped off the pedal" were two of the most popular ones. Nevertheless, it was only in the 1990s, when the school had updated to Vauxhall Formula Junior cars that the system, which had stood the test of time so well, was finally discarded.

Patrick Neve was a countryman of Claude Bourgoignie and had met Jim when he was running Claude in a Belgian Formula Ford race. He was very enthusiastic about motor racing and Jim had told him that, when he was ready, he should come to the school. About a year later, he came to Snetterton. He arrived when everyone was at lunch so, looking around, he found an unlocked window and climbed in When they returned, Jim and John found him sitting there. Jim was convinced that his enthusiasm would make him into a good instructor while John, who didn't think much of Patrick's 'breaking and entering', wasn't so sure. Of course, he stayed Later, after training, he was added to the instruction staff and, on and off, he was with the school for about ten years. He was always getting into hot water for one thing or another and, on the road, he only had two speeds ... fast and very fast. Consequently, he was forever damaging cars yet, with his natural boyish charm and broken English, he managed to get out of trouble both with the Police and Jim In fact, he got away with much more than other members of staff and even managed to persuade Jim to supply him with a Formula Ford to start his racing career.

Later on, of course, he moved up through Formula III and into Formula I where he was one of the first to drive for Frank Williams who was then struggling to get a foothold in Grand Prix racing.

It was in 1970 that John Webb, seeing the success of the school at Snetterton, suggested to Jim that he should open a branch at Mallory Park. The idea was discussed and everyone saw the sense in having a school in the Midlands. The added bonus would be that they would have a second venue for school races and, even more importantly, they could now comply with the RAC stipulation that applicants for full race licences were required to have signatures from at least two circuits.

Very soon, it was set up and David Waring moved over to take charge. They had the use of the circuit on three Saturdays a month. Within a few months, there were quite a few of the Mallory students ready for the next stage. With an interchange of senior students taking the advanced courses, they were able to qualify and race at both the school's circuits. By the following year, the race programme included both venues. Once again, the Jim Russell School had a unique feature which no other school could offer. Nick Masters joined that year as Manager of the Mallory school.

At that time, author Douglas Rutherford was writing novels with a strong motor racing theme. He decided to get closer to the subject and came to Snetterton to do the full course. Drawing on his experiences, his next novel was called 'Gunshot Grand Prix'. It was based on Snetterton and the school but he changed the names of the corners. Probably to give them more glamour, he used the corner names at Monaco.

152

Patrick Neve seemed to manage to 'hang in there' despite his numerous accidents. On one occasion, he was driving the transporter back from Thruxton and, when he arrived at Snetterton, Jim spotted damage to the roof. "What has happened?" demanded Jim. "I 'itaplant" said Patrick. Everybody fell about before finding out that he had actually driven through an avenue of trees hitting the taller branches as he went Later, when the roads were covered with snow, Patrick drove Ralph's Cortina because Ralph had lost his licence. Going around the back of the circuit, Patrick lost it completely and the car ended up on its roof ,as Ralph climbed out of his side door, he was verbally set upon by three women calling him all the names under the sun. Anxious not to be blamed, Ralph was shouting, "It wasn't me, it wasn't me, it wasn't me ... it was him", while Patrick stayed out of sight.

That was only one of several experiences for Ralph in those days. He and Dave Walker were regular fellow commuters back and fro to the workshops from Crimplesham where Ralph had a flat and Dave and his wife Jan, lived in a cottage next door. On one occasion, they nearly ran over a sheep which had obviously just been killed by another motorist. Without a moment's hesitation, Dave jumped out of the car and heaved the sheep into the boot. As soon as they reached his cottage, he lifted it out and took it straight into the bathroom. Jan, who came from Australian farming stock, knew what to do and within minutes had skinned it in the bath. With blood, wool and skin everywhere, they jointed the carcass and before long, the fridges at Ralph's and Dave's were full of lamb Not only that, there was enough for Jim's brother Peter, who lived nearby, to have some as well. They all lived on the free lamb for weeks.

On one occasion, when Claude was racing at Zolder, Jim and Ralph took his race car on a trailer behind Jim's Vauxhall Ventura. All went well and, after the race, they drove down the road to a small Cafe/Bar for an overnight stop. Naturally, they stayed in the bar until late and before long, Jim was looking for "South of the Border" on the jukebox. Unfortunately, it wasn't on there but "I Left My Heart in San Francisco" was. So, in went the coins for that one again and again. Jim, now very happy, kept saying, "San Francisco" to Ralph who had to keep feeding the machine and playing it all evening.

The next morning, they set off for the ferry with the car and the trailer. Little did they realise that they weight of the loaded trailer was affecting certain things on the car. In fact, it was doing no good at all to the brake pipes as it was pulling them out of their connections As they went down a hill towards some traffic lights, Ralph thought that Jim was leaving his braking rather late and yelled, "Brake, Jim, brake" to no avail. Jim's foot was hard to the floor and the car slowed not one iota sailing through not one, but four sets of lights, they led a charmed life as nothing hit them and Jim, completely unperturbed and still partially under the influence of the previous night, drove serenely on.

It took the rest of the journey for Ralph's heartbeat to come back to normal.

Mike Warner had originally worked at Lotus but had left to start his own business in the mid-1960s. Colin Chapman wanted him back to run Lotus Components, so in typical Chapman fashion, he bought out Mike's company to be able to re-employ him. Mike was given the job of negotiating with Jim when the school was buying new cars after the existing school cars had been used in the 'Grand Prix' film. Mike has vivid memories of his first dealings with Jim. "He had a great charm and charisma, similar to Chapman. He was screwing every last penny out of me and, despite the fact that my profit was floating away, I was actually grinning Can you imagine?, I was actually enjoying the fact that he was persuading me to sell him the cars at far too low a price".

At that time, Lotus needed success in Formula Ford. Following on the many successes of the Russell-Alexis, Merlyn had taken over and become the leading marque. Mike saw an opportunity to use the Jim Russell School Racing Team and their hungry young graduate drivers, under Jim's direction, to get Lotus back on top in Formula Ford.

Jim agreed to his suggestions and approached John Reid of Holbay to provide the engines. In order to stress the alliance, a colour scheme very similar to the Lotus green and yellow was chosen for the cars. Although the green used was lighter than Lotus, there was no mistaking the connection. Always immaculately turned out, the cars were immediately a force to be reckoned with. One of the drivers was Mo Harness, very quick but inclined to crash fairly regularly. Nevertheless, his successes were sufficient for him to be kept in the team. His team mate was Bernard Vermilio, from Essex, who was a consistent front runner. When Dave Baldwin, Mike Warner and others at Lotus were looking to make their cars different, they hit upon the idea of making the Lotus 61 look like a smaller version of an Indycar, The resultant wedge-shaped car looked vastly different from anything seen before and when it was immediately a winner in the hands of Mo and Bernard, other drivers started placing their orders. Although the special design gave the car no advantage whatsoever, it proved to be a very successful marketing ploy.

The 1969 season continued in the same winning vein, with Dave Walker and Claude Bourgoignie joined from time to time by Mo Harness. Dave was going all out for the British FF Championship while Claude had his eyes on his own Belgian National Championship.

In June that year, the first ever Italian Formula Ford Race was organised by Goodyear Tyres, Ford Italiana and the Automobile Club of Rome. This prestigious event was held at the

Vallelunga circuit and a class field was assembled. The often erratic Mo was unlucky that day, having to retire with an engine problem, but Dave won the race and Claude was third. They were split by a young Brazilian named Emerson Fittipaldi, who had parried their every move throughout the race and had beaten Claude to the finishing line. After the awards, he was briefly introduced to Jim.

About a week later, Emerson turned up at Snetterton. He asked Jim to manage him. "Certainly", was the reply, "But not in Formula Ford. You're too good for that and, in any case, we're leading the Championship. You need to be in Formula III". "How can I manage that?" was the puzzled Brazilian's reply. "Well", said Jim, "You sell your Formula Ford and equipment and then we can get you a Lotus FIII rolling chassis for about £2,000. I will supply the engines and Ralph Firman will be your mechanic".

JR School graduates all ... Emerson leads Mo Harness and Ian Ashley in a Snetterton Formula Ford race 1969.

Off went Fittipaldi to sell his car and equipment while Jim went to see John Reid again at Holbay engines. He put a unique deal to John – Holbay to supply and keep two engines in race condition throughout the season and Jim would sign a Bankers Order on the spot to pay John a set amount every month. To his knowledge, no-one had ever done that before and it worked like a charm as it was in Holbay's own interest to ensure that the team always had race fresh engines.

Very young Russell children, Amanda, Robert and James, with Emerson Fittipaldi, Ralph Firman and Chico.

Shortly after, there was a cocktail party at Mike Warner's home in Bunwell near the circuit. Jim said to Colin Chapman, "I've got a young Brazilian driver who could well be driving your Formula I car in a couple of years". "I've heard it all before Jim", said Chapman. "Ah, but not from Jim Russell", was the instant reply. Chapman looked at Jim for a moment before saying, "You'd better talk to Mike, then".

155

Last minutes instuctions.

A few days later, Mike and Jim were standing on the bridge at Snetterton watching Emerson lap the circuit. Very soon Mike said, "You're absolutely right, Jim, this one is very special. Come on, let's do business". Soon afterwards, they had struck a deal for Emerson's new Lotus 69 rolling chassis and the package was complete. That really was the start of something big.

Fortunes weren't quite so good for Mo Harness, who had continued his erratic way in Formula Ford throughout the season. He realised that his constant crashes were seriously endangering his seat in the Jim Russell team. Then, nearly at the end of the season, after he had crashed for the eighth time, he jumped out of the car, leapt over the bank, and was last seen hurrying away across the fields. He obviously couldn't face Jim after that one.

As far as the school was concerned at that time, the overseas courses continued to grow and more and more pupils took part. From Canada came two students who were destined to be part of the school's worldwide activities from then on. Little did anyone realise at the time, but Jacques Couture and Dave McConnell were so impressed that, after training and racing

156

with the British school, they asked Jim about opening their own following discussions, a deal was done to enable them to open a Canadian Jim Russell School. They were both racing at that time in the Canadian Formula B series and the school, opened in 1969, was initially a part-time effort. Nevertheless, they operated a limited programme while Jacques raced in, and won, the CASA Championship and also won the very first North American Formula Atlantic Championship. This was, of course, later won by two of his school graduates from the famous Villeneuve family, the brother Gilles (1976 & 77) and Jacques (1980).

With those successes under his belt, Couture retired from racing to give all his attention to the school which they were operating at Le Circuit Mont Tremblant, St Jovite Nr Montreal, which would continue to be the home of the Canadian Jim Russell School from then onwards.

Dave continued to race for a while, coming back to England for the FIII Championship and racing in the Australian Tasman series, before also retiring to instruct at the school where Gordon Rae also joined the staff.

The 1969 Lombank sponsored British FIII Championship was well under way before the new team got started and they knew they had a lot to do in half a season. Emerson's first ever FIII race was at Mallory Park on July 13th where, despite having gearbox problems he finished a creditable fifth, in a race which had been dominated by the Gold Leaf Team Lotus pairing of Mo Nunn and Roy Pike. From there, they went to Brands Hatch for the next round on August 3rd, where they found that the main opposition was Bev Bond in a Brabham B28. The 22 year old Brazilian was now showing his true potential and a terrific scrap developed between the two of them. Neither gave an inch, staying absolutely tied together throughout the entire race. Side by side, they came out of Clearways on the last lap and Bond just managed to take the win by a mere two tenths of a second It was no surprise to anyone that they had shared the fastest lap record of 50.6 seconds. This had been the first of a three week sequence for the FIII racers and, therefore, just a short week later, they were back at Mallory Park. This time, the GLT Lotus effort was thwarted when Mo Nunn crashed in practice so Emerson's main rival was again Bev Bond. This time, there was no question of a scrap between them. 'Fittipaldi Flies' was the banner headline after he had dominated from the front all the way and equalled the lap record of 48 seconds whilst doing so.

Emerson takes the lead out of Bottom Bend in front of the famous Brands Hatch South Bank.

"As you're teetotal ... I'll keep the Champagne!"

It was back to Brands Hatch the following weekend and this proved to be another 'neck and neck' tussle, this time with Roy Pike in the Gold Leaf Team Lotus. Pike never once gave up the struggle but Emerson was up to every move and held the lead to the finish. Another sign of the closeness of these two was yet another shared fastest lap. They jointly broke the lap record leaving it at exactly 50 seconds

Emerson was now very much a threat to the others in this FIII Championship. He had been scoring points all the way and his biggest test was coming up at the next round. This was the prestigious Guards Trophy, again at Brands Hatch, this time on the long circuit. In addition to his usual protagonists in the Championship, several drivers who had been contesting the European FIII series had entered. Chief amongst them were the Scandinavian pair, Ronnie Peterson and Reine Wisell. It made no difference to Fittipaldi when the flag dropped. He was soon in the lead and, despite the constantly attacking Peterson and Wisell, he was still leading as they entered the last lap. Down out of Druids they swept and, on the short Bottom Straight, Emerson suddenly spotted an oil slick. Up went his arm to warn the others but, with only one hand on the steering wheel, he became the victim of the oil himself. Quick as a flash he had spun letting both of them by before he could restart. He had no time to rectify the position and had to be content with third place that day.

158

After a couple of week's respite, a two meeting weekend saw them at Crystal Palace on Saturday September 13th. There were two heats and a final and Emerson took second place in his heat. In the final on the tricky little mile-long circuit, where overtaking was always difficult, he started from the second row behind Roy Pike and Charles Lucas and alongside Howden Ganley. Passing Pike took him into third spot behind leader Lucas and Ganley. The three of them pulled away from the rest and at the end of 5 laps, Emerson had moved up another place to be second to Lucas. Two laps later, he was in the lead but Lucas was not to be easily beaten. He took back the lead a couple of times before Emerson re-established himself at the front of the 10 lap mark to control the 15 lap race to the finish. No less than four drivers, including the winner, shared the fastest lap after the hectic race.

A jubilant Russell team then headed for Brands Hatch and the next day's race. There was so much morning fog that it looked at one time as if the meeting would be cancelled. However, after a three hour delay, practice eventually started and Emerson qualified third. Starting from the outside of an all Lotus 59 front row, Bev Bond having changed to one by then, he swept past Bond to follow pole man Nunn into Paddock Bend. It only took him one more lap to oust Nunn and take over the lead. From then on, it was another case of everyone chasing Fittipaldi who went on to take the Dartford Cup in the fastest ever FIII race on the Brands Hatch Club Circuit. He was really closing up in the points table by now having equalled Pike's total to share second place with Alan Rollinson still leading.

The next round was at Mallory Park on 2nd October but there was also an International FIII race at Cadwell Park the same day. Emerson urged Jim to let him go to Cadwell and his family, who had been over with him all the time, also tried to persuade Jim. Even brother Wilson seemed not to realise that the FIII Championship round was the most important race for their boy. Jim was adamant and insisted that they went to Mallory Park. The Lincolnshire International attracted most of the top runners and Jim entered a second Lotus 59 for Dave Walker to have his first real FIII outing. Emerson had broken his own lap record in practice but, in the race, he had no need to extend himself. The important win, however, took him to within one point of Championship leader, Alan Rollinson. With just the final round to go in a couple of week's time, they took time out for Emerson to have his first race on the continent. Appropriately, it was at Montlhery, the scene of Jim's record breaking runs and his Coupes De Salon FII triumph a decade earlier. The trip proved worthwhile. Ronnie Peterson was on pole in the March but Emerson shot into the lead he was never to lose. Poor Peterson's race ended with a nasty crash on the second lap, putting him in hospital for a couple of weeks. For a while, Tim Schenken chased the leader but he also went off and Emerson cruised home to record his, and the team's, first continental race win.

Rollinson, who had been leading the Championship all season, suffered a slipped disc which prevented him from racing in the final round at Brands Hatch. There were plenty of other drivers trying to foil Emerson's efforts that day. One of them was team mate, Dave Walker, who had taken the Formula Ford title and was determined to prove himself ready for the next season in FIII. A spin dropped him down the order but he drove back well to finish third. Up front, however, Emerson was holding off a very determined Bev Bond all the way and by winning this last round became the 1969 British FIII Champion.

He had always been willing to listen to 'Mr Jim', his regular name for Jim, and always adhered to Jim's teachings including walking every new circuit before trying to drive on it. He was a useful engineer, always willing to roll up his sleeves and help out when necessary. He had, of course, prepared his Formula Ford Merlyn with the help of his faithful friend, Chico, who put his Quantity Surveyor's job on hold to come to Europe to help and support him.

The news quickly spread to Brazil as Fittipaldi senior was a TV and Radio reporter who regularly broadcast race commentaries live to their home country through the season. He continued to do so throughout Emerson's racing career in Europe.

Jim personally had a lot of satisfaction from Emerson's Championship title especially thinking back to one of their first visits as a FIII team to Brands Hatch. It was then that Les Leston and Peter Jopp, standing at the back of the pits with big smiles on their faces had said in loud voices, "Oh look, there's Jim Russell ... the working class Ken Tyrrell". Jim thought to himself, "I've proved what a 'working class' team can do and it was in only half a season".

There was plenty to celebrate at the Jim Russell School as, in addition to Emerson's FIII title, Dave Walker was the Formula Ford Champion and Claude Bourgoignie had won his home series to become the Belgian FF Champion. Jim quickly dubbed 1969 The Championship Year and plans were formulated to run Emerson in FII in 1970.

Jim was invited to one of Les Leston's cocktail parties and Walter Hayes, the Ford Motorsport Manager, came over to him. "I've been watching your young Brazilian driver, Fittipaldi and he looks quite promising. What are your plans for him?" When Jim told him that he was going to run Emerson in FII in 1970, Hayes immediately said he would like Ford to help. He followed up by promising £2,000 towards the next season's expenses. Considering that Ford had only given £500 to Ken Tyrrell towards Jackie Stewart's expenses a couple of years before, Jim was over the moon. Also present that evening was Keith Duckworth, the 'worth' of Cosworth. Jim told Keith about his special bankers order deal he had with John Reid of Holbay in FIII and that he had a similar arrangement agreed with Brian Hart for FII engines in 1970. Keith was very impressed and commented, "What a super system ... on those terms, I'd do your engines myself".

Two days later, a letter arrived from Walter Hayes confirming his verbal promise to Jim. Ford asked for only two conditions. One was that Emerson be willing to make certain promotional appearances for them and the other that he would not drive anything but a Ford or a Ford engined car without their agreement. Otherwise, he stressed, they made no

160

demands for victories saying, "We don't mind if he uses the £2,000 to lose every race as long as he is gaining experience". "You can't be fairer than that", thought Jim.

Then came the 1969 JRRDS Dinner Dance and Prize Giving. It was moved to one of the best known venues in the locality – the Swan Hotel at picturesque Lavenham, which was quite a leap forward from the Snetterton Cafeteria This was, incidentally, the first Dinner Dance which the writer attended. Guest of Honour was Mike Warner, who had played quite a part in Emerson's career so far. He set a precedent for suitable guests of honour from then on. The event was so popular that by the next winter of 1970, the Swan Hotel wasn't big enough for the numbers wishing to attend and the Norwood Rooms in Norwich became the venue for a couple of years.

Things became very busy before that social event. Plans were being made to run a winter Formula Ford Series in Brazil in February the following year and, naturally, Emerson was invited to take part. He was also keen for Jim to accompany him back home before then to help his promotion efforts.

The day after the very successful Dinner Dance they flew off to South America. They had already arranged for the new Lotus FII car and Ralph Firman was left to help build it at the factory while they were away. As they sat back in the plane and commenced their long journey to South America, Jim quietly said to Emerson, "Remember that International meeting at Cadwell Park you wanted to do a few months back and the way I insisted that you did the Mallory Park round of the Championship instead?" "Yes, I do, Mr Jim", was the reply. "Well, who won that International, Emerson?" "I do not remember", he said. "So, who is British FIII Champion? asked Jim. "Emerson Fittipaldi" was the proud reply. "You wouldn't have been if you had gone to Cadwell and missed that Mallory Park round", stressed Jim. "You're so right", admitted Emerson. "And I'm so glad you insisted, Mr Jim. Thank you."

Wanting to change the subject, Emerson started talking about food and asked Jim what he would miss most while he was away. Jim replied that it would probably be a meal like roast beef and Yorkshire pudding and then posed a similar question to the Brazilian. "No question – what I missed most was the lovely big pizzas we have at home. When we get to Sau Paulo, I'll collect Super Baby and we'll take you for the biggest pizza you've ever had in your life." Super Baby turned out to be a girlfriend at that time and they did get to enjoy the pizza.

Emerson's faithful friend Chico had stayed around, generally helping out and giving his loyal support throughout the 1969 season. He was already back home and joined them most of the time. Jim had a blockage with his name and kept calling him Mike, much to everyone's amusement.

As soon as they arrived, they were into a hectic round of press conferences and radio interviews. Obviously, Papa Fittipaldi's connections had helped setting many of them up. On the Sunday night, they were featured on an hour long prime time National TV chat show. All the

Fittipaldi family plus Chico were there. There was a lady interviewer and during the programme, Jim proudly talked about the school saying, "There are two things you can't take away from England ... the Jim Russell Racing Drivers School and Rolls Royce". A month later, Rolls Royce went into liquidation! Following the chat show, everyone they met had seen the programme and they had super service everywhere they went.

On one occasion, they went to a practice day at the Rio de Janeiro circuit. Jim was amazed at the bizarre collection of vehicles practising. There seemed to be all kinds of road and race cars, plus some vans Walking down the pit road, he couldn't believe his eyes ... there was a mechanic with a lighted cigarette in his mouth, calmly pouring petrol from a can into the tank of a car When he expressed his extreme concern, Emerson's laconic reply was, "Don't worry about it, the fuel is very poor here".

After that, Jim was glad to spend a lazy day on the beach. Emerson took him to the beautiful Guaraja Beach where Jim loved the Casa Grande Hotel right on the edge of the sand. He said to Emerson, "That's where I'm going to stay next time I'm here". Ten years later, he did.

Emerson was staying for the special five race Temporada Formula Ford series early in 1970 and Jim was due to fly home for Christmas. Suddenly, the ex-Governor died and there was a week of mourning with everything closing down. Off they went to the Government Offices where, despite an enthusiastic greeting by the Governor, there was no way he could arrange Jim's papers for his return. He talked keenly about the school and even suggested that he would send his chauffeur along for a much-needed tuition. However, after the week's mourning, everything went back to normal and Jim got his papers signed in time to get home for Christmas. A local flight took him to Rio de Janeiro. The plane hadn't been airborne long when a stewardess, recognising Jim from the TV show, came along to introduce herself to him. Her name was Marie Helena and she had obviously taken a shine to Emerson. She told Jim she would love to meet his protégé and in typical Jim fashion the reply to that was, "Get me another Scotch and I'll see what I can do" It didn't take long for that request to be granted and he found himself answering questions about Emerson to this very attractive young lady. He told her that the young driver had just celebrated his twenty-second birthday and lived with this brother, Wilson. She was so keen and insistent that, before the flight had ended, he had finally given her their address and telephone number before wishing her good luck. Dismissing her as another 'starry-eyed' fan, he put the matter out of his mind.

Emerson was soon embroiled in the February 1970 special Formula Ford series which had been organised by Motor Circuit Developments, as the company who ran Brands Hatch and other places was now called. They had sent the experienced Jackie Epstein to run things and he found it a gigantic task. Firstly, the distances that the teams had to travel between consecutive weekend races were daunting and the second most important problem was the heat. The British drivers, which included school graduates, Sid Fox and Ian Ashley, the initial Formula

162

Ford winner Ray Allen, Tom Walkinshaw, Tony Lanfranchi and the two ladies, Gabrielle Konig and Liane Engeman, were constantly finding the very high temperatures distressing. Antipodians, Vern Schuppan and Peter Hull were also suffering.

It wasn't quite so bad for the locals who, in addition to Emerson, included his brother Wilson, Luis Bueno, Ricardo Ashcar and Marivaldo Fernadez. Despite that there was some exciting racing, albeit in very scary conditions caused by the almost non-existent crowd control. No doubt about the winner though. Emerson continued to show his worth, and become more and more a national hero, by winning the series handsomely with the Lotus 61M. He won three of the races, was second in another and suffered fuel problems in the remaining one. Ian Ashley finished second in the table to make it a Jim Russell one-two.

Dave Walker had been scheduled to also take part by failed to arrive. He had previously taken the chance to race at Sebring just after Christmas. He drove a 'works' prepared Lotus Formula F car in the special Grants 8 Championship at the Sebring Continental Series L & M Grand Prix. His efforts, after a good practice, expired with an electrical problem. Then, when he was expected in Brazil, he appeared at the Daytona Grand Prix for Formula Fords. Once again, after qualifying fifth in practice, another electrical fault, this time a broken battery lead, caused his retirement from third place.

Despite the fact that it was winter time, there was plenty of activity by Russell graduates. In addition to Brazil and the USA, there was racing at home. Unusual for those years, a meeting was held in February at Brands Hatch. The featured race was for Formula Fords and Claude Bourgoignie again flew the Russell flag well, winning both his heat and the final. Second to him, at that time in a Merlyn, was Bernard Vermilio.

Jim had met Carlos Pace in Brazil and arranged for him to drive the Jim Russell car in FIII alongside his plans for Emerson in FII.

Jim had asked Emerson to be back in England as soon as possible after the Temporada series had finished. Towards the end of February, he appeared at Snetterton. Standing in the doorway of Jim's office, he shook his clenched fist at Jim in mock anger saying, "You bugger, Mr Jim. Look ..." as he indicated behind him with his thumb. There stood a smiling Marie Helena Sure enough, she had contacted Emerson and their first meeting had led to more, so much so that she had given up her job as an Air Stewardess and joined him on his travels. It wasn't long before they were married in Norwich. They were probably unique in so much as they were actually married three times In addition to the first marriage in Norwich, they repeated the process in London and, finally, for the folks back home, again in Brazil Jim soon hurried Emerson up to the Lotus factory to see his new race car which Ralph had just about finished. One of the staff came up to Emerson and told him that Colin Chapman would like to see him. Excusing himself, he was ushered into Chapman's office. About an hour later, he came out and, rather sheepishly said to Jim, "Mr Chapman has offered to make me a Lotus 'works' driver in FII in 1970 and then straight into Formula I. What shall I do?" "No question. You've got to take the opportunity – it's too good to turn down." "Well", said Emerson, "Mr Chapman says he will buy the FII outfit from you, so that you won't lose out". Very shortly afterwards, Fred Bushell paid over the cheque which Jim sent to the Lotus Bank in Wymondham for special clearance. The Lotus people waited at Snetterton to take the transporter away but Jim, taking no chances, had sent Ralph Firman into Attleborough with it. He was waiting in the Griffin Hotel for Jim's call The Bank Manager couldn't get the cheque cleared, He was so determined to complete the deal for Jim that he stayed on at his desk well after time. In the meantime, Emerson, seeing the funny side of things said, "I think I've been hi-jacked, Mr Jim" Then, at 7 pm, just when everyone was ready to give up for the day, word came from the persistent Bank Manager that the cheque had finally been cleared. Ralph was very relieved to get the call to bring the transporter back. As it disappeared towards Hethel, Jim was rather sad to reflect that he would no longer be looking after the brilliant Brazilian but knew that the move was right for Emerson.

Ralph took the transporter to Hethel. He handed it over and was immediately 'frog-marched' off the premises, Despite this, he did in fact help the FII team through their first two or three races before deciding to run his own team. Thinking about the move, he asked Jim's opinion. "Well", said Jim after deliberating for a while, "I suppose it'll either be good, or otherwise it will be bad" "That's a lot of help", thought Ralph as he took his first step into the world of the self-employed.

A young passenger eagerly awaiting for Jim to take off ...

Emerson's first race in Formula II was at Hockenheim in Germany. Derek Whyborn, the circuit caterer, Brian Feltham, the circuit manager, and Jim were discussing this in the Snetterton clubhouse one evening. After a few drinks came the suggestion, "Why don't we charter a plane and fly out to watch Emerson?" Everyone seemed to think it was a good idea and Brian said that he would make enquiries. The very next morning, Jim saw a Cessna flying around the circuit and soon it landed on the back straight. Over strode the pilot. "I'm looking for Jim Russell", he said. Jim replied,

... airborne from Snetterton.

"That's me". "Well, I've brought a plane for you to see", was the astounding reply. "Now I know I've got a hangover", thought Jim. Nevertheless, he agreed to have a test flight and afterwards the pilot told him the price. Jim thought, "I can't waste his time", so offered him £1,000 less. As an afterthought, he added that a pilot had to be supplied to fly them to Hockenheim. Much to his surprise, this offer was taken seriously and, following a phone call to his office, the deal was done "Now what do I do?" thought Jim. "I've got a plane and can't fly".

However, before that there was Hockenheim. The pilot duly arrived on the Friday morning to pick them up. Derek had a large picnic hamper with plenty of food and drink. Off they went and had a fantastic weekend, eating, drinking and watching Emerson's race. On the Monday morning, they flew back and Jim immediately rang the Norwich Flying Club to arrange for a course of flying lessons. Like everything else in his life, he gave it 100% and got his licence at the age of 50. He continued to fly regularly from his Bardwell home, where he kept the plane hangered and an airstrip prepared. He was soon using the local Honington Air Force control for the latest updates on weather conditions and their operations. It was imperative that he kept them informed of his movements considering that their flight paths crossed, He did everything 'by the book' and, consequently, had a trouble-free flying history. He actually logged over 400 flying hours in nearly 15 years until, at the age of 65, he decided to give up and sell the plane.

165

When weather conditions were good, he very often used the plane to go the short distance from his home to Snetterton circuit. He would fly over the Norwich Straight when they were preparing for a lesson day, 'waggle' the plane's wings and the instructors would move the cones over so that he could land the plane. On one occasion, the instructors pretended not to understand Jim's signals. As he passed over them, they waved back enthusiastically but made no attempt to move the cones. Around flew Jim another couple of times getting the same response and eventually flew off, never to be seen again that day No-one ever told him that it had been a deliberate 'wind-up'.

After Jim had sold his plane, he started to think about getting a boat. Like most people involved in motor racing, he took his holidays in the winter. Since his children had been very small, the family had been going to the Canary Isles. Over the years, he had watched the various ocean-going powerboats and taken trips on them from time to time. He decided that he would like a boat of his own kept out there for the more frequent holidays he was now taking.

He talked to Jack Brabham about it and was nearly put off the idea by the Australian. Jack said, "You'll get just two days pleasure from a boat ... the day you buy it and the day you sell it".

Despite this, Jim went off to the Earls Court Boat Show and, coincidentally on the same day as Nigel Mansell, he bought one. In typical Jim Russell fashion, he made the salesman work very hard and pushed for every bit of discount off the price before saying, "OK, it's a deal, as long as you deliver it". This was agreed and the salesman sat down at his desk to complete the paperwork.

"Now, Mr Russell, the delivery address ... somewhere on the Norfolk Coast?" he enquired. "No ... lower", replied Jim. "Oh, the South Coast is it?" "No ... lower than that." "Not Europe?" "Keep going", said Jim, as the salesman's mouth dropped open. "Try Gran Canaria" Instant panic ensued and the poor salesman, not knowing what to do next, ran in to see his boss. Out they came together but Jim was adamant. A deal was a deal and he insisted that they either delivered the boat to Gran Canaria or they could forget the sale. Faced with losing out completely, they had no option. Jim signed up and the boat was delivered to Las Palmas.

▷ *Another Japanese course with John Paine.*

Chapter 13   *The Bumper Years*

By now, students were coming from all over the world and America supplied a regular proportion of them. The numbers seemed to increase when their country was engaged in a Far East war. This was because the Americans had realised that taking 'further education' in England was preferable to fighting a war. They could legitimately call the training at the racing school 'further education' but that was all. Some of them extended their stay for much longer than the course, even when it was taking 14 days. One such student was called Joe. He was obviously anxious to keep out of the States and stayed around a long time. He made sure to make himself useful to such a degree that Jim eventually appointed him Overseas Advertising Manager The appointment was to prove to be short-lived. Before he could actually take up his new position, the next Saturday's race meeting was interrupted by the police. They turned up

Jacques Couture presents an award to Alan Mertons.

Classroom instruction from John Paine.

during morning practice looking for Joe and his mate who had 'bummed' their way around East Anglia, leaving a trail of debts behind them, How he had been able to pay for his races became clear at that point Joe had pre-paid for his race that day and John Paine pleaded successfully for him to be allowed to race. The novelty of the situation appealed to the law enforcers who agreed to wait around and watch Joe race. They sat there watching and waiting before walking over to Joe's race car as he returned to the paddock and arresting him as he stepped out of the car. With a brief farewell and thank you to John, he was 'whisked' away, never to be heard of again.

Many students took a long time to complete their training, primarily because of their lack of cash. Alan Mertons was one such student. He took over a year, constantly saving up to pay for the next stage but, as he says, from the day he first came to the school, he was 'hooked' on motor racing. He had, like so many others, stumbled upon racing and the school when a friend loaned him a copy of Motoring News. The school's advert therein fired his imagination and life was never the same again. His was a familiar story. He worked at anything he could get, working evenings and weekends in a bar and a garage to supplement his daytime earnings so that he could get his next 'fix' at the school. Eventually, he was racing with the school and successfully competing in the school's Championships. To this day, he thanks Jim Russell for giving him the cheapest and best opportunity to start motor racing. Like so many others, he didn't survive in public racing but the good grounding he had at the school held him in good stead for the career he carved out when he started his world famous Galmer Engineering. Over a quarter of a century later, he still retains a great interest in the Jim Russell School and still says that his student days training and racing were some of the happiest of this life. That says a lot for the man who was the winning constructor at the 1992 Indy 500, does it not?.

John Paine used to run the place like the proverbial Sergeant Major, sometimes feared but invariably respected for his dedication to the job. Mind you, his serious attitude to the job meant that some employees took the opportunity to 'wind him up'. One of the culprits was Pete Merrylees who joined as a mechanic to replace Ken Thoroughgood in 1971. He was always pulling tricks on the rest of the staff. One day, for instance, he cut up an Autolite sticker, reforming the letters to read 'Toilet' and stuck them on a tree over a bucket John was not at all pleased, pointing out that some of the visiting students with a poor knowledge of English could take the sign seriously, It was probably a relief for John when Pete left in 1972 to help Ralph set up the new Van Diemen factory, For many years John's secretary, more of a personal assistant, Val, was there to look after the students with their paperwork and the hundred and one things that cropped up throughout the day. The over-sexed adoring young students, says Alan Mertons, worshipped her from afar.

Alf Lilford was a part-time instructor who commuted from Stevenage when he was required and was always wanting to be a full-time member of the staff. One day in 1971, his wife was present and she said to Jim, "Buy a hotel for students to stay and Alf and I will sell up, move up here and run it" Actually, Jim had been thinking that way for some time and so he started to look around for a suitable place. He was talking to the matron of a local old people's home. She was a regular visitor to the Doric bar and mentioned that she wanted to close the home down and sell the large house. Jim took David Waring with him to look round and within days he had bought the large house in Bunwell for £25,000. It didn't take long to convert and very quickly, the Bunwell Manor Hotel opened with Mrs Alf Lilford in charge while Alf became a full-time instructor. Alf was never stuck for an answer to students. It was quite usual for the instructors to use their own road cars to show students the lines around the circuit. On one occasion, he was doing that and was asked, "Alf, are you supposed to ride the curb on the inside of that corner?" "Of course not", he replied straight-faced. "I've just had half an inch wider tyres fitted and forgot to make an allowance".

Just after buying Bunwell Manor, Jim and John Paine went to Japan. John had been talking to BOAC about a deal for Japanese students to get cheap air fares to

John, Jim and Dave Walker master chopsticks.

A later promotional unit.

Britain. He had approached them at the right time as, apparently, they needed to improve their image in that country having upset the Government earlier. Jim and John took advantage of the offer of BOAC's free flight to investigate the possibility of opening a school in Japan. They had only been there a few days when Dave Walker arrived to join them He was trying to get a deal together to do FII in 1972 and wanted to get Mitsubishi to supply him with some free engines. That meant that he socialised with Jim and John most of the time but failed to get his engines. They also enjoyed various Japanese restaurants, having great fun coping with chopsticks for the first time. They found that sitting on cushions on the floor, as was traditional, proved to be very different to chairs It had certain advantages, however ... when John felt the need to warn Jim that the Saki wine was very potent and said, "Be careful – don't drink too much of that stuff". Jim, already getting quite happy replied, "Why not? I haven't got far to fall, have I?".

Later, they went to the Suzuki circuit by train. John, as usual, was carrying two heavy briefcases packed with school brochures. His motto, like the Scouts was "Be Prepared". As they took their seats on the train, he complained to Jim that the weight of the cases would probably make his arms a couple of inches longer after the trip. At that moment, Jim looked out of the window to see a local actually carrying a small piano on his back up the platform "You should worry", he said. "Look at that guy ... now he's got something to really complain about".

170

When they arrived at Suzuki, they found a very disorganised saloon car school in operation and couldn't believe the lack of control and poor safety measures. Discussions took place about starting a Jim Russell School there before they left but, getting embroiled in the home schools on their return meant that the idea was shelved until a later date. Unfortunately, that date never came.

Although pupils were still being booked into Bunwell Manor, the smokers among them didn't take kindly to the "No Smoking" signs in the dining room. They had been there since the place was an old people's home and Pam Lilford had decided to leave them up. Things came to a head on Jim's return from Japan when he went in for a meal one evening. His trade mark for many years, until he finally gave up smoking, was his tin of tobacco complete with Rizla papers. He tackled Mrs Lilford and ordered the signs to be taken down. When she argued, Jim said, "It's my hotel and I will make the rules. If it was your hotel, you could make the rules ... fair enough?" He continued by asking if she would like to buy the place. "I'll tell you what ... you can buy for £30,000". She took up the offer and, within a few days, was the owner. So, Jim Russell Hotelier, lasted just a few months but he had made a quick profit and students could still be booked into the hotel.

When the school were running trials on the Norwich Straight, the staff brought the cars back to the pits the shortest way. This meant that they drove back in an anti-clockwise direction. Alf, in his usual manner, was driving much faster than necessary and at Sear Corner, he under-steered straight off into the cabbage field. As the car hit the rough, so it flipped and ended up upside down with Alf still in it. Someone ran back to the office saying, "Get an Ambulance, Alf's upside down in a car at Sear" Jim, overhearing this, got his priorities right and asked, "Is the car all right?" Luckily, neither Alf or the car suffered much damage.

Visiting the Japanese Touring Car School ...

... and presenting the awards.

Colin Campbell. Val, Peter Mackintosh and Patrick Neve get a technical lecture from David Loring.

The fame of the school was spreading rapidly. An example of this was provided when comedian Dick Emery's writers contacted the school about filming one of his outrageous programmes around a motor racing theme. A full day's filming was arranged and the TV crew turned up bright and early to set things up. The star arrived accompanied by Graham Hill, who had been 'roped in' for good measure. The school staff had a great time with the hilarious script and situations. Strangely enough, Graham, who had never driven a Formula Ford before, had great difficulty with the clutch on his car. It was much heavier than a Formula I clutch and, after a while, he asked for help. John Paine came to the rescue. Donning one of Graham's helmets, he became his 'stand-in' (or should it be 'sit-in?'), for some of the scenes. During one of the breaks, they were all having a cup of coffee when Graham turned to Jim and said, "I'll bet you're making a packet out of this, aren't you Jim?" Quick as a flash came the reply, "No, Graham, I'm doing it for nothing just as you are".

Following Emerson's success, there was a steady flow of Brazilian students. Generally, they arrived in groups and very often rented a house in Attleborough for their stay with as many as nine or ten living together, Most of them stayed on for months in order to race with the school after training. It was, and in some cases still is, normal to find young men so eager to get into motor racing that they would make all kinds of creature comfort sacrifices and put up with the barest of essentials. Many of them couldn't even afford to rent a room and either slept in a tent behind the school or in their cars, which were invariably 'old bangers'.

172

When John advertised for another instructor, he received an interesting application from the former manager of the famous Red Arrows – the RAFs crack display team. Naturally, he was intrigued and asked the young man to attend for an interview. Peter Mackintosh arrived and was given the job.

He was introduced to Jim, who immediately asked, "How many flying hours have you got?" "Oh", replied Peter, "About 3,600" "Well", Jim said, "That's about 3,500 more than me. See that bush that's interfering with the wind sock ... get a saw and cut it down", Peter's mouth dropped open but he said nothing before turning and carrying out his first task at the school later, of course, he was trained as an instructor and became a worthwhile member of the team.

During a lapping session one day, John was puzzled by the big gaps that appeared between cars. Normally, the cars stayed relatively close throughout the session but this day there were bunches of cars separated by unusually large gaps. After a while, John decided to take a look and when he got to the Norwich Straight, he found Alf Lilford and Fred from the Snetterton Service Station trying to move a herd of cows off the circuit. The pupils, determined to have their complete 10 laps of lapping, were slowing down and threading their way between the cows who were steadfastly going across at their own pace.

The Dinner Dance that year was moved to the larger Norwood Rooms in Norwich and the Guest of Honour was Chris Lowe of Motor Circuit Developments, the school's landlords.

Early in 1971, a young Tiff Needell won a national newspaper competition which was the envy of everyone trying to get into motor racing. He not only won a Lotus 69F Formula Ford, he also won the trailer, overalls, helmet, plus a full training course at the school. This he booked for April and set off for Snetterton towing his new racing car behind his old Morris 1000 Traveller. Unfortunately, he hadn't reckoned on the weight of the racing car and trailer combination and he finally limped into Snetterton with the front suspension nearly pulled out of the Morris Luckily, Jim saw his problem and his Morris was repaired in the school's workshops. Tiff recalls with pleasure the instant camaraderie of students arriving from all over the world, all burning with desire to become racing drivers. He must have impressed Jim through his training course as his first public races were paid for by the school.

Unfortunately, his first major accident happened in front of everyone at Snetterton. Touching another car going through, would you believe, Russell Bend, he cartwheeled down the finish straight and his prize car was a sorry mess The good news was that, once again, the school workshop came to the rescue. He was able to use it and get valuable assistance from the staff which helped him to rebuild the car at a minimum cost. Going on to become one of the most versatile drivers of his time, Tiff has a motto which sums up his attitude – "Unluckier than a few – luckier than thousands".

Around this time, Jim introduced his bonus scheme for graduates in public races. It was simple enough. Those graduates who carried the school's stickers on their race cars, were able to claim a bonus when they finished in the first three places. Tiff and others remember just how successful this was with well over half the cars in Formula Ford emblazoned with "Jim Russell International Racing Drivers School" along each side Tiff was among the many who regularly claimed their bonuses.

Later that year, Danny Sullivan enrolled at the school but his arrival was in stark contrast to that of Tiff. He had been driving a taxi in New York when, by sheer chance, he picked up a certain Dr Frank Falkner. It turned out that the good doctor was involved with the Formula I Elf Team Tyrrell and was so impressed by Danny's driving that he promised to help him get into motor racing. Sure enough, before long, the ex-taxi driver found himself at the British Grand Prix At Silverstone courtesy of Ken Tyrrell and Jackie Stewart. That wasn't all. Dr Falkner insisted that Danny should go to the Jim Russell School and not only arranged the booking but also the very special transport from Silverstone to Snetterton. So it came to pass that Danny arrived in style, flying into the school in Colin Chapman's Gold Leaf Team Lotus plane and then going on to his Attleborough hotel in the GLTL car, As Danny recalls, "Hardly the unobtrusive low key way to turn up to meet your fellow novices. I looked like some spoilt rich man's kid, instead of a hard-up taxi driver".

The next day, on the first morning of the course, Jim opened with his usual procedure which entailed everyone standing in a line while he walked along, greeting them and asking each one to introduce themselves. When he got to Danny, he said, "No need to tell me who you are. I've already had Ken Tyrrell and Jackie Stewart on the phone asking me to look after you", Danny wished for the ground to open up and swallow him but, despite the initial embarrassment, everyone took it in good part and very soon they were all getting along on the usual friendly terms. So much so that Danny has very happy and grateful memories of his time at the school saying, "It was a great experience at a fabulous school which really was the launch of my career".

When he won the Indy 500, he sent a photo of himself holding the massive trophy on which he wrote, "Just look where the Jim Russell School helped to put me".

Jim wanted to fly to the Clermont Ferrand circuit in France. By then he still hadn't got an instrument rating for such a journey, so he asked Peter Mackintosh to go with him. Peter plotted the route and, except for occasionally giving instructions about their direction, made no comment about Jim's flying. On their way back, they stopped at a small airfield to refuel and set off towards home. Gradually, the cloud began to thicken and Jim began anxiously watching the worsening conditions. They were flying down a valley and he noted that the clouds were now only a couple of hundred feet above them. All the time he was glancing up at the threatening clouds, he expected a comment from Peter but none was forthcoming. By then Jim was beginning to wonder if Peter had been fooling him. "Perhaps he can't fly at all", he thought, worrying to himself. All the time, Peter was sitting next to him looking completely

Danny Sullivan's message from the Indy 500 podium says it all.

relaxed with the map on his knees. The very quietly he said, "OK, I'm in control now", as he leaned forward, took the controls and immediately banked the plane to turn round and head back to the little airport for the night. "Better safe than sorry", he said to Jim as they landed They found some accommodation and the next morning as they boarded the plane, Jim said, "Right, you do some flying now". Peter took over and flew the plane back to Le Touquet before handing the controls to Jim for the final leg to Southend and home.

There were increasing numbers of students who weren't old enough to get a driving licence but still enrolled for the courses. Age didn't matter as long as they could drive but, without a road licence, they were not able to race. James Weaver was one such youngster. He was still at school when he found out about the Jim Russell Racing Drivers School. At the age of 16, he persuaded his mother to enrol him. She had to bring him back and forward to the school and he completed the course. It was several years before he had his first race and became known as the 'bridesmaid' due to continually finishing second. He did, of course, put paid to that nickname a few years later. He established himself on the American sports car racing scene before being recognised in Europe. He has overcome many setbacks in what has proved to be a very successful sports car career highlighted by becoming Champion.

Wally Ward, having returned from America, was still not settled. Eventually, he came up with another idea. This time he was thinking about Austria and, having taken a look, he asked Jim's permission to open a Jim Russell School at the Osterreichring Circuit. Jim had never been there so, before he gave his blessing to the project, he decided to have a look for himself. By now, he had his instrument ratings so off he flew to Austria. With certain reservations, he gave his permission and Wally took a few cars over to start up. After a while, disturbing reports about the way it was operating started to worry Jim. The last thing he wanted was for a school bearing his name to be below his own high standards. Luckily, he had no need to take any action as Wally soon realised that it wasn't going to be profitable and closed it down, much to Jim's relief.

When Peter Mackintosh decided to move on in 1972, another advert was placed in the Daily Telegraph. It was read with interest by a young Scottish driver who had run out of money. He was looking for an interesting job to keep him going until he could save enough money to resume his racing. His name was John Kirkpatrick and little did he know that applying for the position of 'trainee instructor' at the Jim Russell Racing Drivers School was to change his life forever. An interview with Jim and John got him the job and he was soon getting the meticulous John Paine training. He never forgot the attention to detail which was John Paine's hallmark and remembers with gratitude the way he was helped. With that and his natural aptitude, he was upgraded to senior instructor later the same year. He had, in fact, found his true vocation and, as time went on, his plan to return to motor racing as a career gradually faded until it was gone forever.

A few Israelis, fresh from their war, attended the Overseas courses around that time. They were, in the main, difficult to control, especially two ex-tank commanders who seemed to have a built-in death wish. When John Kirkpatrick questioned them, they shrugged their shoulders and one said, "Back home we see sunrise ... but no sunset." Another one, Ran Sade, arrived in the dead of winter and proceeded to live in an old Cortina with a Calor gas heater for warmth. As the weather deteriorated, everyone worried about him. One very bad night, John K was worrying so much that he got up from his warm bed and drove to the circuit so that he could open the school building for Ran to sleep on the floor.

It wasn't only at night that the weather caused problems. It had become almost a matter of pride that they wouldn't let bad weather stop the training. Jim and the two Johns would very often use a tractor and shovels to physically clear the circuit to allow them to start.

Later in 1972, Ralph Firman and Ross Ambrose decided to form a race car manufacturing business across the road from Snetterton. Ross was from Tasmania, known as Van Diemen land, so they decided to call their Formula Fords by that name. The school had been using Merlyns for some time and were contemplating getting new cars. Jim showed his faith in Ralph by giving him an order for a dozen new cars to be built and delivered the following year. This, of course, was a tremendous start for the new company and, although the partnership with Ross was short-lived, Ralph never looked back. He was forever grateful to Jim for that initial order which led to an on-going supply situation ever since. The first batch of Van Diemen RF73 cars were augmented with RF74s and RF75s which were kept through the next couple of years. It was the RF78 which proved to be even more successful as a school car than its predecessors. So much so that it was used continually until the arrival of the Van Diemen built Formula Junior in the late 1980s at the British School. Both the American and Canadian schools continue to use them until the present day. It was generally acknowledged that the car was ideal for all the school's activities with a generous cockpit allowing it to accommodate almost everyone, Ease of maintenance also helped with its popularity.

Van Diemens at Snetterton.

Chapter 14
Graduates Do The School Proud

The highlight of 1972 was, of course, Emerson Fittipaldi winning the Formula I World Championship ... the school's first International title. Emerson was quick to acknowledge all the help he had received from Jim. Backing this up in fine style was Frank Gardner being named the British Champion Driver of the Year and Jean Pierre Jassaud finishing second in the European Formula II Championship.

In addition to Mallory Park, another even bigger operation opened at Silverstone in 1973, which was to become the school's headquarters for the next decade. The very successful innovative County Championship was launched, followed by the World Scholarship and the unique skid control circuit was laid down at Snetterton. These were exciting years with student numbers exceeding all expectations.

During these years, the school's race meetings continued to thrive with well over 100 students regularly taking part, many of them staying on for several seasons just competing at

Jim, Emerson, Marie-Helena and Peter Warr of Lotus celebrate after the end of season Brands Hatch meeting to honour Emerson's 1972 World Championship win.

The Merlyns outside the Silverstone school.

school races. When they were established at Snetterton, Silverstone and Mallory Park, the school's race programmes encompassed all three circuits giving the student racers even more experience than ever before and this certainly increased the grounding for the many who progressed to public racing.

Jimmy Brown was responsible for the move to Silverstone in 1973. He was the manager of the circuit at that time and had been watching the ever increasing popularity of the school. He said to Jim, "How would you like to run a school at our Grand Prix Circuit?" Jim agreed a deal and the school opened its third operation, in this country, later that year. It soon attracted a lot of the British students but the Overseas courses still remained at Snetterton. Within a year the school's race programme increased to 18 meetings, taking in all three circuits.

Over in Canada, Jacques Couture who had retired from active racing, was joined by new instructor, Bob Butte, who like Jacques had trained at Snetterton. Dave McConnell also instructed when he wasn't racing. The Overseas courses varied in length according to circumstances, sometimes extending to as long as three weeks A special Course for South Africans was tied in with BOAC who were then sponsoring the school. The itinerary included visits to race car manufacturers, sightseeing tours in London, visits to a London night-club plus several free days off aimed at giving them a holiday around the full training course, One day was always given to skid control. Since the early days, this had meant taking the students by coach to the Brands Hatch Skid Pan and, in their discussions, Jim and John Paine would often talk about the possibility of a skid pan at Snetterton. Firstly, they investigated other skid pans. John Paine and John Kirkpatrick visited the Hendon Police College set-up and were not at all impressed with the dirty oil surface. The same applied to Brands Hatch and the common view was that there must be a better way. Eventually Jim thought about a different form of surface and felt that this was the way to go. Instead of the conventional skid pan with its traditional old engine oil to induce a slippery surface, it only needed clean water, The secret was in the special bitumen emulsion used to paint a very smooth asphalt surface. Furthermore, by laying down an oval shaped circuit, the skid training would simulate road driving much more effectively. Unfortunately, MCD, the circuit owners, were not so impressed and refused to pay for it to be built. They had no objection to Jim having one at Snetterton, as long as he paid for it, The decision was made and the work was put in hand. Very soon the country's first and only skid circuit operating with clean water only, was in use. To start off, they used old road cars with well-worn smooth tyres. Soon they found a local tyre company who could produce new 'slick' tyres which did the job well. Before long, Jim had persuaded Alfa Romeo, for whom he was a dealer at Downham, to supply two of their cars for the skid school and this method continued with other manufacturers over the years.

Further changes at the three outlets of the school saw New Zealander, Mark Carew, join David Waring's instruction team at Mallory Park and John Paine was spending more time heading things up at Silverstone.

In 1973, Jim was approached by BOAC to go to South Africa. They had been pleased with the outcome of the Japanese visit a year or so earlier, and wanted him to run a one-off school for the locals in their own road cars for South Africans at the Kylami Circuit.

The trip was arranged for the day after the Annual Dinner Dance and Prize Giving which was at the Holiday Inn in Leicester. After a very enjoyable evening, a large crowd decided that they would get their swimming things and go downstairs to the hotel's indoor pool. Soon there was quite a crowd in the pool with others, including Jim and Jennifer, standing watching their antics. Suddenly, some unknown, probably a little the worse for wear, ran up and pushed Jim, fully clothed, straight into the water. While several swimmers quickly came forward to help him out, he was much more concerned with keeping his tobacco and cigarette papers dry, Unfortunately he was wearing a brand new suit which was absolutely ruined by the chlorinated water. We all returned with him to his room where, after changing, he proceeded to empty the sodden notes from his wallet and hang them to dry on a hastily erected line in the bathroom, The culprit was never discovered and, no doubt, in the cold light of day would have been too ashamed to own up.

Jim and John flew off to South Africa the following morning where they ran a very success-ful four day course. On one occasion, as the cars were lapping, Jim thought he saw a fanbelt fly off one of the cars. He shouted to John who went to investigate. He almost picked it up but stopped himself in time ... it was a snake They also used the opportunity to look at the possi-bility of a Jim Russell School there. That idea was provisionally shelved and never did get taken further. One of the reasons was just lack of time. With everything going on and new ideas to develop at the three British Circuits, it was no wonder that further expansion overseas was put on hold. Silverstone was attracting more and more students, the lure of the name making it the most popular school with many of them. Gerry Corbett joined the instruction team for both Silverstone and Mallory Park and was to stay for a number of years.

Meanwhile, the Canadian school was going from strength to strength. Rob Swartout, who followed the same route as the others and trained at the Snetterton school, had now joined the instruction staff. Preparations were being made for Canadian students to come to Snetterton and experience training at 'headquarters' the following year. During that year they started an association with what was to become a very famous French-Canadian family named Villeneuve. Giles, whose brilliant career was cut short when he was killed in Formula I, was first to be trained. He was followed by his brother Jacques and, much later, Giles' son Jacques brought fame to the school by becoming World Champion in 1997 Back in England, a unique new Championship was inaugurated in 1973 when the school launched its County Championship. Its concept was simple. Students were asked to nominate their county, either by birthplace or residence, and score points at all the

The winning Lincolnshire County Championship team. Terry Gibbons on the left.

race meetings for their team. The size of the team didn't matter as, by dividing the points scored by the number of team members, every team had an even chance. It was an instant success. Registrations came thick and fast so that no less than thirty counties were represented in that first year. Everyone gained from this idea. The school sent out press releases to all the regional newspapers and had a tremendous amount of exposure while the same happened for the students with their local papers eagerly following the fortunes of 'their' own county team and its members. It soon became a regular feature on sports pages around the country. With press releases after each of the twelve rounds of the Championship the school and its students were always in the news. The end result of that first County Championship was a perfect example of the way the scoring system worked as the smallest team won. Lincolnshire County represented by just three drivers, Andy Roughton, Terry Gibbons and Graham Rhodes, became the first County Championship winners while Rhodes took the school's individual Championship. Nottinghamshire took second place and Norfolk was third.

Don MacLeod won the British National Formula Ford Championship and Teddy Pillette won his first British Formula 5000 Championship.

That year, the Annual Dinner Dance and Prize Giving moved to the more central location of the De Vere Hotel in Coventry and the proud little Lincolnshire team received their trophies from Stuart Turner, by then the Ford Director of Competitions for Europe, who was Guest of Honour and shared the prize giving duties with Derek Bell. Stuart Turner was very late arriving that evening much to everyone's surprise. He eventually turned up to explain that he had gone to Coventry Street in London by mistake

The 1974 County Championship saw victory go to the Berkshire team with Yorkshire and Warwickshire very close together in second spot. It had been even bigger and better than the year before with 42 teams taking part. Alan Smith from the winning team took the individual prize.

Jackie Stewart was again responsible for introducing someone to the school later that year. He had met up with

Stuart Turner presents the Trophy to 1973 school champion, Graham Rhodes.

Fernando Perrado at a special reception in London. He was the Uruguayan who had led a small party over the awesome Andes, and survived, to get help to his team mates after his national football team's plane had crashed on the wrong side of the mountain range. The whole story, of course, was made into a film called "Alive" in the early 1990s.

In conversation with him at that reception, Jackie had realised that Fernando was more than a little interested in motor racing and took him along to the Monaco Grand Prix. Nando, as he was called by nearly everyone, had asked Jackie where he might try his hand at motor racing. This led to him being introduced to Jim and he came to Snetterton to do the Overseas course that Summer. He may not have scaled the heights as a racing driver but he certainly appreciated the training as witness his comments in the school's visitor's book ... "I would have lost many precious time if I hadn't done the course. Now I know what to do and where to go. Your help and advice are great."

During the 1970s graduates were regularly winning races and championships. Consequently

182

many of them were taking advantage of the Jim Russell Bonus Scheme. John Paine's desk had a healthy input of letters claiming cash from these successful graduates.

The Canadian school organised a unique business and pleasure trip during the Summer of 1975. They managed to fill two aeroplanes with students eager to race in England as well as see the sights. The trip was arranged around the time of the British Grand Prix and the new fleet of Van Diemens for the school were collected before they did their series of three races at Snetterton, Mallory Park and Silverstone. They were all booked into the Post House at Norwich and John Kirkpatrick arrived well before their coach. When he walked into the bar, he found Mario Andretti there. He was then driving for Parnelli Jones who, at that time, had a place at Griston, near Snetterton. John saw an opportunity to score points for the school and asked Mario to do him a favour. "Would you make it appear that you are here specially to talk to this bunch of Canadian students?" "Sure", said the easy going American driver. Shortly afterwards fifty-six Canadians walked in, just about every one of them looking astonished as they saw Mario there He was brilliant, talking to them all for about an hour. They were late for dinner but no-one minded and they were never told that it had been a coincidence that just about the most famous American driver had met them that evening.

The 1975 Canadian visitors greeted by John Kirkpatrick (left) and Guenda Eadie (third from right). Jacques Villneuve (uncle of the World Champion of the same name) is the laughing attendee fourth the left.

John K, Jim and Guenda on the unique skid crcuit.

Skid control action.

After Mallory, they all went to Silverstone to watch the British Grand Prix and stayed over for the special Jim Russell race meeting the following day. Much to their surprise, the very English Clerk of the Course said, "I'll tell you the same as I told the chaps yesterday" The Canadians thought that was really neat.

Between their race meetings, they spent a few days in London, losing two of their party in Soho for 48 hours. Continuing to gain numbers and support, the 1975 County Championship, which had previously only included English Counties and the lone Renfrewshire team from Scotland, now had teams from the Isle of Wight, Gwent and three Scottish teams. One of them, Dunfriesshire, won the title and their Captain, Graham Wilson, took the Individual award.

Graduate success continued. That year Derek Bell won at Le Mans and Teddy Pillette won the European F5000 Championship.

Then came the idea of a Jim Russell World Championship. Having carefully sorted out the rules and regulations, press releases announcing its launch were sent out. Almost immediately an urgent call came from the FIA, pointing out that they had exclusive rights to the "World Championship" title So, even before it had started, the name had to be changed to the World Scholarship. Up until then there had been an individual championship which was continued. In the meantime, John Paine had moved his office permanently to Silverstone which became the school's headquarters in 1975 leaving John Kirkpatrick in charge at Snetterton where they concentrated on the ever popular Overseas courses.

Pupils were also sent from Mallory Park and Silverstone to Snetterton for skid control tuition. The Skid Circuit was getting so busy that it need a full-time operator. From the applications received, they were intrigued to interview a young Scottish lady, Guenda Eadie, who had been making a name for herself in rallies. She convinced them that she could do the job and she certainly proved to be the right choice. Not only did she impress as a skid control instructor, she also made an impression on the media. So much so that there were constant features about this 'female skid instructor' in all kinds of news outlets especially women's magazines. She was, very soon, encouraged to take a Jim Russell training course taking to racing as she had to rallying.

There were 132 entrants for the World Scholarship that year, including 20 from overseas, and just three of them were female. When the final ten were announced, Guenda was the only woman to make it. A good indication of the International aspect of the school was that the finalists comprised of two from England, Guenda from Scotland, two from America and one each from Greece, Spain, Sweden and New Zealand. The star studded panel of judges comprised Colin Chapman, Derek Bell, Jack Sears, Patrick Neve, Innes Ireland, Alan Henry and Chris Witty ,This set the quality of judges for future years. Guenda was undaunted by this array and was soon being looked at as a possible outright winner. With the outcome in doubt, the November fog came down and the final runs had to be abandoned. The very consistant Brian Househam was given the verdict and the prize of a new Van Diemen FF, priced those days at £3,250, but Guenda had done enough to take the second place cheque for £250.

With a full time instructor, every effort was made to get the maximum use of the skid circuit. Over the years many attempts were made to encourage road driving schools to include a skid control lesson in their driving courses without success. Although everyone thought it an excellent facility, Jim felt it should have more use. Then came the idea of a winter skid challenge. It was an instant success. Again it was a simple formula. Teams of four people could enter in various categories. Apart from the obvious motoring clubs, there were special sections for young farmers, bank employees, rotarians and many others. It was run on a timed laps principle and ended with a special award ceremony. Normally, the school's sponsors ... Esso, Shell, Firestone, Imperial Leather and BOAC were some over the years ... would put up the top prize and there were trophies as well as cash for the winners. It was another brilliant idea. It kept the skid circuit busy in the winter and, apart from providing a fun competition, it also introduced many people to the very necessary art of controlling a skid.

In 1977, the Canadian operation was reorganised to enable Jacques Couture to move into America. He opened a school at the Ontario Motor Speedway in California. He took Bob Butte with him, leaving Dave McConnell to run the St Jovite school, where he was joined by another Jim Russell England graduate, Vince Loughran. Because the Kastners were still running their unofficial Jim Russell school at Willow Springs, Jacques had to call his new operation The British School of Motor Racing for the next few years

Although there was a reduced number of counties and drivers in the County Championship that year, the competition was closer than ever. A good example of student racers who came back to race with the school on a regular basis was the Individual Champion, Chris Pilborough. He was one of the staunch bunch of graduates who came back regularly to compete in the school race meetings. He did so well into the 1980s. He was a convincing winner that year but, despite his good performances, his county team of Essex were only able to finish second behind the London team.

Bullfighter come racing driver, Kelly Tipps.

Probably the most unique student to arrive during the late seventies was Kelly Tipps. This little American earns his living as a Professor of Classic History in Florida but for a long time, he was a part-time bull fighter and came to Snetterton to learn to be a racing driver. From that two week course, he became a regular racer with the school, continuing to commute from America when duties allowed, so that he could do a school race. From the beginning, he respected the dedicated instruction of John Kirkpatrick whose only reaction when Kelly crashed on the third day of his course was to throw his clipboard, with great force, at the pit wall Kelly was quite sure it was going to be thrown at him. Not only was he relieved and impressed that he was let off, he was even more impressed at Jim's barbecue. When he thought he had better own up and said to his host, "I was the one who shunted the car this week", the only response from Jim was, "I heard there had been a prang", before he changed the subject, He recalls the way John used to stand at Riches watching the students driving through the corner and he was not happy at the way Kelly was missing the clipping point. Finally, John stood right on the curb and pointed vigorously at his feet. The next time round Kelly made sure he got it right as John jumped back very quickly. It was the American's moment of satisfaction but no-one is more a champion of the school and particularly of John's dedication to training and encouraging young aspirants. As Kelly says its that feature of the school which has kept him coming back and striving to do a little better every time. He has carried on racing with the school over the years, interspersed with some public racing. Without a doubt, he has made his mark in the school's history by being the longest consistent racing returnee of all.

A young Brazilian made a lasting impression on Jim and his staff around that time. Firstly, his unusual and improbable name which was, would you believe, Julius Caesar Penheiro That would surely have ensured plenty of publicity if he had continued in a racing career. More importantly, he had the most fantastic driving talent which should have taken him all the way to the top. Like so many of the Brazilians to come over, he spoke his own charming brand of English at the time even though he was working at Harrods. When asked what he sold there, he replied, "Mackavites", which puzzled everyone until they realised that he meant McVities biscuits

Everybody, especially John Kirkpatrick, was convinced that they had another star in the making but, unfortunately he went home to Brazil and was never seen again. No doubt he became one of the many who couldn't raise the sponsorship he needed and yet another talent was wasted.

About this time, another possible project came under consideration. Following a discussion with Speedway star, Tommy Price, it was decided to jointly build a speedway stadium just outside the Snetterton circuit. Unfortunately, the existing speedway establishment at Norwich didn't take kindly to the idea and, following their strongly voiced objections, Jim decided to drop the idea.

Another young lady to make her mark in the seventies was Juliette Slaughter, a vicar's daughter who, in addition to having natural driving talent, certainly knew how to promote herself. By doing so, she also promoted the school. After her training course she proceeded to land herself all kinds of drives and sponsorship deals. Her very feminine, and mostly skimpy, clothing in the paddock made sure that her photos were regularly featured in the press. Consequently, her media coverage rivalled that of Guenda during that time.

The annual Dinner Dances continued to be held at the De Vere Hotel in Coventry until the late seventies. Unbeknown to John, when he had first decided to approach that particular hotel, he was already known by the Assistant Manager, Herbie Waser, who immediately recognised John and said, "You're the man who gave me a good rollicking when I was a pupil of yours at Mallory Park" Although John couldn't actually remember the incident, it did cement the relationship which kept the annual event there for quite a few years. Then in 1980, Herbie Waser moved to the Bell House Hotel in

Juliette Slaughter (nee Scott-Gunn).

△ Stan Thomas, Steven Lancefield, Jim and Ralph Firman at the 1976 dinner.

△ Patrick Neve is the recipient at the same dinner.

▷ "Is the mike on?"

Beaconsfield, where he had been appointed Manager. He suggested that the school might like to move the Dinner Dance with him and this was agreed.

Possibly the first ever coloured American driver, Willy T Ribbs, came through the school and, before returning home, won the 1977 BRSCC Dunlop Star of Tomorrow FF Championship. Around the same time, the first ever Greek student, Ilias Efessios, came to the school and, after training, continued as the only Greek driver in Formula Ford for several seasons before business requirements took priority over racing. Richard Noble, while gaining all the experience he could before making his land speed record attempt, came to the school for training. He stipulated that his visit should be kept free from exposure and this request was obviously upheld. Naturally, the school staff followed his progress with more than a little interest after that. Other personalities who came in for tuition included show jumping star, Ann Moore, singer Vince Hill, Noel Edmunds and Pink Floyd drummer, Nick Mason.

John Kirkpatrick was by now getting very friendly with Guenda and, for some time, had tried to arrange a weekend away. This was proving to be difficult with the school operating most weekends. When he had to instruct Mallory Park one Saturday, followed by Snetterton on the Sunday, he saw his chance and arranged to meet Guenda at the Holiday Inn in Leicester on the Saturday night.

John arrived at about 8.30 pm. He saw no sign of Guenda so he booked a room and had a lonely dinner before finally giving up and going to bed. When he next saw Guenda on his return to Snetterton he asked her where she had been that night. "Oh, I was at the Holiday Inn", she replied. "Where were you?" "I was there, too" said a perplexed John. She had arrived mid-afternoon and taken a room. As far as she was concerned, John didn't show. It transpired that they had stayed in rooms two floors apart.

Roberto Guerrero, a young Colombian doing an engineering course, went to the Mallory Park school but was frustrated by his once monthly lapping sessions. With his natural talent, he wanted to race. By chance, he met John Kirkpatrick at the British Grand Prix that year. "I want to race", he said. "No problem", replied John. "Come to Snetterton for the full treatment". Within days, he had arrived in Norfolk and very soon he was racing. Without telling his family back home, he gave up his engineering studies and moved into the local house which was John's home. There he joined another lodger, Thierry Tassin. It wasn't long before he was spotted by Ralph Firman, who signed him to drive for Van Diemen the following year and his career, which led to Formula I and Indycars, had begun

Later that year came the first truly International World Scholarship when the best of the Canadian and American schools were sent over to compete. For the first time, there were separate sections for Overseas and British students. Another star studded judging panel was assembled which included Derek Bell, Jack Sears, Patrick Neve, Alan Henry and Nigel Roebuck. After all the tests, lapping and interviews by the judges, Canadian Gilbert Pednault won the

"Turn right at Riches' John K. appears to be saying.

Overseas section and a young Scot, Anthony Reid, was the winner of the British section. Their prizes were identical. They had both won a free season of Formula Ford races, driving Van Diemen RF78s in the 1978 Esso Championship. Both were also continuing a very active association with the schools as instructors alongside their racing careers.

The team was run by Gerry Corbett from the school's Silverstone workshop and both drivers acquitted themselves well, getting into the prize money several times despite the very strong opposition which, that year, included such people as graduates Mike Thackwell, Jim Walsh, David Sears, Roberto Guerrero and Cameron Binnie to say nothing of Kenny Acheson and Michael Roe.

This was the year that the American Indycar drivers and cars visited this country for the first time. They had two race meetings, one at Brands Hatch (hence the reason for the short circuit to be called the Indy circuit) and one at Silverstone. One of the star drivers, Tom Sneva, thought he would come over early and take a look at Silverstone before anyone else arrived. He got talking to the school and the outcome was that he learnt the circuit in one of the school's Van Diemens, giving the pupils an exciting afternoon.

Jim had begun to wake up in pain with both his wrists which soon developed into a lack of circulation in his hands. Eventually he went to his doctor who sent him to a consultant. This led to an x-ray and, after examining the result, the consultant said, "Have you been in an accident? You've got two fractured wrists" Jim was flabbergasted and recalled that the only accident was at Le Mans twenty years ago. "Well", said the consultant, "You damaged your wrists then and you've been like it ever since It's not unusual for people to get aches and pains for the rest of their lives after a major accident. Never mind, a minor operation will sort that out". It did.

Also in the seventies came the success of school graduates in the Grovewood Awards. These were set up in 1963 and ran until the eighties. Grovewood Securities put up the cash awards and the Guild of Motoring Writers were given the task of selecting the most promising up-and-coming young British and Commonwealth drivers each year.

Bernard Vermillio had the honour of being the first graduate to get a commendation in 1971, followed by Bob Arnott in 1972. The first major award was the following year when Don McLeod was third. Then Tiff Needell was commended in 1975 followed by getting the major award of £1,000 the following year. After Phillip Bullman's third place in 1977, Mike Thackwell emulated Tiff by getting a commendation in 1978 and taking the top award in 1979. That year no less than three of the five names were from the school as James Weaver and David Sears were also commended

Judges Derek Bell, Alan Henry, Jack Sears, Patrick Neve and Nigel Roebuck with the 1978 World Scholarship winners Gilbert Pednault and Anthony Reid.

The 1978 World Scholarship again attracted a large contingent from across the Atlantic with American Jon Beekhuis, who had trained at the Canadian school, taking the Overseas prize. It hadn't looked that way prior to the event as John Kirkpatrick had been forewarned by Nigel Roebuck and Alan Henry that, another Canadian, Jacques Villeneuve, brother of Giles, would be the man. They had seen him win the Formula Ford race supporting that year's Canadian Grand Prix and had been very impressed with his performance. He certainly drove well in this World Scholarship but he was a little too sharp but, then again, John K was a little sharper. Jacques pulled into the pits having slipped out of his seat belts and John suspected that the French-Canadian had done so to be able to reach and zero the 'tell-tale' needle on his rev counter. He was right and Jacques was automatically excluded from the results.

The British prize winner was Alan Dunn. The London team won the County Championship and Les German was the school's individual Champion. Dave McLelland had been over to successfully race, finishing runner-up in one of the National Formula Ford Championships. Jim Walsh did likewise in the main Esso FF series.

The following year another American, Robert Stevenson, took the Individual Championship racing for his adopted Norfolk team, but it was the Middlesex team which won the County Award.

"There's the clipping point ... David Sears is standing on it".

This World Scholarship judging panel has Colin Chapman and Innes Ireland (second and third from the left) while Derek Bell looks more interested in the car!

Alan Dunn and John Beekhuis after winning the 1979 World Scholarship surrounded by the judging panel including Patrick Neve, Peter Mackintosh (third left) Jack Sears and Nigel Roebuck.

Jim's BBQ room. Jacques Couture and John Paine extreme left. Jim, in the background, cooks the steaks.

Skid Instructress, Guenda Eadie, managed to combine her demanding job at the school with competing in the National Faberge sponsored Ladies Fiesta Championship and winning it convincingly. Naturally, this brought even more publicity for both the talented lady and the school. Rick Whyman won the Northern Ford Championship while Thierry Tassin was runner-up in the European Townsend Thoreson FF Championship. James Weaver did the same in the like sponsored British FF Championship. The hotly contested World Scholarship had an Argentinian winner, Enrique (Quique) Mansilla and Chris Oxley took the British Award. As was the custom, the prize presentation took place later in the evening at Jim's Bardwell Manor home. He had earlier converted the old stable block into a very attractive function room with a built-in barbecue in the corner. Jim would happily prepare the barbecued meats for his guests while Jennifer and helpers looked after the rest of the food. It had become a regular, and very popular, feature of the Overseas courses for all the students and instructors to be entertained there one evening during their training. On this World Scholarship occasion, however, something went wrong. One of the main guests, namely the Overseas winner, failed to appear. Mansilla was last seen going back to his hotel to change before going to Bardwell. As the time went on, everyone began to worry and they were right. Instead of enjoying a super party, he was laying in a hospital bed. His exuberant road driving had put him off the road and although he wasn't badly hurt, that is where he stayed that night.

The American school moved in 1979 to Riverside Raceway and, by then, the Kastners had closed their Willow Springs operation. At last, Jacques Couture could use the Jim Russell name again.

Patrick Neve had been racing in everything from Formula Ford upwards and still worked at the school during the seventies. For 1979, he formed a team to run Quique Mansilla in the National Formula Ford Championship and by the end of the year, Patrick had persuaded Jim to form a partnership team to be called Russell Neve Racing. They had spotted another young Brazilian graduate, Bolivar de Sordi, and signed him up for 1980. Unfortunately, despite getting Jim to accompany him back home during that winter, he was unable to get sponsorship and Jim flew home alone.

While Jim was booking into the Hilton hotel in Sao Paulo, he found himself standing next to Bernie Ecclestone who said, "Hello Jim ... what are you doing here?" Jim told him that he was there to try and help a young school graduate get sponsorship just as he had done for Emerson Fittipaldi a decade or so earlier. Bernie asked how the school was going. "Oh, we've got 5 outlets now", replied Jim proudly. "We'd better get together when I get back", said Bernie, but they never did. Jim listed that as one of his all time regrets.

The short-lived Russell Neve team was soon disbanded and it was decided to run a Jim Russell Racing team from the Downham Market racing workshop, which was already in being. John Kirkpatrick was made team manager. They ran three cars that year, retaining the exuberant, but erratic, Mansilla who was joined by a very talented Brazilian, Luis Schaffer, and a rather overweight American, Peter Cramer. They probably picked one of the most competitive years of Formula Ford with drivers including Brazilians Roberto Moreno and Raul Boesel plus Irishman Tommy Byrne and the British doctor Jonathan Palmer taking part. These were halcyon days for the formula with no less than four National Championships (RAC, Townsend Thoreson, Esso and P & O Ferries) plus several more regional series as well. While the major pickings went to Moreno, Boesel and Byrne, the Jim Russell star was Schaffer who regularly featured in the leading bunch. He finished third in the P & O Ferries Championship and fourth in the RAC, where returnee David McClelland was a fine second. Jim Walsh added further honours to the school by taking the Esso Championship for the second year running and Andy Wallace started his illustrious career by winning the Pre-74 Formula Ford Championship. Roberto Guerrero and Thierry Tassin were front runners all season in the FIII Championship finishing third and fourth respectively. James Weaver finished a fine second in the Sports 2000 series and Glenn Eagling was similarly placed in Clubman's B Championship.

Despite some good results, the overheads and extra work entailed in running the team alongside the school's heavy programme, meant that a decision was made to wrap up the racing operation at the end of that season. Although Mansilla stayed in the country to step up to Formula III, Schaffer, regrettably went back to Brazil and a very promising career was effectively concluded.

There were many occasions when personalities wanted to come along and get a drive in a racing car. This was particularly so in the case of people in other sports. Unfortunately they were very often prevented from doing so for insurance reasons. Footballers and boxers couldn't get permission from their managers who feared accidents. In 1980, Joe Bugner and Dave Boy Green were in that category. Bugner was particularly keen and tried very hard to overcome his manager's objections to no avail.

When Emerson Fittipaldi retired from Grand Prix racing in 1981, the Ford Motor Company threw a special party to mark the occasion at the Carlton Tower Hotel in Knightsbridge.

Enjoying Emerson's retirement (from Formula I) speech with Marie-Helena and Frank Williams.

It was a very exclusive affair with just 20 guests including such luminaries as Walter Hayes, Keith Duckworth, Pat MaClaren and Frank Williams. Apart from Emerson and Marie-Helena, they invited people who had helped him during his career. Jim and Jenny, Ralph and Angie Firman were joined by FF engine tuner, Denny Rowlands and his wife. Unfortunately, Colin and Hazel Chapman were unable to attend at the last moment. Nevertheless, it was a great evening with Emerson proving himself to be a funny after dinner speaker When the Russells and the Firmans arrived in the afternoon and had checked in, they ordered tea for four but nearly collapsed when they got the bill for £78. It was the same with the very high bar prices and to top it all, the party went on into the early hours and they realised that they had eventually paid £120 per head for about two hours in bed. Still, they were all thrilled to have been at that special evening for Emerson. Mind you, it wasn't long before he was making the headlines again in Indycar racing, winning the famous Indy 500 and adding that Championship to his list of successes in 1983.

Throughout all the years since it was launched, they still had the advantage of the only skid circuit in the country. Amazingly, despite many visits from other operators including the Hendon Police School, no-one else had actually copied Jim's unique idea. Furthermore, over the many years he and his staff had been unable to convince the road driving school industry

196

that the inclusion of a skid control lesson in their course would be a major step forward. Jim always regretted that this hadn't happened. However, several advanced driving schools did use the facility. John Lyon, who had graduated from the school before the skid circuit had been laid down, was a regular user throughout its entire existence. His highly respected advanced road driving courses, which he operates on a one-to-one basis, invariably included a concentrated skid control lesson. It very often entailed a long drive to bring his pupils to Snetterton but he felt it was the best possible place to teach skid control.

It was still an all year round operation as the Winter Skid Challenge was still in a very healthy state and now included a junior section which attracted entries from many colleges and high schools. Guenda had stayed as the Chief Instructor right through until 1982 but then, after meeting and marrying a school graduate who had a business in Liverpool, she became Mrs Colin Palmer and moved away.

Freddy Dack, whose early days at the school were some twenty years before, returned to join the staff and train before taking over as her replacement.

Due no doubt to the continued attraction of training at the Silverstone Grand Prix circuit, less and less students were opting for Mallory Park. It was only a matter of time before the decision was taken to close the school there and concentrate on the Silverstone Headquarters School. Here, with John Paine in charge, they mainly catered for British students wile continuing to operate the Overseas courses at Snetterton where John Kirkpatrick was still in charge.

For many years, the school used the British Grand Prix as a marketing opportunity. Apart from the fact that there were always graduates racing that weekend, the established 'Parade of Flags' gave the school centre stage before the Grand Prix. This entailed equipping the fleet of school cars with flag poles from which each car flew a different national flag of one of the partaking GP drivers. Instructors and senior students drove a slow lap of the circuit during the lunch break. This, coupled with editorial in the programme, ensured good promotion for the school.

As they reached the end of the school's ten year agreement with Silverstone, the powers that be offered to renew but wanted a massive rent increase. After much discussion and consideration, Jim decided that it would not be a viable proposition with the greatly increased overheads. Very reluctantly, the school was closed and everything returned to Snetterton. Of course, the really big downside of all of this was the loss of two circuits for the school's race meetings. The Jim Russell Racing Club, placed in a different position, decided to put the County Championship on hold while the school consolidated at Snetterton. This was meant to be for one year only but it soon became clear that lots of things were changing in the eighties and the heady days of the seventies had gone.

To add to their problems, Jim heard from John Webb that there would be no weekend dates available for the school's race meetings at Snetterton in 1983. This really was a major problem. How could they continue the full courses, especially for the overseas pupils, if they couldn't even give them the traditional race at the end of the course? Looking at various options, they decided to

△ *Dropping the cherquered flag for the finish of the very last JRRDS race at Snetterton before the move to Donington.*

◁ *They've now grown and become School graduates ... James, Amanda and Robert Russell.*

try to revert back to a similar operation to the one with which they had started. They needed to arrange for a couple of races within a public race programme. It was decided to approach the BARC, who were then running a big proportion of race meetings at Snetterton. To this end, John Paine went down to their headquarters at Thruxton for a meeting with Sidney Offord who was then running the Club. John successfully arranged for the school to have two races at every BARC meeting at Snetterton that year and, upon his return, a list of courses was drawn up to fit into the schedule. So, at least for a couple of years, the school's training programme could continue. However, despite this new

Dr. Frank Faulkner and Danny Sullivan with the Russells during the school's 30th Anniversary party at Laguna Seca.

arrangement, the future looked less certain than at any time in the school's history. The school continued to attract students from all over the world to fill the ever popular courses and the trial and super trial days remained as popular as ever. Nevertheless, Jim and John Paine were feeling ready to let go of the reins. When Jim reached the age of 65, in 1985, he decided that this was a good time and made the most important decision to hand over control of the school to an Australian graduate, Graham Peake. He also decided to give up flying his own aircraft and sold the plane. Both actions were a personal wrench but, in the case of the school, he was soon partly involved again when it passed into the hands of the American school at Laguna Seca after a year or so. It became part of the American/Canadian/British group and they immediately asked Jim to

A far cry from 1957... some of the Jim Russell School at fleet Donnington in 1997.

The Jim Russell School at Laguna Seca Circuit. U.S.A.

become their Chairman. Within 12 months the founding school had moved from its long-time home at Snetterton to Donington Park. With the logistical problems of controlling it from so far away, the Americans began feeling the strain of so much Atlantic commuting, and proved receptive when John Kirkpatrick made them an offer in 1987. Once again, the school was completely British owned and Jim was happy to continue operating as Chairman.

During this time, Jim Russell Management came into being. This was formed by the directors of the British, American and Canadian schools, under the chairmanship of Jim himself, in order to promote the Jim Russell operation in further areas of the world. This has been so successful that, when the school celebrated its 40th anniversary in 1997, there were further schools or agencies in Spain, Portugal, Mexico, Brazil, Japan, Malaysia, Thailand, Australia, South Korea, Sri Lanka, The Scandinavian Countries and Russia.

The real secret of the school's longevity is simply that everyone has continued to operate the straight-forward, safe, step-by-step tuition laid down by Jim from the very beginning.

As Colin Chapman wrote in the school's visitors book way back in 1974 ... "Congratulations to the Jim Russell Racing Drivers School ... the foundation of British Motor Racing".